LABOR LAW

Brent E. Zepke

Member of the
Bars of:

DISTRICT OF COLUMBIA
NEW JERSEY
PENNSYLVANIA
TENNESSEE

1977

LITTLEFIELD, ADAMS & CO.
Totowa, New Jersey

Copyright © 1977
by
LITTLEFIELD, ADAMS & CO.

Library of Congress Cataloging in Publication Data

Zepke, Brent E.
    Labor law.

    (Littlefield, Adams Quality Paperbacks;
    No. 325)
    1. Labor laws and legislation--
        United States.
I. Title.
KF3369.Z46   344'.73'01   77-4022
ISBN 0-8226-0325-X

PRINTED IN THE UNITED STATES OF AMERICA

Preface

The objective of this text is to explore and present labor law in the most concise, understandable manner possible. The method of presentation enables the book to be used for a course within a college of business administration or as a supplemental text in law schools. However, its effectiveness is not limited to formal education, as it would also be worthwhile reading for the plant manager or union leader. In short, it will be valuable to anyone wishing to learn or review labor law.

The topic of labor law is so complex that the author must establish certain parameters in which to frame his approach. The typical one is to differentiate the study of unions from the other topics which might be considered in the employer-employee situation. This study follows that approach and presents primarily topics that involve unions. Even when the study is restricted to unions, a certain amount of editing is necessary in order to fit the concepts into one volume; i.e., by necessity an opinion of the status of the topics explored and of their relative importance is expressed by their inclusion or exclusion within the parameters discussed previously.

Statutes form the basis of the study of unions, so a summary of the key statutory provisions is presented in the chapter entitled "Statutory Regulation." The subjects outlined in that chapter, along with other key topics, are explored in depth in other chapters, with each chapter presenting the relevant parts of the applicable statute, complete with a discussion of the aims and applications of the sections. Within each chapter the text is usually followed by legal cases. The text discusses the principles and offers many case citations that would lend themselves nicely to assignments for additional research. The cases at the end of the chapters present some factual situations that have been litigated and the actual language used by the courts. These have by necessity been condensed, and assignments towards exploring the entire cases would be appropriate.

Because of the significance of the Labor Management Relations Act of 1947, as amended, it is presented in full in the Appendix and is referred to throughout the text as "the Act," or by the initials "LMRA," or merely by section number, such as "8(a)(1) provides." Key legislation is sometimes referred to by the name of the elected official who sponsored it in Congress, so the LMRA is sometimes called the Taft-Hartley Act.

The National Labor Relations Act of 1935, designated by the initials "NLRA," sometimes called the Wagner Act in honor of its sponsor in Congress, established the National Labor Relations Board, sometimes called the Labor Board or merely the Board. This is another key act but its provisions have been merged into the LMRA.

I would like to thank my son, Chad, for being himself and thus providing the inspiration for my efforts.

Table of Contents

1. Introduction

This presentation will consider the principles and procedures that govern the integration of the philosophies of organized labor with the goals of management.

The emphasis of the presentation is governed by the definitions of employer and employee under the Labor Management Relations Act. An "employer" includes any person acting as an agent of an employer but does not include the United States or any wholly owned government corporation, or any person subject to the Railway Labor Act, or any labor organization when acting as an employer. Governmental employees are covered under the chapter bearing that title and the Railway Labor Act is discussed in the "Historical Development" chapter.

The term "employee" includes one whose work has ceased as a consequence of a current labor dispute but does not include an agricultural laborer, or one in domestic service, or one employed by his spouse or parent, or anyone having the status of an independent contractor, or anyone employed as a supervisor, or anyone employed by an employer subject to the Railway Labor Act.

There is an increasing concern that individuals may be injured by the union that represents them, so the chapter "The Individual and the Union" will consider this situation.

The historical development chapter should assist one in ascertaining some of the "wrongs" which have been the target of rules. The wrongs are particularly important because it is less difficult to define some forbidden conduct than it is to define exactly the manner in which one should conduct himself. Thus, there is considerable emphasis placed on the wrongs or unfair labor practices.

The issues involved in labor disputes are vital and as fundamental as the right to earn a living and the right to control one's property. Disputes can be violent, affect third parties, and almost always be expensive. An article in the *Wall Street Journal*, September 9, 1975, indicates just how expensive even a slight dispute may be:

> "A Chicago management consultant calculates the average employer loses $124 per worker during the course of a union representation vote run by the NLRB. Even if the management wins the vote, consultant Woodruff Imberman figures legal costs, productivity lapses, and lost worker and supervisor time add

up. A union organizing drive, he warns, 'is hard to smother and is quite expensive.'

"The $124 cost total is reached by adding an estimated $19 a worker to hire special legal talent; $27 for worker pay and overhead during anti-union meetings on company time; $58 for an average 8% dip in productivity while campaigning goes on; and $20 in executive pay for fighting the union. The estimates assume a four-week campaign in an average-sized U.S. plant paying $4.50 an hour in wages and benefits.

"For larger plants, of over 1,000 workers, the cost is less—about $102 a worker."

The aim of labor laws is to provide for a freedom of choice for the employees on whether or not to organize. If they organize, collective bargaining in good faith is the objective and the method to accomplish this is to balance the interests involved.

"The law is not an end in itself, nor does it provide ends. It is preeminently a means to serve what we think is right."

William J. Brennan
Opinion, *Roth* v. *United States*
354 U.S. 476 (1957)

2. Historical Development

General. In all areas of the law, the date on which the legal opinion on the case under consideration was handed down is an important factor in evaluating the holding. Perhaps in labor law the date is even more important than in most other areas, as its evolution has been a series of attempts to balance the forces of labor and management. The "balance" has tipped first in one direction and then, with the advent of the corrective measure to this first tipping, in the other direction, and then the procedure is reversed.

Most areas of the law have experienced a certain amount of swaying and balancing, but there appears to have been more of this motion in labor law than in most areas. A variety of factors are responsible; the number of people involved in the result, the critical nature of the subject matter (wages, working conditions, etc.), the financial strengths of the parties, and the lack of constitutional guidelines are but a few of the complicating, emotion-producing factors.

Therefore one should note the date of any case cited as authority and remember that a given case may or may not still represent the current status of the law; more research is necessary to effectively decide the result. Every effort has been made in this presentation to indicate the current status, with the exception of the historical development described in this chapter. Because of the nature of labor law, a knowledge of historical development is a prerequisite to an understanding of the current theories and controlling doctrines, so this is presented in the following pages.

It is interesting to observe how the critical issues of jurisdiction and remedies arose time and again and how they evolved into their current positions. Whether one is dealing with legislative or court actions, the initial determination must be whether the organization has the authority to pass rules or judgments that will be binding on the relevant parties. For instance, in labor law, it was at one time felt that the U.S. Congress could not pass laws that dealt with labor problems. If this were still believed, the scope of labor law would certainly be different today. With respect to remedies, the remedy for a strike has evolved from being primarily a criminal charge to being primarily a civil action, and currently a criminal charge is imposed for a strike only in unusual circumstances. A good example of the effect of the combination of jurisdiction and remedies is the altering of the status of injunctions. As the power to obtain injunctions changed, so did the relative strengths of the parties.

Early Developments. In the early years of this country, here as well as abroad, the production system consisted of craftsmen who performed a job from start to finish, such as a carpenter building an entire house. Each man had to do everything necessary for life by himself until the emergence of the idea that it was more efficient to divide the work up and share the results. Craftsmen tended to work in small groups and because of the specialization, among other things, they became known by their trades and hence the origin of names such as "Taylor" and "Smith" (wonder what a Zepke did?).

To control their trade, craftsmen used slaves, indentured servants, and apprentices, with the latter becoming the most popular. The Philadelphia printers' action in 1786 is usually considered the first "strike"; as might be imagined, it involved a wage problem where the printers wanted a minimum wage of $6.00 per week.

Localized labor organizations sprang up around the country, but judicial reaction to them was not favorable as they were considered a criminal conspiracy. The danger of being labeled a criminal via a criminal conspiracy was a tremendous hindrance to union members and leaders.

The depressions of the 1830's and the late 1850's hurt the attempts by unions to organize significant numbers of employees. The attempts in the early 1850's survived and were the first beginnings of national unions. The Civil War was a difficult time for labor as was the depression of the 1870's.

One of the few unions that survived the combination of these events was the Noble Order of the Knights of Labor, organized in the late 1860's by the tailors. The Knights tried to combat the evils of the new industrial society through size of membership, for they equated size with power. In the 1880's the Knights grew to 700,000 members by incorporating local unions of all types into a higher organized confederation at the national level. Ironically, the philosophy of accepting such divergent groups that caused the Knights to grow so large eventually caused its decrease in membership during the 1890's, because the leaders could not satisfy all the factions within the Knights and this, along with some other factors, led to the downfall of the organization. By 1900 it had in effect disappeared.

The AFL. Samuel Gompers had been one who had disagreed with the Knights' philosophy of representing such divergent interests. He was instrumental in combining some national craft unions into the American Federation of Labor in 1886, with himself as president. This initial step is indicative of the strong influence that Gompers had on labor relations for almost forty years.

The AFL's philosophy was to rely on the collective bargaining process to achieve gains through negotiations, and to make the negotiations more effective, exclusive jurisdiction for each union was attempted. Each member union represented a single skilled craft only (to prevent one of the problems that arose with the Knights' attempts to represent everyone). Thus, the AFL was a federation of craft unions, and the federation acted in matters of common interest to all members.

Judicial Action. The criminal-conspiracy doctrine that had been applied to unions was limited by *Commonwealth* v. *Hunt* (4 Metc. (Mass.) 111), an 1842 case stating that justifiable objectives legitimated the union's attempt to gain a closed-shop requirement. Limiting and eventually removing the stigma of being labeled a criminal for labor activities was a big step in the evolution of labor law.

In the 1880's, the courts began to recognize civil rather than criminal remedies in actions against unions. The unions' actions were permitted as long as they were not "inimical to the public welfare," did not involve the use of force to compel membership, or were not for an improper objective, where the court decided what was proper. The injunction (a court order to cease a given activity) arose as a powerful tool, as it was an enforceable court order to prevent certain union actions. Judges evaluated the objectives of the unions in light of antitrust laws and local statutes, and they might issue an injunction against the union, perhaps even ex parte (where one party is not even present). The controlling factor was the objectives of the unions, and the classic case was *Vegelahn v. Guntner*, 167 Mass. 92, 44 N.E. 1077 (1896), because the decision illustrated the thinking of the times and the dissent represented the thinking of the future. The case is presented at the end of this chapter.

Legislation before 1920. In the late 1800's labor had begun to achieve some changes by lobbying, and although the changes were not tremendously comprehensive, they did indicate labor's concern and showed that its efforts towards legislation would be expanded. The Sherman Antitrust Act of 1890 was aimed at business and was an attempt to stop monopolization and restraint of trade, but ironically the Act was initially applied against labor organizations. The Act specifically applied to "groups of persons," and unions were held to be "groups of persons," whereas the legal fiction that an entire corporation is a single "person" (thus not a group of persons) protected corporations.

Railway legislation was an important step and was caused by several strikes between 1886 and 1894, which spurred action by the federal government and Congress. During one strike (the Pullman strike), the Attorney General obtained an injunction against the union to prevent interference with the workers "by threats, persuasion, force, or violence," and the Supreme Court (*In re Debs*, 158 U.S. 564) in 1895 upheld the right of the federal government to intervene under the commerce clause and the power to establish post offices. This was a very important step as it gave the U.S. government jurisdiction in certain instances. Congress passed the Erdman Act of 1898 which applied only to employees engaged in the operation of interstate trains and also included a provision for voluntary arbitration. In 1908 the Supreme Court held the Erdman Act unconstitutional (*Adair v. U.S.*, 208 U.S. 161) because among other reasons it felt that the commerce clause did not empower Congress to regulate employer-employee relationships (as they did not affect interstate commerce). It is important to note that railroads had been given special legislation, and this concept is continued today via the Railway Labor Act of 1926.

Regarding those not involved in railroads, the "Danbury Hatters" case (*Loewe v. Lawlor*, 208 U.S. 278) in 1908 discouraged unions by declaring that the Sherman Antitrust Act prohibited "any combination whatever to secure action which essentially obstructs the free flow of commerce between the States." Following this Supreme Court case, many lower courts prohibited all union activity and thus helped to provide the impetus for the Clayton Antitrust Act of 1914 which labor hailed as its "Magna Charta." The Clayton Act provided that the antitrust laws should not be construed to prohibit the existence of labor organizations or to prevent them from "lawfully carrying out the legitimate objects thereof." The Act also barred the use of injunctions by federal courts in actions between an employer and employees if the terms of employment were involved. Thus the powerful weapon of the injunction was limited.

The Labor Movement, 1900–1920. In the early 1900's the AFL grew rapidly and achieved a membership of almost 2,000,000 by 1913. Union membership in general grew from approximately 2,500,000 in 1914 to 5,000,000 in 1920, partly thanks to the Clayton Act of 1914. Federal controls enacted during World War I helped labor, but the violent coal and steel strikes of 1919 caused unions to suffer a setback. Over 300,000 steel workers went on strike and public sympathy was heavily on the side of management. The strike was broken within three months. This result plus the adverse publicity slowed the expansion of unions to almost zero.

The 1920's. During the early 1920's there was a recession which, when combined with management's activities, led to a decrease in the size of the AFL but an increase in company-dominated union membership. Management's activities included commencing programs such as group life insurance, medical plans, and improved grievance procedures, and when these were integrated with high wages, some of the incentives for unionization decreased. Management tried to become fairer in its approach to situations by becoming less subjective and more objective. There were also managers who became more scientific in their approach to management and introduced time and motion studies as well as standards for many jobs.

In the 1920's the Supreme Court severely limited the effect of the Clayton Act by segregating the antitrust standards applied to business from those applied to labor. In 1925 the Court upheld an injunction against a union's activities by holding that a secondary boycott was not trying to achieve a legitimate objective (*Duplex Printing Co.* v. *Deering*, 225 U.S. 443). The Court also held that the Clayton Act did not legalize the activities of a labor combination that was otherwise unlawful and that to be protected the parties had to be in a proximate relation to a controversy, which parties to a secondary boycott were not.

In *Bedford Cut Stone Co.* v. *Journeymen Stone Cutters Association* (274 U.S. 37) the Supreme Court in 1927 permitted some actions by management that it had rejected as applied to unions. An injunction was permitted against a legitimate union goal by finding that the union's tactics violated the Sherman Antitrust Act by restraining interstate commerce.

The Railway Labor Act of 1926. The interstate character of the railroads and the difficulties experienced by the industry spurred passage of the first peacetime effort to spell out detailed rules and regulations for union-management bargaining, with the aim being to encourage the bargaining process by providing stimulants for it. The Railway Labor Act imposed a duty on both parties to make and maintain agreements, and if this failed, there was created a mediation board with the power to serve and to offer voluntary arbitration. If the President felt that a dispute would interfere with essential rail service, he could appoint an investigatory board.

In 1930 the Supreme Court upheld the constitutionality of the Railway Labor Act (*Texas & N.O. Ry.* v. *Brotherhood of Railway & S.S. Clerks*, 281 U.S. 556). With some amendments today, the Act is still controlling in the railroad and airline industries (via a 1936 amendment).

Labor from the 1930's. The Knights of Labor had had difficulties in trying to represent both skilled and unskilled labor, and the AFL consequently had limited itself to skilled members. The shift to a more industrialized economy caused an increase in unskilled workers who were not represented, so spokesmen such as John L. Lewis arose to try to organize these unskilled groups. These leaders challenged the two key principles of national union autonomy and and exclusive jurisdiction that were important to the AFL. National union autonomy is the right for each union to govern itself. Exclusive jurisdiction is when the unions establish rules whereby a single union, in order to prevent fighting among the unions, is given the exclusive right to organize a given labor force; often the unions will enter a "no-raiding agreement" to prevent other unions from trying to organize the same labor force.

At the 1935 AFL convention, the factions that wanted to keep the AFL the same had a split with the new groups that followed Lewis. After a vote won by the former, the Lewis group formed the "Committee for Industrial Organization," within the AFL structure. The Committee was charged with violating the AFL constitution and was suspended from the AFL, so in 1937 the ▸Congress of Industrial Organizations (CIO) was formally organized as an independent structure of unions. As might be expected with such a start, there was feuding between the unions which caused problems internally and with the regulatory agencies. Further problems arose as the Communist Party was able to reach positions of power in several CIO unions.

Several factors, including the Depression, World War II, and the common bond of representing labor to management, tended to draw the AFL and the CIO closer together. In 1955 the AFL-CIO confederation drew up a constitution that completed a merger which had been approaching since the early 1950's.

The two issues, autonomy and exclusive jurisdiction, that caused the CIO to be formed, were dealt with in the new constitution. Presently, the national union autonomy is preserved, yet the Executive Council of the AFL-CIO can suspend member unions where corruption or Communist influence exists. Racial discrimination is prohibited, but for this latter restriction the remedy of suspension is not available. Exclusive jurisdiction was a difficult topic for which to enact a set of operating rules, so no-raiding agreements became mandatory and yet the craft and industrial unions were both recognized. Problems continue to arise as new jobs are created, or worse yet, as old jobs represented by two different unions are combined into one job. An example of this is where carpenters used to hang doors and metalworkers work with metal, so who should work with the new metal doors? There are more disputes that arise out of this type of problems, called jurisdictional disputes, than out of any other aspect of unions' conduct towards each other.

With the exception of governmental employees or those covered by the

Railway Labor Act, today there are four basic acts that control management-union relationships. These four acts are discussed in the following four sections.

The Norris-LaGuardia Act. The Norris-LaGuardia Act was passed in 1932 (during the Depression) to assist unions. Legislators felt that they, and particularly the judicial system, had not sufficiently aided the bargaining process. Some of the key provisions of the Act were to remove the power of federal courts to enjoin coercive activities by unions which did not involve fraud or violence, and to exempt certain labor activities from federal antitrust laws. Since this Act, antitrust laws are used against unions only where a collusion between labor and management exists. The aim of the Act was to make the workers free to decide on whether or not to organize. Although there were no affirmative obligations placed upon employers to negotiate with unions, the Act was effective in removing many of the prohibitions that had been used to prevent unions from exerting economic pressures.

The National Labor Relations Act. The National Labor Relations Act, commonly known as the Wagner Act (20 U.S. Code, §151-166), was passed in 1935 to equalize the bargaining power between employers and employees. The Act came during the Depression and was meant to restrict the employer's powers, which were felt to be too great. A major criticism has been that this Act went too far by making only an employer's acts unfair practices. The National Labor Relations Board was created to administer the Act, and with some changes this Act and the Board are still a principal factor in most labor disputes.

The Labor Management Relations Act. The Labor Management Relations Act, commonly known as the Taft-Hartley Act, was passed in 1947. The aim was to again try to balance the forces of labor and management. Many of the provisions of the 1935 Act that permitted various union conduct, such as a closed shop (union membership required for employment), were repealed. Unions were also held to be able to commit unfair labor practices.

The 1935 Act, as amended in 1947, is the basic labor law for employee-employer relationships with respect to organizing and subsequent bargaining. This Act is covered in detail in this text, and it is important to emphasize that the aim is to provide rules and regulations for the organizational process and the resulting relationships, so the coverage is almost completely restricted to activities involving unions.

The Act (hereafter when "the Act" is referred to, the reference is to the 1935 Act as amended in 1947) had two aims. First, to guarantee employees the right to organize and bargain collectively through representatives of their own choosing or to refrain from such activities. Second, to keep that right inviolate by declaring certain acts of employers and unions to be unfair labor practices.

The rights of the employees are set forth in Section 7, which reads as follows:

"Employees shall have the right to self-organization, to form, join, or assist labor organizations, to bargain collectively through representatives of their own choosing, and to engage in other concerted activities for the purpose of collective bargaining or other mutual aid or protection, and shall also have the right to refrain from any or all of such activities except to the extent that such right may be affected by an agreement requiring membership in a labor organization as a condition of employment as authorized in Section 8(a)(3)."

These broad principles are defined more closely in other parts of the Act, sometimes in terms of what is permitted conduct and sometimes in terms of what is not permitted. An example of the latter is the most cited portion of the Act, Section 8, which lists unfair labor practices.

This Act and its amendments are outlined in the chapter entitled "Statutory Regulation" (Chapter 3).

Labor Management Reporting and Disclosure Act of 1959. The Labor Management Reporting and Disclosure Act of 1959 had several aims, with the following being the major one:

> "The Congress . . . finds, from recent investigations in the labor and management fields, that there have been a number of instances of breach of trust, corruption, disregard of the rights of individual employees, and other failures to observe high standards of responsibility and ethical conduct which require further and supplementary legislation that will afford necessary protection of the rights and interests of employees and the public generally as they relate to the activities of labor organizations, employers, labor relations consultants, and their officers and representatives.
>
> "One of the means used by Congress for accomplishing the goals of the Labor-Management Reporting and Disclosure Act is the requirement of reporting to the government on various union affairs and on certain transactions between unions and management. The reporting requirements apply to unions, union officers, union employees, union trusteeships, employers, employer associations, and labor relations consultants.
>
> "The other means used by Congress to gain the ends sought by the law is the regulation of various internal union affairs. Such regulation covers union elections, rights of union members, misappropriation of union funds, imposition of trusteeships, and personnel of union staffs."

The provisions of this Act are included throughout this text in the relevant subject matter, with the chapter on a member's rights within the union being one of the principal places in which coverage appears. The Act is important in that it empowers the Secretary of Labor to become involved, and it permits the National Labor Relations Board (hereafter called the Board) to delegate its authority in election cases to regional directors.

Cases. The legislators pass statutes with general wording so they may be applied to a variety of situations while maintaining the intent of the legislators. The courts interpret the statutory language in light of the legislative intent and apply this to specific situations, so the interpretations of the courts are vitally important. To present these interpretations and to illustrate the type of reasoning and actual language used by judges, cases on some of the topics included in the chapter are presented at the end of the chapters. These cases do not alter the law as presented within the chapter, but rather merely illustrate some specific applications by the courts.

Space requirements dictate that the cases be summarized in a sentence or two in the body of the chapters, condensed at the end of each chapter, or if particularly important and/or short enough, then the case is presented in its entirety at the end of the chapter. The emphasis of condensed versions of the cases is on the points relevant to that chapter, and the omissions may include all or any part of the facts, the opinions, or the dissent.

Vegelahn v. *Guntner et al.*

167 Mass. 92, 44 N.E. 1077 (1896)
Supreme Judicial Court of Massachusetts
Suffolk, Oct. 27, 1896

Held: In this case, decided in 1896, the majority's opinion reflects the thinking of
    that time, when it was a crime to exert economic pressure by picketing, and
    while there is some discussion of threats of personal injury, the case turned on
    the picketing.

    By granting an injunction, the courts prohibit the conduct in question
    and if the injunction is violated then the violating party may be held in contempt
    of court and fined or jailed. Because injunctions are so effective in stopping the
    conduct in question, the permitted uses of them has varied widely over the
    years as legislators have sought to establish fair guidelines for their use by the
    courts. Today injunctions are permitted but only if irreparable harm will result
    if an injunction is not issued.

    Justice Holmes, who wrote many opinions that are still cited, wrote the
    dissent in this case and this more truly represents the modern approach of
    permitting but regulating the right to picket.

Opinion:
Injunction—Conspiracy to Injure Business
    The maintenance of a patrol of two men in front of plaintiff's premises, in
furtherance of a conspiracy to prevent any workmen from entering into, or continuing
in, his employment, will be enjoined, though such workmen are not under contract
to work for plaintiff. Field, C. J., and Holmes, J., dissenting.
    ALLEN, J. The principal question in this case is whether the defendants should
be enjoined against maintaining the patrol. The report shows that, following upon a
strike of the plaintiff's workmen, the defendants conspired to prevent him from
getting workmen, and thereby to prevent him from carrying on his business, unless
and until he should adopt a certain schedule of prices. The means adopted were
persuasion and social pressure, threats of personal injury or unlawful harm conveyed
to persons employed or seeking employment, and a patrol of two men in front of the
plaintiff's factory, maintained from half past 6 in the morning till half past 5 in the
afternoon on one of the busiest streets of Boston.
    The defendants contend that these acts were justifiable, because they were only
seeking to secure better wages for themselves, by compelling the plaintiff to accept
their schedule of wages. This motive or purpose does not justify maintaining a patrol
in front of the plaintiff's premises, as a means of carrying out their conspiracy. A
combination among persons merely to regulate their own conduct is within allowable
competition, and is lawful, although others may be indirectly affected thereby. But a
combination to do injurious acts expressly directed to another, by way of intimidation
or constraint, either of himself or of persons employed or seeking to be employed by
him, is outside of allowable competition, and is unlawful.
    HOLMES, J., dissenting:
    The policy of allowing free competition justifies the intentional inflicting of
temporal damage, including the damage of interference with a man's business by
some means, when the damage is done, not for its own sake, but as an instrumentality
in reaching the end of victory in the battle of trade. In such a case it cannot matter
whether the plaintiff is the only rival of the defendant, and so is aimed at specially,
or is one of a class all of whom are hit. The only debatable ground is the nature of
the means by which such damage may be inflicted. We all agree that it cannot be

11

done by force or threats of force. We all agree, I presume, that it may be done by persuasion to leave a rival's shop, and come to the defendant's. It may be done by the refusal or withdrawal of various pecuniary advantages, which, apart from this consequence, are within the defendant's lawful control. It may be done by the withdrawal of, or threat to withdraw, such advantages from third persons who have a right to deal or not to deal with the plaintiff, as a means of inducing them not to deal with him either as customers or servants. *Commonwealth* v. *Hunt*, 4 Metc. (Mass.) 111 (1842). I have seen the suggestion made that the conflict between employers and employed was not competition. But I venture to assume that none of my brethren would rely on that suggestion. If the policy on which our law is founded is too narrowly expressed in the term "free competition," we may substitute "free struggle for life." Certainly, the policy is not limited to struggles between persons of the same class, competing for the same end. It applies to all conflicts of temporal interests.

If it be true that workingmen may combine with a view, among other things, to getting as much as they can for their labor, just as capital may combine with a view to getting the greatest possible return, it must be true that, when combined, they have the same liberty that combined capital has, to support their interests by argument, persuasion, and the bestowal or refusal of those advantages which they otherwise lawfully control. I can remember when many people thought that, apart from violence or breach of contract, strikes were wicked, as organized refusals to work. I suppose that intelligent economists and legislators have given up that notion today. I feel pretty confident that they equally will abandon the idea that an organized refusal by workmen of social intercourse with a man who shall enter their antagonist's employ is unlawful, if it is dissociated from any threat of violence, and is made for the sole object of prevailing, if possible, in a contest with their employer about the rate of wages. The fact that the immediate object of the act by which the benefit to themselves is to be gained is to injure their antagonist does not necessarily make it unlawful, any more than when a great house lowers the price of goods for the purpose and with the effect of driving a smaller antagonist from the business.

3. Statutory Regulation

General. This chapter is aimed at providing an overall understanding of the Labor Management Relations Act of 1947. A significant portion of the rest of this text will analyze in detail the general principles presented in this chapter, and the appendix contains the Act in full. One should obtain from this chapter an awareness of the nature of the behavior which the Act seeks to regulate and the scope of the Act in general. Notice that in this chapter the outline form used throughout the rest of the text is disregarded and the actual labeling used within the statute is used. This labeling is to prevent confusion when referring to the sections of the Act and to assist one in becoming familiar with the section numbers, so that if an 8(b)(4) violation is referenced one might have an easier time remembering what type of violation was committed.

National Labor Relations Board. The National Labor Relations Board has final authority over representation and unfair labor practice questions, subject to judicial review in some circumstances.

UNFAIR LABOR PRACTICES. If a Regional Director refuses to issue a complaint, an appeal to the General Counsel is possible. Usually a Regional Director will be the first to make a ruling with respect to a given situation. Once the General Counsel decides whether or not an unfair labor practice complaint shall be issued, there is no review of his decision.

To obtain enforcement, the NLRB must petition the appropriate court of appeals.

REPRESENTATION QUESTIONS. NLRB certifications of a union in a representation proceeding are not final orders, and hence since a court will review only final orders, a court review is not obtainable. However, if the employer does not obey the NLRB order, the certification can be tested by the Board filing a charge of a refusal to bargain against the employer.

National Labor Relations Act. It is worthwhile to outline the provisions of the Act to present its scope and an overview of its provisions. (Again, please note that the labeling of the items is as they appear in the Act, also that this is a short form and in some places ideas are presented which are not given as complete sentences but are meant merely to demonstrate what the Act deals with.)

SECTION 1 (under Title I). The policy of the statute and its constitutional basis.

SECTION 2. Definitions.

SECTIONS 3-6. The operation of the NLRB.

SECTION 7. The rights of the employees.

SECTIONS 8(a) and 8(b).

a. *Employer Unfair Practices.* The unfair labor practices are set forth in Section 8. Employer unfair practices, virtually unchanged from the original (Wagner) Act, may be summarized as follows:

8(a)(1). To interfere with the rights guaranteed in Section 7.

8(a)(2). To dominate or interfere with a union or to contribute support, financial or otherwise, to it.

8(a)(3). To encourage or discourage membership in a union by discrimination in regard to hire or tenure of employment.

8(a)(4). To discharge or otherwise discriminate against an employee because he has filed charges or given testimony to the NLRB.

8(a)(5). To refuse to bargain collectively.

b. *Union Unfair Practices.* Union unfair practices may be summarized as follows:

8(b)(1). To restrain or coerce either employees in the exercise of the rights guaranteed in Section 7, or an employer in the selection of his bargaining or grievance representatives.

8(b)(2). To cause an employer to discriminate against an employee in violation of Section 8(a)(3), or against an employee to whom membership in the union has been denied or terminated on some ground other than nonpayment of dues.

8(b)(3). To refuse to bargain collectively.

8(b)(4). To engage in strikes and boycotts for purposes proscribed by the Act.

8(b)(5). To exact excessive or discriminatory fees or dues under union-shop contracts.

8(b)(6). To exact compensation from an employer for services not performed or not to be performed.

8(b)(7). To picket or threaten to picket to force an employer to recognize or bargain with a labor organization.

SECTION 8(c). The employer free speech provision: An employer may express his views so long as his message does not contain a threat of reprisal or promise of benefits.

SECTION 8(d). The parties must bargain in good faith, but they need not reach an agreement.

SECTION 8(e). Entering into a hot cargo agreement is an unfair labor practice for both the employer and the union. Hot cargo refers to items produced by an employer with whom the union has a disagreement, so the union tries to influence another employer to treat the items as "too hot to handle" or as hot cargo.

SECTION 9. Representation procedures are covered in this section.

SECTION 10.

a. The Board has power to prevent unfair labor practices listed in Section 8.

b. The Board can call a hearing of a complaint within six months.

c. The Board may take more testimony or may rule.

d. The Board can change its mind until a charge with transcript has been filed in court.

e. The Board can petition a court for backing of its rules.

f. A person can petition the court against the Board.

g. Commencement of proceedings (e) or (f) shall not operate as a stay of the Board's order.

h. This Act shall not limit equity courts.

i. Petitions filed under this Act shall be heard expeditiously, if possible within ten days.

j. The Board shall have the power to petition a court upon filing of a complaint to seek a temporary injunction.

k. The Board is directed to hear a charge under 8(b)(4)(D) (a charge of forcing an employer to assign work to one union rather than another union).

l. The Board shall petition, if preliminary investigation warrants, the courts for an injunction if the charge is an 8(b)(4)(A), (B), or (C), or 8(e), or 8(b)(7).

SECTIONS 11-12. Additional NLRB procedures.

SECTION 13. Guarantees the right of employees to strike.

SECTION 14. Section 14(b) authorizes the states to enact statutes that outlaw union shops.

TITLE II SECTION 202(a) establishes the Federal Mediation and Conciliation Service.

TITLE III SECTION 301 allows suits to enforce collective bargaining agreements in federal or state courts.

TITLE III SECTION 303 allows one injured by a violation of 8(b)(4) to maintain an action in federal court.

Miscellaneous on Unfair Practices. Section 7 establishes a broad principle that is difficult to define exactly, so Congress described in Section 8 conduct that does not meet the Section 7 principle and hence is an unfair labor practice. Thus, the approach is that it is easier to define what does not conform to Section 7 than to issue a complete definition of the principle. A considerable amount of this presentation will deal with Section 8 and what constitutes an unfair labor practice.

4. Resolving Disagreements

Procedures

GENERAL. Both parties often commence discussions with aims and views different from each other's—resolving these differences is what the bargaining process is all about. So it is worthwhile to consider the techniques developed to assist the parties in reaching an equitable solution to disputes that arise before or under the collective bargaining agreement. Remember that the purpose is to provide a vehicle for enabling the parties to reach a solution which is mutually satisfactory via collective bargaining, so a third party is employed only when the parties fail to resolve the issues on their own. The type of mechanism applied to the disagreement depends on several variables, such as the industry (the Railway Labor Act has its own procedures), the effect on third parties (a secondary boycott may call for expedited action), the effect on the community (a strike by garbage workers may be held to be an emergency), the action taken by the parties (violence), the collective bargaining agreement (it may call for binding arbitration), and a variety of other factors that in theory are not controlling but in a given situation may assume paramount importance. The one-party actions such as strikes are not covered here as they are covered elsewhere in detail, and they are also not means of solving disputes but pressure tactics to force one of the other means.

NEGOTIATIONS. The preferred method of reaching agreement on the issues is to negotiate. The aim of the labor laws is to promote the procedure of negotiations, and agreements reached will usually be given great weight unless they violate a law or public policy.

MEDIATION AND CONCILIATION. Mediation is where a third party (the mediator) participates in the dispute negotiations in order to assist the parties to resolve their disagreements. The mediator may meet with the parties separately or jointly and he tries to find areas of possible compromise. The mediator makes no decisions for the parties but rather he acts as a neutral expert to bring the parties together and sometimes to act as a fact-finder, but his recommendations do not bind the parties.

If the third party who intervenes in the labor dispute has the power to impose his decision, then the procedure is arbitration, and if the third party can only suggest a solution then the procedure is conciliation.

The Labor Management Relations Act created the Federal Mediation and Conciliation Service (FMCS) as an independent federal agency to assist in the process, and many states have similar agencies. The FMCS usually deals with two major types of cases: (1) disputes affecting national health or safety and (2) other serious disputes between unions and employers engaged in activities affecting interstate commerce. Typically, the parties will request the FMCS's assistance but if the dispute causes a "substantial interruption" to interstate commerce, then the FMCS may extend its facilities upon its own motion (LMRA, Section 203(b)).

The National Mediation Board (NMB) was created by the Railway Labor Act and applies to the railway and airlines industries. Although the NMB's decisions are not enforceable by court action, there is emphasis placed on this means as a way to prevent the potentially damaging effect on third parties of self-help tactics in the transportation industry. If the mediation fails, the mediator must induce the parties to arbitrate, and if the parties refuse, and the dispute may cause major disruptions to transportation, then the mediator must advise the President of the United States, who may create an emergency board to investigate the dispute (Railway Labor Act, Section 10).

The National Mediation Board may become involved with: (1) disputes concerning rates of pay, rules, or working conditions; or (2) interpretation of agreements reached through mediation; or (3) to a limited extent, representation disputes among employees.

VOLUNTARY ARBITRATION. Voluntary arbitration is a method of resolving disputes by empowering a neutral third party to investigate, hear witnesses, and render a binding opinion on the parties. The aim is to provide a relatively speedy and inexpensive procedure for settling disputes without the parties resorting to self-help, and it is also very useful in resolving minor disputes which are troublesome but not of the magnitude to generate more drastic methods. "Voluntary" refers to the agreeing to arbitrate the situation, but once the arbitration procedure is agreed upon, then the arbitrator's decision is binding and, unless he abuses his discretion, the courts will enforce his decision.

The National Labor Relations Board usually defers to the arbitrator's decision but retains the ultimate power, and in the "Steelworkers Trilogy," a series of cases handed down the same day by the Supreme Court and all involving the steelworkers (363 U.S. 564, 363 U.S. 593, 363 U.S. 574, all three June 20, 1960) the Court held that a federal court, in determining the enforceability of arbitration awards, may not inquire into the merits of the awards. The arbitrator is supposed to restrict himself to interpreting the contract and the courts will not investigate the merits to ascertain whether his interpretation was correct, even if the contract has expired, as it had in one of the Trilogy cases. The Courts favor arbitration as Justice Douglas said in one of the Trilogy cases:

> "An order to arbitrate the particular grievance should not be denied unless it may be said with positive assurance that the arbitration clause is not susceptible to an interpretation that covers the asserted dispute. Doubts should be resolved in favor of coverage."

Meeting this test in order not to arbitrate is very difficult in light of the Court's refusal to look at the merits of an arbitrator's decision. Some of the restrictions on an arbitrator's powers are discussed in the Collyer decision at the end of this chapter. An arbitration is less formal than a legal trial and the arbitrator's decision is enforceable by a court.

Almost anyone can be selected as an arbitrator, but most contracts call for one certified by the American Arbitration Association (AAA) or the National Academy of Arbitrators. Sometimes tripartite boards are provided for in the contract, but this is unusual.

Arbitration is a creation of the grievance procedure to permit the unions to give up their right to strike in exchange for arbitration, which is a replacement for a strike and not a law suit.

Three things are necessary for arbitration to occur:

a. A contract must provide that one party can take the grievance to arbitration. If two parties are necessary to take to arbitration, then the process is not effective.
b. The contract must have a clause that limits the power of the arbitrator to terms of the contract. This is important as the arbitrator may only apply the contract and not modify it or exceed its scope.
c. The contract must have a very precise method for selecting an arbitrator, for if a party can continuously object to the selections, then he can make the arbitration clause not effective.

Almost any dispute under the contract may be arbitrated, including whether or not a particular dispute should be arbitrated, and many contracts permit the employer to utilize the process. Arbitration is an important tool, and if the contract provides for it, then a party may bring a law suit to force the other party to arbitrate.

COMPULSORY ARBITRATION. Compulsory arbitration is arbitration compelled by state or federal statute, rather than under contract as in voluntary arbitration. The arbitrators' decisions are also binding, as in voluntary arbitration, but in order for the statute to overrule the principle of not forcing the parties to bargain, the dispute must have major consequences for third parties. Voluntary arbitration occurs much more frequently than compulsory.

ADMINISTRATIVE ACTION. The dispute may be of such a nature that an administrative body has been given jurisdiction by Congress, either federal or state, to deal with it. The administrative bodies are empowered by Congress to fact-find and to reach a binding decision enforceable by court action. More details of administrative actions are provided throughout this text, usually by citing the major agency involved in labor disputes, the National Labor Relations Board. Agencies are becoming more numerous at the federal, state, and even city level. For instance, there is an Equal Employment Opportunity Commission at the federal level, and a Human Relations Commission at the state and in some instances also at the city level. So the same person may bring several actions arising out of the same incident.

COURT ACTION. Court action is in most conditions a last resort for the parties, with some exceptions where court action may occur before other remedies are exhausted. The exceptions are very few and must be specifically provided for by statute or court case.

The injunction (an order to cease a given mode of conduct) is a court action that has generated a great deal of controversy over the years because it effectively terminates the other party's principal means of protest.

LEGISLATION. Either party may on a continuing basis lobby for its cause, and when it convinces enough legislators that it is correct, then there are some legislative changes enacted. There obviously have been too many statutes to discuss them here, so the sole purpose of this section is to remind the reader that legislation is a method of settling disputes even though it is rarely used for a single dispute; it is used for large ongoing disputes or as a reaction to a dispute.

Hierarchy of Rules

THE CONSTITUTION. When the English settled "the colonies," they brought with them their concepts and experiences concerning law. So the original American law was based on English law, much of which was decided by courts rather than legislatures, the other main source of laws. The English case law was controlling, even after the Revolutionary War, because the American judges adopted it as an available, developed form of rules that had a rational basis. Even after the adoption of the U.S. Constitution, the English law was followed so long as it did not conflict with the Constitution. The Constitution is the supreme law of the land and any rule that conflicts with it will be held to be unconstitutional and hence invalid and will not be enforced. However, the Constitution, in order to represent the people in so many aspects of life over so long a period of time, had to be sketched in general terms and hence is subject to different interpretations by reasonable persons, and this is where so much controversy arises. No judge will uphold something he feels is unconstitutional, but the ultimate test of constitutionality lies with the Supreme Court.

LEGISLATION. The legislatures, within the bounds of the Constitution, have the power to pass laws which, under the theory of separation of powers, the courts interpret and the executive branch enforces. If the legislators have not passed any statutes that deal with a subject, then if the case law (called common law) is constitutional it is controlling. After the legislature passes a statute, there will develop a series of cases in which the courts interpret the statute in light of the very specific circumstances in which cases arise. These cases will be decided by attempting to ascertain the intent of the legislators, and if these later cases conflict with the cases from prior to the statute, the later cases will control if the statute is constitutional. The theory is that the legislature has the power to pass laws which must be followed, but if they have not passed any directly in point on an issue, then all that the courts have on which to base their finding is prior case law.

In order to deal with such a variety of concepts as they must, the legislature will sometimes pass a statute that establishes guidelines for legislative intent as applied to some particular area of concern, and also establishes an administrative agency to enforce the legislative intent. The National Labor Relations Act established such intent and an agency to enforce it—the National Labor Relations Board.

EXECUTIVE BOARD. The executive branch expresses the President's wishes either by an Executive Order or by an order emanating from a presidential appointment in either a staff or agency position. For instance, the Equal Employment Opportunity Commission can issue orders that have executive enforcement. The orders from the executive branch can be tested in court and possibly held invalid as exceeding the power of the issuing party.

ADMINISTRATIVE AGENCIES. Administrative agencies are sometimes thought to be quasi-legislative or quasi-judicial in that they possess the power to investigate the conduct and also have an internal process to pass judgment on it. If the defendant does not agree with the outcome, he can petition a Federal Appellate Court for a review of the holding.

Such a right to appeal is either based on the Act creating the agency or, if this is silent, the Administrative Procedure Act has been held to grant this right, but the right is limited to be used only after the internal administrative procedure has been exhausted (with an exception provided if this will cause harm or be futile), and the court review is limited to ascertaining whether the administrative body has exceeded its authority.

Note that the appeal is not to the lower federal court which weighs and establishes facts, but to the appellate court which accepts the facts as developed by the agency and rules on the agency's dealings with the law and facts. If the agency has not exceeded its discretion, then the ruling stands.

The agencies are very powerful and fighting a holding can be very costly and time-consuming. The court may return a case to the agency, which may again do something that the defendant appeals to the court, which may again return it to the agency. The agencies may make rulings, but they must look to the courts to enforce them if they are challenged.

THE COURTS. The federal court system permits actions to be brought at the trial level if a federal law is involved. The case proceeds through the federal system, but if an appeal of a federal agency is the style of the action, then the appellate court is the court system's first contact. The Supreme Court either refuses to hear a case, in which event the lower court ruling stands, or if a constitutional issue is involved, the Court may hear the case, which is referred to as "granting certiorari." The Supreme Court is the final word on any court action and sometimes must decide cases where on similar facts two different Appellate Courts (called circuit courts in the federal system) have reached different conclusions, both of which the respective courts feel are the correct interpretation of the status of the law.

STATE V. FEDERAL. The Constitution gives the federal Congress the right to control matters affecting interstate commerce, and by implication the power to control the rest of business activities is left to the states. The Congress's and courts' interpretation of what affects interstate commerce has been expanding, especially in the 1960's when civil rights activities were prevalent. Discussions of whether something affects interstate commerce are often found in cases, especially in the earlier cases of labor law. If the federal Congress passes a law, then this preempts the state law if the two conflict, but state law can be used to supplement federal law.

The same preemptive principle applies to agencies created by federal or state legislators or executive branches. Concerning agencies, it is interesting to note that if an alleged discrimination occurs, then the alleged aggrieved party can bring a complaint under both state and federal agencies for the same incident and thus have it investigated twice.

SUMMARY. The courts decide the interpretation of any of the following and they are listed in descending order:

 a. Constitution
 b. Statute
 c. Supreme Court
 d. Lower Court
 e. Administrative Bodies

The state level is similar, with the preemptive doctrine between state and federal being as previously stated.

Remedies of the NLRB. The NLRA is not a criminal statute but is a remedial law that is intended to prevent and remedy unfair labor practices rather than to punish the person responsible for them. The Board is authorized by Section 10(c) "to take such affirmative action including reinstatement of employees with or without back pay as will effectuate the policies of the Act."

The Board's aims are to eliminate the unfair labor practice and to undo the effects of the violation. The Board has considerable discretion in selecting a particular remedy or set of remedies, and some typical ones issued to employers are:

 * Disestablish an employer-dominated union
 * Offer certain named individuals reinstatement and back pay
 * Bargain collectively with a certain union as the exclusive representative of the employees

Some typical orders to unions are:

 * Refund dues illegally collected
 * Bargain collectively upon request

The Board's orders usually include a direction requiring the posting of notices in the employer's plant or union's office notifying the employees that certain conduct will cease and stating any other remedies imposed.

Special proceedings are required in certain types of cases such as jurisdictional disputes under Section 10(k) and injunction proceedings under Sections 10(l) and 10(j). Section 10(k) involves charges of 8(b)(4)(D) violations; the section prohibits unions from striking to compel an employer to assign work to a particular union.

Section 10(1) provides that charges involving certain boycotts, picketing, and work stoppages, as defined in Sections 8(b)(4)(A), (B), (C), all three sub-paragraphs of 8(b)(7) and 8(e), be given priority handling, and if the Board finds a reasonable cause to believe that a charge is true then the Board is required to petition the U.S. District Court for an injunction to prohibit the activity until the Board can fully investigate.

Section 10(j) allows the Board to petition for an injunction after complaint has been issued.

If an employer or union fails to comply with an order from the Board, the Board under 10(e) may petition the U.S. Court of Appeals for a court decree enforcing the order.

Section 10(f) provides that a review of the Board's order may be obtained from the circuit court of appeals, and the court may enforce the order, remand it to the Board for reconsideration, change it, or set it aside entirely. If the court enforces the Board's order then failure to comply may be punishable by fine or imprisonment for contempt of court.

Textile Workers Union of America v. Lincoln Mills of Alabama

353 U.S. 448, L.ed.2d 972, 77 S.Ct. 912 (1957)

Held: A suit for a violation of a contract between an employer and a labor organization in an industry affecting commerce may be brought, in a federal court, and in addition to this, 301 of the LMRA also provides that the federal courts may fashion a body of federal law and this need not apply conflicting state law.

Arbitration is a favored technique and is provided for with specific performance, for it is considered the unions' comparable right to managements' obtaining a no-strike clause.

The Norris-LaGuardia Act did not withdraw the federal courts' power to compel enforcement of collective bargaining arbitration.

Opinion:

Mr. Justice Douglas delivered the opinion of the Court.

Petitioner-union entered into a collective bargaining agreement in 1953 with respondent-employer, the agreement to run one year and from year to year thereafter, unless terminated on specified notices. The agreement provided that there would be no strikes or work stoppages and that grievances would be handled pursuant to a specified procedure. The last step in the grievance procedure—a step that could be taken by either party—was arbitration.

This controversy involves several grievances that concern work loads and work assignments. The grievances were processed through the various steps in the grievance procedure and were finally denied by the employer. The union requested arbitration, and the employer refused. Thereupon the union brought this suit in the District Court to compel arbitration.

The District Court concluded that it had jurisdiction and ordered the employer to comply with the grievance arbitration provisions of the collective bargaining agreement. The Court of Appeals reversed by a divided vote. 230 F.2d 81. It held that, although the District Court had jurisdiction to entertain the suit, the court had no authority founded either in federal or state law to grant the relief. The case is here on a petition for a writ of certiorari which we granted because of the importance of the problem and the contrariety of views in the courts. 352 U.S. 821, 1 L.ed.2d 46, 77 S.Ct. 54.

The starting point of our inquiry is §301 of the Labor Management Relations Act of 1947, 61 Stat. 156, 29 USC §185, which provides:

"(a) Suits for violation of contracts between an employer and a labor organization representing employees in an industry affecting commerce as defined in this chapter, or between any such labor organizations, may be brought in any district court of the United States having jurisdiction of the parties, without respect to the amount in controversy or without regard to the citizenship of the parties.

"(b) Any labor organization which represents employees in an industry affecting commerce as defined in this chapter and any employer whose activities affect commerce as defined in this chapter shall be bound by the acts of its agents. Any such labor organization may sue or be sued as an entity and in behalf of the employees whom it represents in the courts of the United States. Any money judgment against a labor organization in a district court of the United States shall be enforceable only against the organization as an entity and against its assets, and shall not be enforceable against any individual member or his assets."

There has been considerable litigation involving §301 and courts have construed it differently. There is one view that §301(a) merely gives federal district courts jurisdiction in controversies that involve labor organizations in industries affecting commerce, without regard to diversity of citizenship or the amount in controversy. Under that view §301(a) would not be the source of substantive law; it would neither supply federal law to resolve these controversies nor turn the federal judges to state law for answers to the questions. Other courts—the overwhelming number of them— hold that §301(a) is more than jurisdictional—that it authorizes federal courts to fashion a body of federal law for the enforcement of these collective bargaining agreements and includes within that federal law specific performance of promises to arbitrate grievances under collective bargaining agreements. Perhaps the leading decision representing that point of view is the one rendered by Judge Wyzanski in *Textile Workers Union* v. *American Thread Co.* (D.C. Mass.) 113 F. Supp. 137. That is our construction of §301(a), which means that the agreement to arbitrate grievance disputes, contained in this collective bargaining agreement, should be specifically enforced.

From the face of the Act it is apparent that §301(a) and §301(b) supplement one another. Section 301(b) makes it possible for a labor organization, representing employees in an industry affecting commerce, to sue and be sued as an entity in the federal courts. Section 301(b) in other words provides the procedural remedy lacking at common law. Section 301(a) certainly does something more than that. Plainly, it supplies the basis upon which the federal district courts may take jurisdiction and apply the procedural rule of §301(b). The question is whether §301(a) is more than jurisdictional. . . .

Congress was interested in promoting collective bargaining that ended with agreements not to strike.[1] The Senate Report, p. 16 states:

"If unions can break agreements with relative impunity, then such agreements do not tend to stabilize industrial relations. The execution of an agreement does not by itself promote industrial peace. The chief advantage which an employer can reasonably expect from a collective labor agreement is assurance of uninterrupted operation during the term of the agreement. Without some effective method of assuring freedom from economic warfare for the term of the agreement, there is little reason why an employer would desire to sign such a contract.

"Consequently, to encourage the making of agreements and to promote industrial peace through faithful performance by the parties, collective agreements affecting interstate commerce should be enforceable in the federal courts. Our amendment would provide for suits by unions as legal entities and against unions as legal entities in the Federal courts in disputes affecting commerce."

Thus collective bargaining contracts were made "equally binding and enforceable on both parties." . . .

Plainly the agreement to arbitrate grievance disputes is the quid pro quo for an agreement not to strike. Viewed in this light, the legislation does more than confer jurisdiction in the federal courts over labor organizations. It expresses a federal policy that federal courts should enforce these agreements on behalf of or against labor organizations and that industrial peace can be best obtained only in that way.

To be sure, there is a great medley of ideas reflected in the hearings, reports, and debates on this Act. Yet, to repeat, the entire tenor of the history indicates that the agreement to arbitrate grievance disputes was considered as quid pro quo of a no-strike agreement. And when in the House the debate narrowed to the question

---

[1] "In any event, it is certainly a point to be bargained over and any union with the status of 'representative' under the NLRA which has bargained in good faith with an employer should have no reluctance in including a no-strike clause if it intends to live up to the terms of the contract. The improvement that would result in the stability of industrial relations is, of course, obvious." S Rep No. 105, 80th Cong.

whether §301 was more than jurisdictional, it became abundantly clear that the purpose of the section was to provide the necessary legal remedies. Section 302 of the House bill, the substantial equivalent of the present §301, was being described by Mr. Hartley, the sponsor of the bill in the House:

"Mr. Barden. Mr. Chairman, I take this time for the purpose of asking the Chairman a question, and in asking the question I want it understood that it is intended to make a part of the record that may hereafter be referred to as history of the legislation.

"It is my understanding that section 302, the section dealing with equal responsibility under collective bargaining contracts in strike actions and proceedings in district courts contemplates not only the ordinary lawsuits for damages but also such other remedial proceedings, both legal and equitable, as might be appropriate in the circumstances; in other words, proceedings could, for example, be brought by the employers, the labor organizations, or interested individual employees under the Declaratory Judgments Act in order to secure declarations from the Court of legal rights under the contract.

"Mr. Hartley. The interpretation the gentlemen has just given of that section is absolutely correct." 93 Cong. Rec. 3656–3657.

It seems, therefore, clear to us that Congress adopted a policy which placed sanctions behind agreements to arbitrate grievance disputes, by implication rejecting the Common-law rule, discussed in *Red Cross Line* v. *Atlantic Fruit Co.* 264 U.S. 109, 68 L.ed. 582, 44 S.Ct. 274, against enforcement of executory agreements to arbitrate. We would undercut the Act and defeat its policy if we read §301 narrowly as only conferring jurisdiction over labor organizations.

The question then is, what is the substantive law to be applied in suits under §301(a)? We conclude that the substantive law to apply in suits under §301(a) is federal law which the courts must fashion from the policy of our national labor laws. See Mendelsohn, Enforceability of Arbitration Agreements Under Taft-Hartley §301, 66 Yale LJ 167. The Labor Management Relations Act expressly furnishes some substantive law. It points out what the parties may or may not do in certain situations. Other problems will lie in the penumbra of express statutory mandates. Some will lack express statutory sanction but will be solved by looking at the policy of the legislation and fashioning a remedy that will effectuate that policy. The range of judicial inventiveness will be determined by the nature of the problem. See *Jackson County* v. *United States*, 308 U.S. 343, 351, 84 L.ed. 313, 317, 60 S.Ct. 285. Federal interpretation of the federal law will govern, not state law. Cf. *Jerome* v. *United States*, 318 U.S. 101, 104, 87 L.ed. 640, 643, 63 S.Ct. 483. But state law, if compatible with the purpose of §301, may be resorted to in order to find the rule that will best effectuate the federal policy. See *Jackson County* v. *United States*, supra (308 U.S. 351, 352). Any state law applied, however, will be absorbed as federal law and will not be an independent source of private rights.

It is not uncommon for federal courts to fashion federal law where federal rights are concerned. See *Clearfield Trust Co.* v. *United States*, 318 U.S. 363, 366, 367, 87 L.ed. 838, 841, 63 S.Ct. 573; *National Metropolitan Bank* v. *United States*, 323 U.S. 454, 89 L.ed. 383, 65 S.Ct. 354. Congress has indicated by §301(a) the purpose to follow that course here. There is no constitutional difficulty. Article 3, §2 extends the judicial power to cases "arising under . . . the Laws of the United States. . . ." The power of Congress to relate these labor-management controversies under the Commerce Clause is plain. *Houston, E. & W. T. R. Co.* v. *United States*, 234 U.S. 342, 58 L.ed. 1341, 34 S.Ct. 833; *NLRB* v. *Jones & L. Steel Corp.*, 301 U.S. 1, 81 L.ed. 893, 57 S.Ct. 615, 108 ALR 1352. A case or controversy arising under §301(a) is, therefore, one within the purview of judicial power as defined in Article 3.

The question remains whether jurisdiction to compel arbitration of grievance disputes is withdrawn by the Norris-LaGuardia Act, 47 Stat. 70, 29 USC §101. Section 7 of that Act prescribes stiff procedural requirements for issuing an injunction in a labor dispute. The kinds of acts which had given rise to abuse of the power to enjoin are listed in §4. The failure to arbitrate was not a part and parcel of the abuses against which the Act was aimed. Section 8 of the Norris-LaGuardia Act does, indeed, indicate a congressional policy toward settlement of labor disputes by arbitration, for it denies injunctive relief to any person who has failed to make "every reasonable effort" to settle the dispute by negotiation, mediation, or "voluntary arbitration." Though a literal reading might bring the dispute within the terms of the Act (see Cox, Grievance Arbitration in the Federal Courts, 67 Harv. L. Rev. 591, 602–604), we see no justification in policy for restricting §301(a) to damage suits, leaving specific performance of a contract to arbitrate grievance disputes to the inapposite procedural requirements of that Act. Moreover, we held in *Virginian R. Co. v. System Federation*, R. E. D. 300 U.S. 515, 81 L.ed. 789, 57 S.Ct. 592, and in *Graham v. Brotherhood of Locomotive Firemen & E.*, 338 U.S. 232, 237, 94 L.ed. 22, 28, 70 S.Ct. 14, that the Norris-LaGuardia Act does not deprive federal courts of jurisdiction to compel compliance with the mandates of the Railway Labor Act. The mandates there involved concerned racial discrimination. Yet those decisions were not based on any peculiarities of the Railway Labor Act. We followed the same course in *Syres v. Oil Workers International Union*, 350 U.S. 892, 100 L.ed. 785, 76 S.Ct. 152, which was governed by the National Labor Relations Act. There an injunction was sought against racial discrimination in application of a collective bargaining agreement; and we allowed the injunction to issue. The congressional policy in favor of the enforcement of agreements to arbitrate grievance disputes being clear, there is no reason to submit them to the requirements of §7 of the Norris-LaGuardia Act. . . .

Republic Steel Corporation v. *Charlie Maddox*

379 U.S. 650, 85, S.Ct. 614 (1965)

Held: Federal labor laws, if applicable, preempt state laws, so that if there is an appropriate federal law then one must bring the action in federal court instead of state court, even if there seems to also be an appropriate state law.

Opinion:

An employee sued his employer in an Alabama state court for severance pay which was allegedly due under the terms of a collective bargaining agreement between the employer and the employee's union. The employer was engaged in interstate commerce, and its industrial relations were subject to the provisions of the Labor Management Relations Act. Nearly three years prior to the commencement of the action, the employee had been laid off. The collective bargaining agreement authorized severance pay if the layoff resulted from the employer's decision to close its mine permanently, but the agreement also provided for a three-step grievance procedure, to be followed by binding arbitration. The case was tried on stipulated facts without a jury, and although the employee had made no effort to utilize the grievance procedures which were provided by the collective bargaining agreement, judgment was awarded in his favor for the amount which he claimed was due him. The Alabama Court of Appeals and the Alabama Supreme Court (275 Ala. 685, 158 So.2d 492) affirmed on the grounds that state law was applicable to a suit for severance pay and that, under Alabama law, an employee was not required to exhaust his grievance procedures as a prerequisite to bringing such a suit.

On certiorari, the United States Supreme Court reversed. In an opinion by HARLAN, J., expressing the views of eight members of the court, it was held that federal law, rather than state law, applied, and that, in accordance with the policies embodied in the Labor Management Relations Act, the employee's failure to utilize the grievance procedures provided by the collective bargaining agreement precluded him from being able to sue his employer for severance pay.

BLACK, J., dissented on the ground that the Labor Management Relations Act should not be construed so as to require an individual employee, after he is out of a job, to submit a claim involving wages to grievance and arbitration proceedings or to surrender his right to sue his employer in court for the enforcement of his claim.

27

Connell Construction Company v. Plumbers and Steamfitters Local Union No. 100

U.S. Supreme Court, No. 73-1256 (June 2, 1975)
(Lower court 483 F.2d 1154, 1973)

Held: This case discusses the relationship of labor laws to other laws. Federal antitrust laws provide an exemption for concerted union activities, but do not offer
an exemption for concerted efforts between labor and nonlabor. However, the
courts have provided a limited exemption for concerted efforts between labor
and nonlabor, so the effect is that federal labor laws usually preempt federal
antitrust laws.

In general, federal laws preempt state laws, and federal labor laws do
preempt state antitrust laws.

Opinion:

Respondent union, representing the plumbing and mechanical trades in Dallas,
was a party to a multiemployer collective-bargaining agreement with a mechanical
contractors association. The agreement contained a "most favored nation" clause, by
which the union agreed that if it granted a more favorable contract to any other
employer, it would extend the same terms to all association members. Respondent
picketed petitioner, a general building contractor which subcontracted all plumbing
and mechanical work and had no employees respondent wished to represent, to
secure a contract whereby petitioner agreed to subcontract such work only to firms
that had a current contract with respondent. Petitioner signed under protest and,
claiming that the agreement violated §§1 and 2 of the Sherman Act and state antitrust laws, brought suit against respondent seeking declaratory and injunctive relief.
By the time this case went to trial, respondent had secured identical agreements from
other general contractors and was selectively picketing those who resisted. The District
Court held (1) that the subcontracting agreement was exempt from federal antitrust
laws because it was authorized by the first proviso in §8(e) of the National Labor
Relations Act (NLRA), which exempts jobsite contracting agreements in the construction industry from the statutory ban on secondary agreements requiring employers
to cease doing business with other persons, and (2) that federal labor legislation preempted the state's antitrust laws.

I. The Court of Appeals for the Fifth Circuit affirmed, 483 F.2d 1154 (CA 5
1973), with one judge dissenting. It held that Local 100's goal of organizing nonunion
subcontractors was a legitimate union interest and that its efforts toward that goal
were therefore exempt from federal antitrust laws. On the second issue, it held that
state law was preempted under *San Diego Building Trades Council* v. *Garmon*, 359
U.S. 236 (1959). We granted certiorari on Connell's petition. 416 U.S. 981. We
reverse on the question of federal antitrust immunity and affirm the ruling on state
law preemption.

II. The basic sources of organized labor's exemption from federal antitrust laws
are §§6 and 20 of the Clayton Act, 15 U.S.C. §17 and 29 U.S.C. §52, and the Norris-
LaGuardia Act, 29 U.S.C. §§104, 105, and 113. These statutes declare that labor
unions are not combinations or conspiracies in restraint of trade, and exempt specific
union activities, including secondary picketing and boycotts, from the operation of the
antitrust laws. See *United States* v. *Hutcheson*, 312 U.S. 219 (1941). They do not
exempt concerted action or agreements between unions and nonlabor parties. *UMW* v.
Pennington, 381 U.S. 657, 662 (1965). The Court has recognized, however, that a
proper accommodation between the congressional policy favoring collective bargaining
under the NLRA and the congressional policy favoring free competition in business
markets requires that some union-employer agreements be accorded a limited non-

statutory exemption from antitrust sanctions. *Meat Cutters Local 189* v. *Jewel Tea Co.*, 381 U.S. 676 (1965).

The nonstatutory exemption has its source in the strong labor policy favoring the association of employees to eliminate competition over wages and working conditions. Union success in organizing workers and standardizing wages ultimately will affect price competition among employers, but the goals of federal labor law never could be achieved if this effect on business competition were held a violation of the antitrust laws. The Court therefore has acknowledged that labor policy requires tolerance for the lessening of business competition based on differences in wages and working conditions. See *UMW* v. *Pennington, supra,* at 666; *Jewel Tea, supra,* at 689-690 (opinion of Mr. Justice White). Labor policy clearly does not require, however, that a union have freedom to impose direct restraints on competition among those who employ its members. Thus, while the statutory exemption allows unions to accomplish some restraints by acting unilaterally, e.g., *American Federation of Musicians* v. *Carroll,* 391 U.S. 99 (1968), the nonstatutory exemption offers no similar protection when a union and a nonlabor party agree to restrain competition in a business market. *Allen Bradley Co.* v. *IBEW Local 3,* 325 U.S. 797, 806-811 (1945).

This record contains no evidence that the union's goal was anything other than organizing as many subcontractors as possible. This goal was legal, even though a successful organizing campaign ultimately would reduce the competition that unionized employers face from nonunion firms. But the methods the union chose are not immune from antitrust sanctions simply because the goal is legal. Here Local 100, by agreement with several contractors, made nonunion subcontractors ineligible to compete for a portion of the available work. This kind of direct restraint on the business market has substantial anticompetitive effects, both actual and potential, that would not follow naturally from the elimination of competition over wages and working conditions. It contravenes antitrust policies to a degree not justified by congressional labor policy, and therefore cannot claim a nonstatutory exemption from the antitrust laws.

There can be no argument in this case, whatever its force in other contexts, that a restraint of this magnitude might be entitled to an antitrust exemption if it were included in a lawful collective-bargaining agreement. Cf. *UMW* v. *Pennington, supra,* at 664-665; *Jewel Tea, supra,* at 689-690 (opinion of Mr. Justice White); *id.,* at 709-713, 732-733 (opinion of Mr. Justice Goldberg). In this case, Local 100 had no interest in representing Connell's employees. The federal policy favoring collective bargaining therefore can offer no shelter for the union's coercive action against Connell or its campaign to exclude nonunion firms from the subcontracting market.

III. Local 100 nonetheless contends that the kind of agreement it obtained from Connell is explicitly allowed by the construction industry proviso to §8(e) and that antitrust policy therefore must defer to the NLRA. The majority in the Court of Appeals declined to decide this issue, holding that it was subject to the "exclusive jurisdiction" of the NLRB. 483 F.2d, at 1174. This Court has held, however, that the federal courts may decide labor law questions that emerge as collateral issues in suits brought under independent federal remedies, including the antitrust laws. We conclude that §8(e) does not allow this type of agreement.

IV. Although we hold that the union's agreement with Connell is subject to the federal antitrust laws, it does not follow that state antitrust law may apply as well. The Court has held repeatedly that federal law preempts state remedies that interfere with federal labor policy or with specific provisions of the NLRA. *Amalgamated Association of Street Employees* v. *Lockridge,* 403 U.S. 274 (1971). The use of state antitrust law to regulate union activities in aid of organization must also be preempted because it creates a substantial risk of conflict with policies central to federal labor law.

In this area, the accommodation between federal labor and antitrust policy is delicate. Congress and this Court have carefully tailored the antitrust statutes to avoid conflict with the labor policy favoring lawful employee organization, not only by delineating exemptions from antitrust coverage but also by adjusting the scope of the antitrust remedies themselves. See *Apex Hosiery Co.* v. *Leader*, 310 U.S. 469 (1940). State antitrust laws generally have not been subjected to this process of accommodation. If they take account of labor goals at all, they may represent a totally different balance between labor and antitrust policies. Permitting state antitrust law to operate in this field could frustrate the basic federal policies favoring employee organization and allowing elimination of competition among wage earners, and interfere with the detailed system Congress has created for regulating organizational techniques.

Because employee organization is central to federal labor policy and regulation of organization procedures is comprehensive, federal law does not admit the use of state antitrust law to regulate union activity that is closely related to organizational goals. Of course, other agreements between unions and nonlabor parties may yet be subject to state antitrust laws. See *Teamsters Local 24* v. *Oliver, supra,* at 295-297. The governing factor is the risk of conflict with the NLRA or with federal labor policy.

V. Neither the District Court nor the Court of Appeals decided whether the agreement between Local 100 and Connell, if subject to the antitrust laws, would constitute an agreement that restrains trade within the meaning of the Sherman Act, so we remand for this consideration.

NLRB v. *Fainblatt*

306 U.S. 601 (1938)

Held: The National Labor Relations Act is applicable to relatively small employers
who are not themselves employed in interstate commerce but process materials
which are transmitted by others into interstate commerce. The fact that the
volume may be relatively small is not significant and the NLRA, as amended,
is applicable.

Opinion:

Only the question of the Board's jurisdiction is raised by the petition and in
briefs and argument. It has been settled by repeated decisions of this Court that an
employer may be subject to the National Labor Relations Act although not himself
engaged in commerce. The end sought in the enactment of the statute was the prevention of the disturbance to interstate commerce consequent upon strikes and labor
disputes induced or likely to be induced because of unfair labor practices named in
the Act. That those consequences may ensue from strikes of the employees of manufacturers who are not engaged in interstate commerce where the cessation of manufacture necessarily results in the cessation of the movement of the manufactured
product in interstate commerce, has been repeatedly pointed out by this Court.
National Labor Relations Bd. v. *Jones & L. Steel Corp.*, 301 U.S. 1, 38-40, 81 L.ed.
893, 912, 913, 57 S.Ct. 615, 108 A.L.R. 1352; *National Labor Relations Bd.* v.
Fruehauf Trailer Co., 301 U.S. 49, 81 L.ed. 918, 57 S.Ct. 642, 108 A.L.R. 1372;
National Labor Relations Bd. v. *Friedman-Harry Marks Clothing Co.*, 301 U.S. 58,
81 L.ed. 921, 57 S.Ct. 645, 108 A.L.R. 1375; *Santa Cruz Fruit Packing Co.* v. *National
Labor Relations Bd.*, 303 U.S. 453, 463 et seq., 82 L.ed. 954, 958, 58 S.Ct. 656;
cf. *Consolidated Edison Co.* v. *National Labor Relations Bd.*, 305 U.S. 197, ante, 126,
59 S.Ct. 206. Long before the enactment of the National Labor Relations Act it had
been many times held by this Court that the power of Congress extends to the
protection of interstate commerce from interference or injury due to activities which
are wholly intrastate.

Here interstate commerce was involved in the transportation of the materials
to be processed across state lines to the factory of respondents and in the transportation
of the finished product to points outside the state for distribution to purchasers and
ultimate consumers. Whether shipments were made directly to respondents, as the
Board found, or to a representative of Lee Sportswear Company at the factory, as
respondents contend, is immaterial. It was not any the less interstate commerce
because the transportation did not begin or end with the transfer of title of the
merchandise transported. . . . Transportation alone across state lines is commerce
within the constitutional control of the national government and subject to the regulatory power of Congress. *Gibbons* v. *Ogden*, 9 Wheat. 1, 6 L.ed. 23; *Lottery Case*
(*Champion* v. *Ames*), 188 U.S. 321, 47 L.ed. 492, 23 S.Ct. 321.

Nor do we think it important, as respondents seem to argue, that the volume
of the commerce here involved, though substantial, was relatively small as compared
with that in the cases arising under the National Labor Relations Act which have
hitherto engaged our attention. The power of Congress to regulate interstate commerce is plenary and extends to all such commerce be 'it great or small. . . .

The language of the National Labor Relations Act seems to make it plain that
Congress has set no restrictions upon the jurisdiction of the Board to be determined or
fixed exclusively by reference to the volume of interstate commerce involved. Section
2(6) defines commerce as "trade, traffic, commerce, transportation, or communication
among the several States," without reference to its volume, and declares in subsection

(7) that "The term 'affecting commerce' means in commerce, or burdening or obstructing commerce or the free flow of commerce, or having led or tending to lead to a labor dispute burdening or obstructing commerce or the free flow of commerce." Section 10(a) confers on the Board authority "to prevent any person from engaging in any unfair labor practice (listed in §8) affecting commerce."

The Act on its face thus evidences the intention of Congress to exercise whatever power is constitutionally given to it to regulate commerce by the adoption of measures for the prevention or control of certain specified acts—unfair labor practices—which provoke or tend to provoke strikes or labor disturbances affecting interstate commerce. Given the other needful conditions, commerce may be affected in the same manner and to the same extent in proportion to its volume, whether it be great or small. Examining the Act in the light of its purpose and of the circumstances in which it must be applied we can perceive no basis for inferring any intention of Congress to make the operation of the Act depend on any particular volume of commerce affected more than that to which courts would apply the maxim de minimis.

There are not a few industries in the United States which, though conducted by relatively small units, contribute in the aggregate a vast volume of interstate commerce. Some, like the clothing industry, are extensively unionized and have had a long and tragic history of industrial strife. It is not to be supposed that Congress, in its attempted nationwide regulation of interstate commerce through the removal of the causes of industrial strife affecting it, intended to exclude such industries from the sweep of the Act. In this, as in every other case, the test of the Board's jurisdiction is not the volume of the interstate commerce which may be affected, but the existence of a relationship of the employer and his employees to the commerce such that, to paraphrase §10(a) in the light of constitutional limitations, unfair labor practices have led or tended to lead "to a labor dispute burdening or obstructing commerce."

It is no longer open to question that the manufacturer who regularly ships his product in interstate commerce is subject to the authority conferred on the Board with respect to unfair labor practices whenever such practices on his part have led or tend to lead to labor disputes which threaten to obstruct his shipments. *National Labor Relations Bd.* v. *Jones & L. Steel Corp.*, 301 U.S. 1, 81 L.ed. 893, 57 S.Ct. 615, 108 A.L.R. 1352. . . .

Here, although respondents' manufacturing business is small, employing from sixty to two hundred employees, its product is regularly shipped in interstate commerce. The Board's finding that respondents' unfair labor practices have led and tend to lead to labor disputes burdening interstate commerce and interfering with its free flow is supported by the evidence. Moreover, the Board has found specifically that respondents' unfair labor practices in attempting to prevent the unionization of their factory did in fact lead to a strike in respondents' tailoring establishment, with a consequent reduction of about 50 per cent in respondents' output. These findings are not challenged.

The threatened consequences to interstate commerce are as immediate and as certain to flow from respondents' unfair labor practices as were those which were held to result from unfair labor practices in *National Labor Relations Bd.* v. *Jones & L. Steel Corp.*, 301 U.S. 1, 81 L.ed. 893, 57 S.Ct. 615. . . . That the volume of commerce affected is smaller than in other cases in which the jurisdiction of the Board has been upheld, for reasons already stated, is in itself without significance.

Reversed.

National Labor Relations Board et al. v. Sears, Roebuck & Co.

89 LRRM 2001—U.S. Supreme Court (April 28, 1975)

Held: This case presents the procedure used by the Labor Board when it processes
a complaint which involves an allegation of an unfair labor practice. The Labor
Board used to keep the details of its internal procedures from the public, but
this case, which was brought under the Freedom of Information Act, required
that the processing procedures be disclosed to Sears, so now the public may
ascertain the various steps pursued by the Board in processing a claim, and
also obtain copies of certain of the Board's internal reports.

Opinion:

Mr. Justice White delivered the opinion of the Court.

The National Labor Relations Board (the Board) and its General Counsel seek
to set aside an order of the United States District Court directing disclosure to
respondent, Sears, Roebuck & Co. (Sears), pursuant to the Freedom of Information
Act, 5 USC §552 (the Act), of certain memoranda, known as "Advice Memoranda"
and "Appeals Memoranda," and related documents generated by the Office of the
General Counsel in the course of deciding whether or not to permit the filing with the
Board of unfair labor practice complaints. . . .

Crucial to the decision of this case is an understanding of the function of the
documents in issue in the context of the administrative process which generated them.
We deal with this matter first. Under the Labor Management Relations Act of 1947,
29 USC §151 *et seq.*, the process of adjudicating unfair labor practice cases begins
with the filing by a private party of a "charge," 29 USC §§153(d) and 160(b); 29
CFR §101.2; *Auto Workers* v. *Scofield*, 382 U.S. 205, 219; *NLRB* v. *Indiana and
Michigan Electric Co.*, 318 U.S. 9, 17-18. Although Congress has designated the
Board as the principal body which adjudicates the unfair labor practice case based
on such charge, 29 USC §160, the Board may adjudicate only upon the filing of a
"complaint"; and Congress has delegated to the Office of General Counsel "acting for
the Board" the unreviewable authority to determine whether a complaint shall be filed.
29 USC §153(d); *Vaca* v. *Sipes*, 386 U.S. 171, 182. In those cases in which he decides
that a complaint shall issue, the General Counsel becomes an advocate before the
Board in support of the complaint. In those cases in which he decides not to issue a
complaint, no proceeding before the Board occurs at all. The practical effect of this
administrative scheme is that a party believing himself the victim of an unfair labor
practice can obtain neither adjudication nor remedy under the labor statute without
first persuading the Office of General Counsel that his claim is sufficiently meritorious
to warrant Board consideration.

In order to structure the considerable power which the administrative scheme
gives him, the General Counsel has adopted certain procedures for processing unfair
labor practice charges. Charges are filed in the first instance with one of the Board's
31 Regional Directors, to whom the General Counsel has delegated the initial power
to decide whether or not to issue a complaint. 29 CFR §§102.10, 101.8. A member
of the staff of the Regional Office then conducts an investigation of the charge, which
may include interviewing witnesses and reviewing documents. 29 CFR §101.4. If, on
the basis of the investigation, the Regional Director believes the charge has merit,
a settlement will be attempted, or a complaint issued. If the charge has no merit in
the Regional Director's judgment, the charging party will be so informed by letter with
a brief explanation of the reasons. 29 CFR §§101.8, 102.15, 101.6, 102.19. In such
a case, the charging party will also be informed of his right to appeal within 10 days
to the Office of the General Counsel in Washington, D.C. 29 CFR §§101.6, 102.19.

If the charging party exercises this right, the entire file in the possession of the Regional Director will be sent to the Office of Appeals in the General Counsel's Office in Washington, D.C. The case will be assigned to a staff attorney in the Office of Appeals, who prepares a memorandum containing an analysis of the factual and legal issues in the case. This memorandum is called an "agenda minute" and serves as the basis for discussion at a meeting of the "Appeals Committee," which includes the Director and Associate Director of the Office of Appeals. At some point in this period, the charging party may make a written presentation of his case as of right and an oral presentation in the discretion of the General Counsel. 29 CFR §102.19. If an oral presentation is allowed, the subject of the unfair labor practice charge is notified and allowed a similar but separate opportunity to make an oral presentation. In any event, a decision is reached by the Appeals Committee; and the decision and the reasons for it are set forth in a memorandum called the "General Counsel's Minute" or the "Appeals Memorandum." This document is then cleared through the General Counsel himself. If the case is unusually complex or important, the General Counsel will have been brought into the process at an earlier stage and will have had a hand in the decision and the expression of its basis in the Appeals Memorandum. In either event, the Appeals Memorandum is then sent to the Regional Director who follows its instructions. If the appeal is rejected and the Regional Director's decision not to issue a complaint is sustained, a separate document is prepared and sent by the General Counsel in letter form to the charging party, more briefly setting forth the reasons for the denial of his appeal. The Appeals Memoranda, whether sustaining or overruling the Regional Directors, constitute one class of documents at issue in this case.

The appeals process affords the General Counsel's Office in Washington some opportunity to formulate a coherent policy, and to achieve some measure of uniformity, in enforcing the labor laws. The appeals process alone, however, is not wholly adequate for this purpose: when the Regional Director initially decides to file a complaint, no appeal is available; and when the Regional Director decides not to file a complaint, the charging party may neglect to appeal. Accordingly, to further "fair and uniform administration of the Act," the General Counsel requires the Regional Directors, before reaching an initial decision in connection with charges raising certain issues specified by the General Counsel, to submit the matter to the General Counsel's "Advice Branch," also located in Washington, D.C. In yet other kinds of cases, the Regional Directors are permitted to seek the counsel of the Advice Branch.

When a Regional Director seeks "advice" from the Advice Branch, he does so through a memorandum which sets forth the facts of the case, a statement of the issues on which advice is sought, and a recommendation. The case is then assigned to a staff attorney in the Advice Branch who researches the legal issues presented by reading prior Board and court decisions and "prior advice determinations in similar or related cases," *Statement, supra,* 3076, and reports, orally or in writing, to a Committee or "agenda" made up of various high-ranking members of the General Counsel's Office. The Committee recommendation is then arrived at and communicated to the General Counsel, together with the recommendation of the Regional Director and any dissenting views in the Committee. In special cases, the General Counsel may schedule special agendas and invite other staff members to submit their recommendations. In either event, the General Counsel will decide the issue submitted, and his "final determination" will be communicated to the Regional Director by way of an Advice Memorandum. The Memorandum will briefly summarize the facts, against the background of which the legal or policy issue is to be decided, set forth the General Counsel's answer to the legal or policy issue submitted together with a "detailed legal rationale," and contain "instructions for the final processing of the case." *Statement, supra,* 3076.

Depending upon the conclusion reached in the Memorandum, the Regional Director will either file a complaint or send a letter to the complaining party advising him of his decision not to proceed and informing him of his right to appeal. It is these Advice Memoranda which constitute the other class of documents of which Sears seeks disclosure in this case.

5. Selecting the Representative

Employee Representatives

THE UNIT. The collective bargaining unit selected is usually the most logical one, but the importance of selecting the appropriate unit should not be minimized. By adding or subtracting members, one can influence the composition of the voting population and hence determine whether the union ever achieves majority status and subsequently becomes "certified." Becoming certified means that the Labor Board officially designates the union as the exclusive representative of the employees, and further means that the union has more protection then if it were only "recognized." For instance, another union has a one-year bar to an election if the union is certified.

Employee representatives that have been "designated or selected for the purposes of collective bargaining by the majority of the employees in a unit appropriate for such purposes, shall be the exclusive representatives of all the employees in such unit for the purposes of collective bargaining" (Section 9(a)). So the key is whether a unit is appropriate, and the resolution of this is left to the discretion of the NLRB. With certain restrictions on the board language "the unit appropriate for the purposes of collective bargaining shall be the employer unit, craft unit, plant unit, or subdivision thereof."

The Board's discretion is limited somewhat by some provisions of 9(b), which provides for the following:

a. The Board shall not approve as appropriate a unit that includes both professional and nonprofessional employees, unless a majority of the professional employees involved vote to be included in a mixed unit.
b. A proposed craft unit shall not be held inappropriate simply because a different unit was previously approved by the Board. A majority of the members of the craft unit must vote against being included in a unit with other employees for the craftsmen to establish their own unit.
c. Guards, because they are hired to regulate employees and customers, cannot be included in the same unit as other employees.

APPROPRIATE UNITS. Generally the entire circumstances of the duties and working conditions are considered and the workers with the most characteristics in common are placed in the same bargaining unit. The aim is to balance the unit's size so that the unit is large enough to exert maximum pressure and yet small enough for the members to have common demands and goals. An example of growing too large to adequately represent the demands of one's members is the Knights of Labor, an organization discussed in Chapter 2. Not only did size and hence diverse interests lead to the downfall of the Knights, but it also led to the dispute that resulted in the forming of the CIO.

Some of the factors considered in the search for the appropriate units are:

a. Any history of collective bargaining;
b. Employees' desires;
c. Employees' current organization, although Section 9(c)(5) forbids the Board to give this factor controlling weight;
d. Any other factor that on a situation-by-situation basis the Board deems relevant.

There is no definite rule as to size or coverage of a unit. There may be many units in the same manufacturing plant or the unit may be a single plant or the unit may be more than one plant of the same employer. Note that the Board has the right to reduce the size of the unit to a point where it becomes manageable. One employer tried to make the unit all of his facilities in several cities, but the Board reduced this to a particular city.

EXCLUSIVENESS. To preserve the strength of the unit, once a representative is elected by a majority of the employees, then this person represents all the members as their exclusive agent. This representative has a duty to represent all employees in the unit equally and fairly without regard to their union membership. Designating the representative an exclusive representative means that an employer may not bargain with another representative or group of employees. Usually the employees must present their grievances through their representative, but there is a provision for an employee to present his grievances directly to the employer, if:

a. The adjustment is not inconsistent with the terms of any collective-bargaining agreement.
b. The bargaining representative has been given the right to be present at such adjustment.

RECOGNITION. Recognition of the union occurs when management is required to "recognize" the union as bargaining agent for the employees. At this point, management must negotiate with the union.

The Act does not require that a representative be selected by any particular procedure, so while an election is the most common form, it is not the only method of recognition. Some of the other methods the union may use to demonstrate that it represents a majority of employees are:

a. Authorization cards. If the union obtains authorization cards from a majority of employees, then the employer may be under a duty to bargain even without an election. This would occur if the employer challenges the cards. *NLRB* v. *Gissel*, 395 U.S. 575, 89 S.Ct. 1918 (1969).

b. Strikes. If a· union calls a strike and a majority of workers strike, then the employer may be under a duty to bargain.

The Elections

GENERAL. If a question of representation exists, the Board must order an election by secret ballot (Section 9(c)(1)). If a majority of employees want a union but if because three or more unions are running, no single union achieves a majority of the votes, then a runoff election between the top two vote getters is held.

An election may be held by agreement of the parties or by order of the Board. If by agreement of the parties, it is labeled a "consent" election and would still be supervised by the Board. If the parties cannot agree, the Board may order an election after a hearing. The Regional Directors can also determine the appropriateness of the unit and certify the outcome, if so empowered by the Board.

WHO MAY VOTE. To vote one must be an employee who worked in the unit during the period of eligibility set by the Board and still be employed at the time of the election. Generally the eligibility period is the last payroll period, but this may be varied to accommodate sickness, vacation, a seasonal industry, or other relevant factors. If the industry is seasonal, other guidelines, such as so many days worked during the last year, may be adopted.

Whether a striker can vote is dependent upon why he is striking. An employee striking over an employer's unfair labor practice is eligible to vote. The determination of whether an employee who is striking over an economic issue can vote depends on the facts, and possibly both he and his bonafide permanent replacement may be able to vote.

Remember that whether an employee on strike may be replaced is dependent upon whether the strike is motivated by an unfair labor practice (cannot be replaced) or an economic issue (can be replaced).

Unless there are some unusual circumstances, an election is held within 30 days after it has been directed. The unusual circumstances might be an unfair labor practice charge, where it becomes the option of the alleged aggrieved party whether to proceed or not. If the complaint is dismissed, an election will be held even though the result may be appealed to the General Counsel.

ELECTION AIMS. The aim of the election procedure is to provide the employees with an opportunity to freely indicate whether they wish to be represented, and if so, by whom. The details of the procedures and standards have generated such a volume of litigation that they will not be covered here but rather will be analyzed throughout this presentation. If any party feels that the standards were not met, then he has five days after the tally of ballots in which to file objections with the Regional Director, whose decision is appealable to the Board unless the election was with the consent of the parties, in which case there is no appeal. Thus, it may be important for a party not to consent to the election.

The Election Procedure. If the union wishes to be certified by an election, a set procedure is followed.

The initial step is the filing of a petition for an election, which is then evaluated by the Board, and if the Board has jurisdiction, then a hearing is set. If the Board decides that an election should be held, it is held and the results are binding. This process is discussed more fully in the following paragraphs.

THE PETITION. There are many different types of petitions, one of which may be appropriate to file in a given situation.

    a. A petition for certification of representatives may be filed by either an employee or an employer, where the latter must allege that someone has made a claim to be exclusive representative.

    b. Employees can petition to determine whether or not they wish to retain their current bargaining representative, and the resulting election is called a "decertification" election.

    c. A petition signed by at least 30 percent of the covered employees can lead to a secret ballot to ascertain whether they wish to continue the authority given to their representative under a union-shop agreement. This may lead to a union-shop deauthorization election.

BOARD EVALUATION. After the Labor Board has received the petition, it conducts an investigation which includes a hearing to determine the following (and perhaps more):

    a. Does the Board have jurisdiction; does the business affect interstate commerce?

    b. Is there a sufficient showing of interest to conduct the election?

    c. Does a question of representation exist; is there a dispute?

    d. Is the unit appropriate or is some other unit of employees more appropriate?

    e. Is the representative named in the petition qualified?

    f. Are there any barriers to an election, such as existing conditions or previous elections?

BOARD CRITERIA. These six factors which are used by the Labor Board to decide whether or not to hold an election will be discussed in more detail in this section.

    a. *Jurisdiction to conduct an election.* The business must affect interstate commerce; this used to limit the number of businesses controlled but since the expansion of the concept of affecting interstate commerce by the courts in the civil rights cases of the mid-1960's, this requirement has had little effect.

    b. *Sufficient interest.* The practice is to require at least 30 percent to favor an election and this percentage is of employees in the appropriate unit. Usually the percentage is determined by the number who sign union cards, but employees should read these cards carefully before they sign them.

Sometimes the employees are told that they are requesting an election, but the card actually states that they are requesting union representation. Thus the employee may feel that both sides will have a chance to campaign if he signs the card, but actually there will be no campaign or election but just union certification. Note that even though only 30 percent are required for an election to be held, at least 50 percent must vote for the union in the event that the union is to be certified in the election.

c. *Representation.* If the employees claim recognition and the employer denies it, then there is a question of representation. A question of representation must exist for an election to be ordered. Even a representative that is currently recognized may petition for an election to become certified, which carries added benefits such as a twelve-month bar to another election by a different union.

A decertification petition also questions representation but this petition leads to an election only if filed by an employee and not by an employer. A decertification election can lead to a decertification of the union.

d. *Appropriate Unit.* This is covered in detail by Section 9 of the Act and on pp. 36–37 of this chapter.

e. *Qualifications of Representative.* The individual representative must meet the criterion of being an employee and not supervisory, for supervisors are not covered by the National Labor Relations Board. With respect to unions, the Board does not look inside the union to see if its internal controls, such as its constitution, permit the union to represent the employees, but rather the key is the willingness of the union to represent the employees. Thus, a union whose constitution holds that it will represent craftsmen will not be barred from representing unskilled workers.

f. *Barriers to an Election.* Generally if the above criteria are satisfied, the NLRB will permit an election unless the employees are covered by a valid contract. Some contracts that will not bar an election are:

> The contract is not in writing or is not signed.
> The contract has not been ratified, if this is required.
> The bargaining unit is not appropriate.
> The contract discriminates between employees on racial grounds.
> The union is unstable or no longer in existence.
> The contract can be terminated by either party at any time for any reason.

Time is obviously an important consideration. For instance, the influence of not meeting the requirement of a written contract would certainly vary depending on whether the oral agreement was reached yesterday or five years ago. There are many specific rules with respect to the timing of elections, with the aim being to prevent a continuous series of elections and yet to insure that the employees are given a fair chance to make their choice concerning representation. It is worthwhile to consider some of the barriers to an election that are related to timing.

A valid contract will prohibit an election for the length of the contract or three years, whichever is shorter. The maximum time restriction is to prevent management or the union from committing the employees to a long-term contract that may in time become unfair. Also, a contract for an unspecified period of time is not a bar to an election. So a prudent party will make the contract for a definite time of three years or less.

Once the contract commences to operate as a bar, no petition will be accepted until near the end of the period of the bar, i.e., three years or less. Petitions filed not more than 90 but over 60 days before the end of the contract bar period will be accepted and can bring an election unless the parties agree to a contract during the "insulated" period. The insulated period is the last 60 days of the contract, and during this time a new contract or an extension of the old one will serve to start the cycle over again. Near the end of this cycle the 90-day 60-day rule would again be applicable. Note that once the contract expires, then an election may be held.

There is a one-year bar to accepting petitions when a representative has been certified by the Board, with the theory being that it might take quite some time for the parties to reach their first agreement. If they do reach an agreement, the previously discussed contract-bar rule applies.

Time Restrictions On Union Activities
12-MONTH BAR TO ANOTHER ELECTION
9(C)(3)

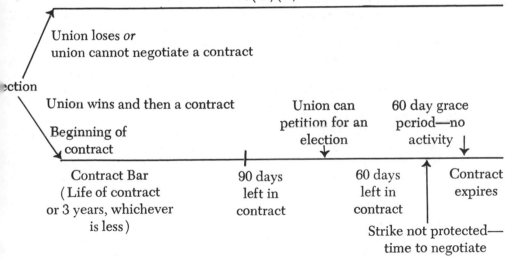

There is a twist to the above, however, and that is that the one-year bar is applicable only with respect to elections involving the same unit or subdivision of it, and the bar is interpreted by the Board as not prohibiting an election in a larger unit. So if the union loses and subsequently can justify a larger unit, then another election may be held. Also, the Board feels that the one-year bar to petitions is applicable only where the union wins and is certified. If there is no certification, then within 60 days of the expiration of the year, petitions may be accepted to order that an election be held immediately upon the expiration of the year.

General Instrument Corporation v. *National Labor Relations Board*

No. 8869. U.S. Court of Appeals Fourth Circuit
319 F.2d 420 (1963)

Held: The primary responsibility for deciding an appropriate collective bargaining unit has been granted to the Board, and review of the decision is limited to a determination of whether there has been a misapplication of law, a failure of substantial evidence, or an abuse of discretion. Thus the Board has virtually complete power in deciding the appropriate bargaining unit.

Opinion:

General Instrument Corporation has several plants, including four within the area encompassed by this Circuit. Involved in this petition is the employer's Thermo-Electric Division at its Newark, New Jersey, plant. The Thermo-Electric Division is devoted to research and development and at the time of the Regional Director's hearing, contained 32 employees, 17 of whom were classified as engineers and 15 of whom were in laboratory classifications. The evidence indicates that the laboratory and the engineering employees work very closely with each other, frequently performing overlapping functions. However, the evidence also indicates that there are several areas in which the groups do not share common interests. The engineers are professionals, whereas the laboratory workers are not; the engineers are generally paid on a salary basis ranging up to $300.00 per week, whereas the laboratory technicians are paid on an hourly basis with rates running up to $3.10 per hour; in general, the engineers are not paid for overtime hours, whereas the laboratory technicians are so paid; most of the engineers have college degrees or the equivalent, or are in the process of obtaining one, whereas none of the laboratory workers have this qualification.

After a hearing, the Regional Director found that a unit of all professional and technical employees would be appropriate, but if the professional employees were to vote under National Labor Relations Act §9(b)(1), 29 USCA §159(b)(1), against inclusion, a unit of laboratory technicians would be appropriate. The Board, reversing the Regional Director, found a unit of laboratory technicians to be appropriate and, therefore, limited the voting count to the ballots cast by these employees. On this basis, a majority of the employees in the unit voted for unionization.

In its analysis of the issues, the Board stated that:

"it is clear that the Petitioner [the union] seeks to represent only the technical employees and does not desire to represent the professionals. Moreover, where as here, the petitioner has no showing of interest among the professional employees, the Board will not direct an election among them to ascertain whether they wish to be joined in the same unit with the nonprofessionals [citing cases in a footnote]. In these circumstances, we find that the requested unit limited to the technical employees is appropriate. . . ."

The employer filed a motion before the Board for reconsideration of the decision, asserting that the Board had allowed the union, by its showing of interest, to determine the appropriateness of the unit. In denying this motion, the Board stated that it

"is of the opinion that the Employer's motion to reconsider should be denied as lacking in merit because the unit of technical employees in the Employer's Thermo-Electric Division, excluding the professional employees, is appropriate for the purposes of collective bargaining."

The employer contends that the decision of the Board should be set aside, since 1) the Board violated NLRA §9(c)(5), 29 USCA §159(c)(5), in that it gave controlling effect to the extent of organization of the employees, 2) the Board failed to perform its duty as imposed by NLRA §9(b), 29 USCA §159(b), to "decide in each case" what the appropriate unit should be, and 3) the Board's unit determination is arbitrary, capricious and an abuse of discretion in violation of Administrative Procedure Act §10(e)(B)(1), 5 USCA §1009(e)(B)(1).

[1] Primary responsibility for deciding whether a unit is appropriate for purposes of collective bargaining has been granted to the National Labor Relations Board. NLRA §9(b), 29 USCA §159(b). Our scope of review of this decision is very limited. *NLRB v. Quaker City Life Insurance Co.*, 319 F.2d 690 (4 Cir. 1963). Misapplication of law, failure of substantial evidence, abuse of discretion—these are the elements upon which a court may rely in reviewing the Board's decision. National Labor Relations Act §10(e) & (f), 29 USCA §160(e) & (f); Administrative Procedures Act §10(e), 5 USCA §1009(e); *NLRB v. Jones & Laughlin Steel Corp.*, 331 U.S. 416, 67 S.Ct. 1274, 91 L.ed. 1575 (1947); *Packard Motor Car Co. v. NLRB*, 330 U.S. 485, 67 S.Ct. 789, 91 L.ed. 1040 (1947); *Pittsburgh Plate Glass Co. v. NLRB*, 313 U.S. 146, 61 S.Ct. 908, 85 L.ed. 1251 (1941); *NLRB v. Quaker City Life Insurance Co., supra*. Absent these, the administrative determination must be supported.

[2] A sufficient basis in substantial evidence on the record as a whole exists to sustain the order presently under attack. The technicals are sufficiently cohesive as a unit and at the same time sufficiently distinct from the professional engineers to permit separate bargaining units. Working conditions, hourly wage scales, job specifications, and advancement opportunities indicate that the technicals have a strong common bond; different levels of education, job specifications, wage basis, advancement opportunities and, significantly, professional status, support a finding that sufficient distinctions between the technicals and the professionals exist to support a separation.

NLRB v. *Dalton Sheet Metal Co., Inc.*

472 F.2d 257 (1973)

Held: To be eligible to vote in a representation election, the employee should be
employed and working on the date on which eligibility is determined, but the
Board may decide on the equities of a given situation and vary the rule slightly
in the event of unusual circumstances.

An example of an unusual circumstance would be a strike, and in the
event of a strike, the Board may or may not vary the employed and working
rule so as to permit permanent replacements, who do not meet the requirements,
to vote in the election.

Opinion:

This suit was filed by National Labor Relations Board under section 10(e) of
the National Labor Relations Act (29 USC §151 et seq.) to enforce its order against
Dalton Sheet Metal Company, Inc. for violation of sections 8(a)(5) and (1) of the
Act in refusing to bargain with the Union (Sheet Metal Workers Local No. 185).

[1] The violation proceedings grew out of a representation election which was
won by the Union on a tally of 42 to 40 votes. The Company challenged a number
of votes in the representation case, and when the Board denied the challenges, the
Company declined to recognize the Union which had been certified by the Regional
Director as the representative of the Company's employees. The Company refused
to bargain, thus bringing about the unfair labor practice charges, since this was the
only way in which the Company could seek review of the Board's decision in the
representation case. *NLRB* v. *Smith Industries, Inc.,* 5 Cir., 1968, 403 F.2d 889, 891.
Under the circumstances, therefore, we review as one both the representation case and
the unfair labor practice case. *NLRB* v. *Ortronix, Inc.,* 5 Cir., 1967, 380 F.2d 737, 739.

On appeal the Company charges that two principal errors were committed by
the Board. First, the Company asserts that the Board erred in refusing to count the
ballots of striker replacements Fulton, Hendrix and King, who it contends were employed as permanent replacement employees prior to the voting eligibility cut-off date
and on the date of the election. Second, the Company contends that the Board erred
in refusing to sustain the challenges to the ballots of employees Parrish, Norris and
Smith, who it contends voluntarily quit employment with the Company and were not
employees on the day of the election. As a corollary to the second charge of error, the
Company avers that the Board erred in granting summary judgment in connection
with the evidence concerning the challenges to the ballots of Parrish, Norris and
Smith, and that a hearing should have been held in regard to these challenges to
make a determination of a substantial and material issue of fact as to whether these
employees voluntarily quit their employment with the Company, and were ineligible
to vote in the representation election.

[2] On the question of the first error asserted by the Company, we sustain the
Board's decision which upheld its Regional Director's ruling that the ballots of striker
replacement employees Fulton, Hendrix and King should not be counted in the
representation election. These three employees were hired prior to the eligibility date
of October 18, 1970, but were instructed by the Company not to report for work
until November 18, 1970, allegedly because of possible picket line violence. They
were, therefore, not working on the eligibility date but were employed and working,
however, on the date of the election on December 3, 1970.

[3] The Board's well-settled, general rule is that an individual must be employed
and working on the established eligibility date in order to be eligible to vote. *Ra-Rich
Mfg. Corp.,* 120 NLRB 1444, 1447 (1958); *Schick, Inc.,* 114 NLRB 931, 934 (1955);

Barry Controls, Inc., 113 NLRB 26, 27-28 (1955). The Company complains that this rule, however, should not be applied by the Board to striker replacements so as to require that they must be both employed and working on the established eligibility date. The Company points to the Board decision in *Tampa Sand & Material Co.*, 129 NLRB 1273 (1961), where the Board held that permanent striker replacements were eligible to vote although not employed on the eligibility date. However, *Tampa Sand* is distinguishable from the present case because the strike began *after* the election was called and the replacements were employed after the eligibility deadline but before the election. *Macy's Missouri-Kansas Division*, 173 NLRB 1500, 1501 (1969); *Macy's Missouri-Kansas Division* v. *NLRB*, 8 Cir., 1968, 389 F.2d 835, 842-845, which involved facts similar to those in *Tampa Sand*. Board counsel, therefore, emphasizes that these exceptions to the general policy pertaining to voter eligibility do not apply in this case because the strike occurred prior to the eligibility date rather than after, as in *Tampa Sand* and *Macy's Missouri-Kansas Division, supra*; that the Union was therefore not in a position to control eligibility by its timing of the strike as it was where the strike occurred after the eligibility date. The Board made its policy clear in this regard by its discussion in *Macy's Missouri-Kansas Division, supra* at 1501:

> "In *Tampa Sand and Material Company*, [129 NLRB 1273] the Board made an exception to its general election eligibility rule—that an employee must have been employed both on the initial eligibility date and the date of the election to be eligible to vote in a Board election—by holding that permanent replacements for economic strikers may vote in an election *where a strike occurs after the direction of the election*. Subsequently, in *Greenspan Engraving Corporation*, [137 NLRB 1308] the Board, although adhering to the rule enunciated in *Tampa Sand*, limited *Tampa Sand* to its specific facts and held that permanent replacements hired for economic strikers after the eligibility date are not eligible to vote in an election *where the strike precedes the direction of election. . . .*
>
> "In both *Tampa Sand* and *Greenspan*, the Board emphasized that the timing of the strike was the controlling factor in determining whether permanent replacements for economic strikers were entitled to vote in a representation election. As the Board stated in *Greenspan*: 'As the timing of the strike [is] peculiarly within the province of the union, rigid adherence by the Board to mechanical standards [the rule that for an employee to be eligible to vote, he must have been employed both on the eligibility date and the date of the election] without regard to the equities of the case would not [be] reasonable.' Accordingly, where, as in *Tampa Sand*, the union called the strike *after* the eligibility date, and it was therefore patently impossible for the employer to hire permanent replacements prior to the eligibility date, the Board held that the equities of the situation required that genuine permanent replacements hired after the eligibility date be entitled to vote. On the other hand, as in *Greenspan* where the union called the strike prior to the eligibility date, and the employer had the opportunity to hire permanent replacements prior to the eligibility date, the Board held that the equities of the situation did not require that such permanent replacements be entitled to vote but that the usual voting eligibility rules should be applicable."

The Company places strong reliance on the Second Circuit decision in *H. & F. Binch Co.* v. *NLRB*, 2 Cir., 1972, 456 F.2d 357, in which that Court sustained a Board ruling which recognized the status as employees of striker replacements upon acceptance by them of vacant positions offered by their employer though the replacements had not actually started to work until after strikers applied for reinstatement. The Court held that actual arrival on the job would not be required for a striker replacement to acquire the status of an employee sufficient to oust the reinstatement of a striker, if an understanding had been reached that actual work would start at a reasonably early date. *Id.* at 362. The Court further held, "The standard established by the Board in earlier decisions appears to have been that a replacement has been obtained if, but only if, both the employer and the replacement understand that the latter has accepted the vacant position before the replaced striker offered to return to work." *Id.* at 362. The recent case of *L. E. M., Inc. d/b/a Southwest Engraving Co. and Towell Printing Co.,* 198 NLRB No. 99 (1972), cited by the Company, is to the same effect. . . .

We are not prepared to nullify the Board's policy on eligibility to vote which requires that striker replacements be both employed and working on the eligibility date since we recognize that "Congress has entrusted the Board with a wide degree of discretion in establishing the procedure and safeguards necessary to insure the fair and free choice of bargaining representatives by employees." *NLRB v. A. J. Tower Co.,* 329 U.S. 324, 330, 67 S.Ct. 324, 328, 91 L.ed. 322 (1946); *Macy's Missouri-Kansas Division v. NLRB,* 8 Cir., 1968, 389 F.2d 835, 842. As the Supreme Court noted in *NLRB v. A. J. Tower Co., supra,* "The principle of majority rule, however, does not foreclose practical adjustments designed to protect the election machinery from the ever-present dangers of abuse and fraud." (*Id.,* 329 U.S. at 331, 67 S.Ct. at 328.)

We can see differences between new hire and striker replacements but not of sufficient substance to cause us to hold that the Board rule requiring both employment and actual working on the eligibility date shall not be applied uniformly both to new employees and replacements. If the Board policy disenfranchises replacements because of the requirement that they also be working on the eligibility date, it also disenfranchises new employees as well. In essence, we can discern no reason why a different rule should be applied to replacements (except in the limited *Tampa Sand* circumstances), than is applied to new employees.

As to the Company's second principal assertion of error, the three employees, Parrish, Norris and Smith, alleged to have voluntarily abandoned employment with the Company prior to the eligibility date, we are unable to tell from the record, the case having been decided on summary judgment, whether their employment ceased voluntarily or not. The issue of fact is sharply contradicted and seriously disputed. The Company, on the one hand, contends that the employees quit their employment without any expectancy of returning. The Board contends, to the contrary, that the facts developed by the Regional Director in his ex parte investigation show they were merely quitting for the time being, until the strike and confusion could subside, and that they had no intention of abandoning their jobs. The Company further asserts that the Regional Director's investigation could not effectively determine whether these employees intended to return to work after the strike and that only after a full hearing can this crucial issue of fact be resolved.

[4] The question does not properly lend itself to disposition by summary judgment and a hearing should have been held by the Board to settle the issue. *NLRB v. Smith Industries, Inc.,* 5 Cir., 1968, 403 F.2d 889; *NLRB v. Ortronix, Inc.,* 5 Cir., 1967, 380 F.2d 737.

Since the Union prevailed in the representation election by only two votes, resolution of this case cannot be finally made until the Board holds a full hearing on the eligibility of Parrish, Norris and Smith to vote in the election.

Remanded for further proceedings before the Board.

6. Unfair Labor Practices—Elections

Employer Unfair Practices (Elections)

GENERAL. The unfair labor practices of employers are listed in Section 8(a) of the Act and those of labor organizations in Section 8(b). Section 8(e) lists the unfair labor practice that can be committed only by an employer and a labor organization acting together.

The aim of an election is to offer employees a fair, unbiased choice as to whether or not they will be represented. If the answer to this is affirmative, then the election should also determine who will be the representative. If the atmosphere of fair or unbiased election is interfered with, by confusion or fear of reprisals, then the Board can set the election aside and order a new one. Conduct is held to interfere even if proof of actual interference is not available, for it is sufficient to merely show that the conduct tended to interfere, a burden of proof much easier to meet.

A balance is sought between conduct which tends "to interfere with, restrain, or coerce employees in the exercise of the rights guaranteed in Section 7" (Section 8(a)(1)), on the one hand, and an employer's right to free speech, on the other hand. An employer's expression of views, "shall not constitute . . . an unfair labor practice . . . if such expression contains no threat of reprisals or force or promise of benefit" (Section 8(c)). The theory of this fine balance is well established but in application it becomes difficult for the decision-maker to achieve a consistent approach when dealing with a variety of fact situations. Sometimes it is particularly difficult for a participant to anticipate how a judge will view a particular act. In spite of the variety of facts that may arise, a basic set of rules has evolved which will illustrate the theory as well as some applications.

HISTORY. Rarely does management want a union, and unions often make antimanagement campaigns, for if the employees are completely happy without a union then the union will not be able to have an election. So the atmosphere of an election is frequently volatile, and it becomes tempting for the parties to promise benefits that can't be achieved or to threaten the employees. Both of these forms of conduct are forbidden for management, but the unions are relatively free to make promises that probably can't be achieved. Unions are prohibited from saying that something has been achieved somewhere else which has not really been achieved. Thus a union can say that it will be able to obtain a pay raise, but the union may not say that it has obtained a raise at plant "X" if this is not true.

The rulings in the early cases held that an employer could literally say nothing, but in 1940 the Supreme Court in the *Virginia Power and Light* case modified this and considered the totality of circumstances. In the 1950's, employers had considerable latitude in what was permitted speech, and in 1969 the Supreme Court ruled for only the second time on this issue. The Court stated that if the occurrence of the events being predicted are in the control of management, then predictions about the possible bad consequences of a union victory are a threat. If the events being predicted are not in the control of management, then predictions by management are permitted. An example of the latter would be that the company might go bankrupt as a similar company did when the union won.

INTERROGATION OF EMPLOYEES. An employer has no duty to turn away and not listen if an employee volunteers anything concerning the union's activities, but the employer's questions concerning unions are subject to close scrutiny. The employer's questions are not unlawful per se (meaning simply because they are asked) but the entire environment concerning the union is evaluated, and the environment may be held to be too antiunion and hence not permitted. So particular questions may be permitted but when considered in light of other conduct may become not permitted.

If the interrogation is in the form of a poll, then it will be considered an unfair labor practice unless the purpose is to determine the validity of a union's claim that it represents a majority. For an employer to be permitted interrogation, the employees must be aware of this narrow purpose and there must be no threat of reprisal. Also, the employer must not have created a "coercive atmosphere." *Strukness Construction Co.*, 165 NLRB No. 102, 1967. If the poll shows that a majority favor the union, then the poll qualifies as an election. The mood certainly seems to be to discourage polls, for if a poll replaces the election, then the employer would not have a chance to campaign prior to the election. Note that the poll does not replace the election if the poll does not favor the union.

SURVEILLANCE. It is an unfair labor practice to use spies or apply surveillance in connection with any phase of the organizational efforts. *Excelsior Laundry Co.*, 186 NLRB No. 129, 1966.

EMPLOYER SPEECH. Congress attempted to balance the employer's right to free speech against the broad power and control that he has over his employees. The NLRA speaks on both sides of the fulcrum by giving the employer certain rights via 8(c) and yet making 8(a) restrictions so broad as to encompass a wide variety of activities. The result is that speech must be evaluated in the totality of its circumstances. *Daniel Construction Co. v. NLRB*, 341 F.2d 805 (1965), cert. denied 382 U.S. 831. This procedure is not too different from the tests used to evaluate speech in other contexts, such as in the "clear and present danger" test of Justice Holmes to decide whether speech leads to an act of violence. If one considers the alternative approaches, this one must win by default if for no other reason. A shortcoming is that unless the conduct is one extreme or the other, then at the time it occurs one is not certain whether or not it is permitted.

CAPTIVE AUDIENCES. An employer may use his property to address his employees during working hours so long as he does not violate some other restrictions, such as a coercive speech or a speech exceeding a restricted time span. The union may be denied an opportunity for equal time. *Livingston Shirt Corp.*, 107 NLRB 400, 1953.

Employees Unfair Practices (Elections)

SOLICITATION AND DISTRIBUTION (EMPLOYEES). This section and the following ones on solicitation and distribution concern areas where considerable controversy has arisen. This is probably in part because of the vital interest to both parties. Unions can reach employees much more easily on the business premises than at home, and the employer is concerned that his employees not be disrupted or distracted during working hours and/or on company property.

Concerning an oral solicitation, the Supreme Court in 1940 drew the distinction between working time and free time, both on company property, and held that some nondiscriminatory restrictions against solicitations may be valid but that management must tolerate some inconvenience. *Republic Aviation* v. *NLRB*, 324 U.S. 793, 1945. An employee may be limited to his free time, for union activities, and if there is a rule that prevents one from being on the premises for any reason when "off duty," then this rule may be applied to persons conducting union activities as well as those conducting other activities. Obviously, there are no restrictions on whether an employee may use his free time when he is not on company property.

Rules limiting distribution of union literature may be valid if the rules do not discriminate against unions as opposed to distribution of other literature. *Mason & Hanger-Silus Mason Co.*, 167 NLRB No. 122, 1970. The rules may limit the union's efforts to nonworking time and in nonworking areas. Thus, an employer may limit the distribution of union literature if he limits the distribution of all literature. With respect to these limitations, one must wonder if this applies to United Fund and similar charities that have enjoyed special status, for if it does and a company solicits for them then the union must be provided equal status—this is undoubtedly not the rule.

SOLICITATION AND DISTRIBUTION (NONEMPLOYEES). If the unions have other means of communicating with the employees, then the employer can prohibit solicitation or distribution by nonemployees anywhere on company property. *NLRB* v. *Babcock & Wilcox Co.*, 351 U.S. 105, 1956. The other means of communicating may require additional effort and expense, but the NLRB feels that this is not a sufficient criterion to permit nonemployees to enter company property. *Dexter Thread Mills, Inc.*, 199 NLRB No. 113, 1972). This is logical if one can imagine the potential security problems of nonemployees en masse on company property, not to mention the increased liability in the event of an accident. The

Supreme Court, in a 1974 case involving Magnavox, held that if the union and the employer agree to prohibit all solicitation on the property, then this would be a violation as it would freeze out any competitive activities by other unions. *NLRB* v. *Magnavox of Tennessee*, 474 F.2d 1269, 1973.

SOLICITATION AND DISTRIBUTION (ON OTHERS' PROPERTY). Shopping centers have been a problem with respect to solicitation, sometimes accomplished by picketing, for the union's aim is usually a store owner in the shopping center and the union usually has no interest in the shopping center owner, so the question of location of the union members' efforts is the key issue. The shopping center owner has a right to peaceful enjoyment of his property while the union feels that its First Amendment guarantee of freedom of expression means that they should be able to present their position on the shopping center property where they can be near the store owner with whom they have a dispute.

The Supreme Court, 965 S.Ct. *Hudgens* v. *NLRB*, 1976, held that the picketing on the property of a shopping center is not protected by the First Amendment and the NLRB should decide the issues by applying their established rules for solicitation and picketing. This case reversed the Supreme Court's own decision in *Food Employers Union* v. *Logan Valley Plaza*, 391, U.S. 308, 1968.

Employer and Employee Unfair Practices (Elections)

COERCION. Giving an activity the status of a "right," such as the much publicized right to remain silent during an interrogation by police, means that one cannot be penalized for asserting it. Similarly, the employees have the right to decide who, if anyone, will represent them and this right cannot be influenced by threats or other forms of coercion.

The right to self-organize would be in jeopardy, as would any other right, if threats of reprisals or force were permitted, so they are not. *Textile Workers* v. *Darlington Mfg. Co.*, 380 U.S. 363, 1965.

Likewise, it is felt that promise of benefits, if timed so as to combat an organizational effort, is also a violation. It may seem strange not to permit an employer to increase his compensation, but the Supreme Court has held that a company's decision to increase benefits can be an unfair labor practice. In one case the company made the decision to increase benefits independently of organization activities and announced it as being unconditional, but gave the announcement just before the election and thus committed a violation of 8(a)(1) as having an unlawful purpose. 8(a)(1) is the only section that requires an unlawful purpose for an unfair practice, as usually the conduct itself is sufficient (note that in this case the conduct of granting an increase would have been permitted). *NLRB* v. *Exchange Parts Co.*, 375 U.S. 405, 1964.

Each party is accorded the right of persuasion and denied the use of coercion. By necessity the union is anticompany and management is antiunion, so it would be an impossibility to expect management to use words of conviction in an effort to persuade an employee to vote against unionization without the presence of "antiunion animus." *NLRB* v. *Colbert Dairy Products Co.*, 317 F.2d 44, 1963. An employer may assert his legal right to "persuade" without being held to have practiced coercion, as the following case, perhaps an extreme example, demonstrates. In this case, the respondent stated in its campaign material that it would "fight the Union in every legal way possible"; that it was "not compelled to agree to a Union proposal or to make a concession to the Union"; that it would engage in "hard bargaining"; that "the only way a Union can force your Company to do anything it is unwilling to do would be to pull you out on strike"; and that "if the Union calls an economic strike you can be permanently replaced." The NLRB found this to be coercive but the Eighth Circuit evaluated each assertion and concluded that the respondent had merely used "hard bargaining" and stated:

> "Inasmuch as respondent did not, in any of the handbills or speeches, state anything more than its legal rights, in an entirely legal manner, we are persuaded to hold that the challenged remarks fall within the protection afforded by §8(c). The conclusion is inescapable that the truthful utterances, protected, as they are, by the First Amendment to the Constitution and authorized by §8(c), were improperly interpreted by the trial examiner and a majority of the Board as a basis for authorizing an unfavorable inference. Accordingly, enforcement of the Board's order is denied." *NLRB* v. *Wilson Lumber Co.*, 355 F.2d 426, 1966.

The dissent in the Court set down the standard for evaluating the NLRB's holdings, and stated:

> "It is often difficult to determine whether certain statements by management constitute permissible forceful argument in support of management's opposition to the advent of a union, or constitute an illegal threat to the employees in the event the union should win the election. In such cases, if the inference or conclusion found by the Board that the statements constituted a threat is a reasonable one, which it was permissible for the Board to make, its conclusion may seem more plausible and reasonable to us." *Surprenant Mfg. Co.* v. *NLRB*, 341 F.2d 756, 760 (6th Cir.), 1965.

Time Ban. There is a ban on certain speeches within the 24 hours immediately preceding an election and a generally more stringent standard for any conduct, the theory being that the other party might be deprived of a chance to reply. The speeches prohibited are those made during company time. *Peerless Plywood Co.*, 107 NLRB 106, 1953.

Truth as a Defense. An employer can make predictions concerning the possible dire economic consequences of a union's being certified. *NLRB* v. *Transport Clearings, Inc.*, 311 F.2d 519, 1963. It is only when the employer goes further and threatens to take economic or other reprisals against the employees that an 8(a)(1) violation may be found. Thus, a prediction that competitive conditions will force a plant to close if a union contract is·signed is protected, whereas a threat to close down in retaliation to unionization is beyond the protection unless the employer goes out of business. *NLRB* v. *Morris Fishman & Sons, Inc.*, 278 F.2d 792, 1960. Going out of business is permitted even if for antiunion purposes. *Textile Workers Union* v. *Darlington Mfg. Co.*, 380 U.S. 263, 1965.

What is not permitted speech is for the employer to make predictions that he cannot objectively support. *NLRB* v. *Gissel Packing Co.*, 395 U.S. 575, 1969. There appears to be no comparable standard for a union's promises but the union cannot assert a factual untruth. An example of a factual untruth would be where the union made a false claim that it had achieved benefits at another plant when it had not.

The standard as to what speech is permissible seems to follow a rule this author has named "Zepke's Rule"—"Truth is a defense so long as you can objectively prove it." The proof is an objective standard, where dire circumstances can be predicted if the union is certified, so long as management can prove that the predictions are based on other occurrences that would support an analogy to the situation at hand. The support could be an employer's factual account of a labor strife, which included violence, so long as the employer also emphasized a willingness to bargain if the union won. *Louisberg Sportswear Co. v. NLRB*, 68 L.C. Par. 12, 599, 1972.

DEFAMATION. States have laws that permit one party to bring a civil action for defamation, and sometimes the attempt has been made to use these laws in a labor strife, but labor laws are federal and hence preempt state defamation laws. So long as the federal law protects the speech in question, which it certainly does if the statements are not coercive and were made without knowledge of their falsity, then the speech is protected. *Linn v. Plant Guard Workers*, 383 U.S. 53, 1966.

MISCELLANEOUS. The NLRB will look at the timing and other general circumstances in order to see if the employees have been able to make an uninhibited choice. The term "laboratory conditions" was coined to represent the desired atmosphere, and this may be held to have been violated by the cumulative effect of activities that singly are permited. Note that any injection of racial prejudice is inherently suspect as it is in other areas of conduct. *Sewell Mfg. Co.*, 138 NLRB 66, 1962.

389 F.2d 835 (1968)

Held: During an organizational drive, an employer may be held to have committed an unfair labor practice for actions that at other times would not be violations and indeed may be beneficial to the employees. Actions such as promise of benefits or transfers, as well as threats, may be held to be an unfair action, so the employer needs to be particularly careful of management's actions during a union drive.

Opinion:

This case is before us on a petition by an employer, Macy's Missouri-Kansas Division, to review a decision and order of the National Labor Relations Board. The Board cross-petitions for the enforcement of its order. The decision and order of the Board are reported at 162 NLRB No. 70. . . .

The scope of our review is limited to a determination of whether the findings of the Board are supported by substantial evidence on the whole record. If the record discloses substantial evidence in support of the findings of an unfair labor practice, the order of the Board must be enforced. *Universal Camera Corporation* v. *NLRB*, 340 U.S. 474, 71 S.Ct. 456, 95 L.ed. 456 (1951).

THREATS, PROMISES AND WAGE INCREASES IN VIOLATION OF §8(a)(1)

Gertrude Cooper was the manager of Macy's main store Ladies' Alteration Department and was stipulated to be a supervisor within the meaning of 29 USC §152(11). While Cooper was on vacation in August 1965 various employees in the department began supporting the Union and signed union cards. Upon her return Cooper made her dislike of unions known. We believe the totality of her expressions could validly be considered coercion, interference, and restraint of employees in the full exercise of their rights guaranteed under the Act. . . .

[2] . . . On at least five occasions it appears that Cooper threatened employees with possible layoff, and, at least by intimation, placed the blame for such layoff on the Union. Cooper was obviously angry at the employees who were supporting the Union and repeatedly indicated that she had been stabbed in the back and betrayed by these employees. She interrogated employees and vilified to others an employee who was a leader in the unionization drive. Finally, on at least one occasion Cooper intimated that an employee would be fired if she did not cease her union activity.

Though not disputing the statements made by Cooper, Macy's contends that the statements were but mild expressions of opinion protected by the right of free speech. We cannot agree. These were clearly coercive remarks, repeatedly made during the course of an organization drive. In their totality these statements constitute what could be considered coercive activity in violation of §8(a)(1) of the Act. *Jas. H. Matthews & Co.* v. *NLRB*, 354 F.2d 432, 439-440 (8 Cir. 1965), cert. denied 384 U.S. 1002, 86 S.Ct. 1924, 16 L.ed.2d 1015 (1966); *NLRB* v. *Byrds Manufacturing Corp.*, 324 F.2d 329 (8 Cir. 1963).

[3] In addition to these threats Cooper made certain promises of benefits. It has often been held that promises of benefit that are calculated to induce employees to foresake the union are unfair labor practices in violation of §8(a)(1). *NLRB* v. *Grand Foundries, Inc.*, 362 F.2d 702, 708 (8 Cir. 1966); *NLRB* v. *Soft Water Laundry, Inc.*, 346 F.2d 930 (5 Cir. 1965).

[4] The evidence indicates that Cooper told employee Franklin that she couldn't do anything about wages at that time "but later on maybe she could do something." Cooper told employee Hinman that the Union couldn't do anything for the employees

that Macy's couldn't do. To employee Butler, Cooper said, "If you will just trust me, Macy's will do more for you than the union."

Though the Board has certainly not made a strong showing that these statements were unfair inducements, we think that taken in the context of the unionization drive, the strong contemporaneous expressions of antiunion sentiment, and the wage increases that were subsequently granted, these statements are a sufficient promise of reward to constitute an unfair labor practice in violation of §8(a)(1).

[5] In addition to the threats and promises the Board found that the granting of $5 to $7 wage increases to three employees were made to discourage union membership in violation of §8(a)(1). The evidence indicates that these raises amounted to about a 10 per cent to 15 per cent increase in salary and were two to three times the average periodic increase.

Macy's argued that these increases were an attempt to keep the salary spreads of senior workers in line with the new minimum wage required to be paid to new workers. The trial examiner was not impressed with this explanation and pointed to the "meteoric raise" in pay scale enjoyed by Harris and Wood that gave them two substantial wage increases within six months. The trial examiner also pointed to the unusual timing of the raises that coincided with the unionization drive and followed assurances from Cooper that Macy's would take care of the employees. Though the employer has presented a plausible justification for the wage increases, we think the Board was presented with a factual issue which was resolved in favor of the General Counsel. As such we believe the finding, having substantial support in the record, is entitled to acceptance by us. *Universal Camera Corp.* v. *NLRB*, 340 U.S. 474, 490, 71 S.Ct. 456, 95 L.ed. 456 (1951).

[6] It is well established that the timely and unilateral granting of a wage increase is an unfair labor practice when it results in employees being induced to forsake the union. "[I]nterferences, accomplished by allurements, are as much condemned by the Act as is coercion." *NLRB* v. *Douglas and Lomason Company*, 333 F.2d 510, 514 (8 Cir. 1964). See also *NLRB* v. *Exchange Parts Co.*, 375 U.S. 405, 409-410, 84 S.Ct. 457, 11 L.ed.2d 435 (1964). . . .

[7, 8] In determining if a transfer constitutes discrimination in violation of §8(a)(3) and (4) we start with the proposition that an employer has a fundamental right to assign employees to positions the employer deems, in the exercise of its managerial discretion, most expedient. The employer generally is allowed to pick the time, place, and manner of employment, and absent contractual restrictions the employee is required to conform with these requirements. See *NLRB* v. *Jones & Laughlin Steel Corp.*, 301 U.S. 1, 57 S.Ct. 615, 81 L.ed. 893 (1937); CCH Labor Law Reporter, §4010 and §4095 et seq. Only if the Board is able to prove that the particular assignment was brought about because an employee exercised his rights guaranteed by the Act will an employer's work assignment be declared illegal.

[9] It is well established, as the Board admits, that the mere coincidence of an employee's union activity and the employee's transfer will not support a charge of discrimination. *Beaver Valley Canning Company* v. *NLRB*, 332 F.2d 429 (8 Cir. 1964). Aside from this coincidence, however, the only positive evidence supporting the Board's finding of discrimination is the fact that Schmidt's immediate supervisor was very unhappy about Schmidt's union activity. Though this is some evidence of discrimination, when viewed in the light of the strong conflicting evidence, we do not believe it is sufficient to support the Board's finding.

To begin, the transfer was not a demotion. Schmidt would receive a higher salary in her new position, and there is nothing to indicate that the work was any less desirable. Schmidt was not deprived of being a member of this Union as the department to which she was transferred was represented by the same Union. Further, other than Cooper's private reaction to the Union there is no particular indication of anti-union animus coming from the company's management. There are unions representing various groups of Macy's employees. On the occasion of this particular campaign the company did not engage in any form of anti-union propaganda or campaigning. . . .

[11, 12] Were we to uphold the Board on this issue, the historical rights of an employer to transfer employees as efficiency demands would almost be eliminated. Once an employee became an active supporter of a union he would remain virtually immune from the directions of his employer. Obviously, such is not, nor should it be, the law. *NLRB* v. *Louisiana Manufacturing Company,* 374 F.2d 696, 706 (8 Cir. 1967). To overcome the inherent right of an employer to assign work to his employees, the Board must make a stronger showing of discrimination than it has shown here. . . .

NLRB v. *Babcock & Wilcox Co.*

351 U.S. 105, 100 L.ed. 975, 76 S.Ct. 679, 1955

Held: This case presents the Supreme Court's analysis of the duty of an employer, under federal labor laws, to permit union activity on his property. The Court's analysis is very thorough and defines and discusses the various combinations of crucial factors, which are: working or nonworking hours, employee or nonemployee, or whether or not discriminatory conduct towards one union took place.

Opinion:

I. In general

§1. Introduction and scope; summary.

[a] Introduction and scope.

The National Labor Relations Act provides that it is an unfair labor practice for an employer (1) to interfere with, restrain, or coerce employees in the exercise of their right to self-organization, to form, join, or assist labor organizations, and to refrain from any or all such activities, or (2) to dominate or interfere with the formation or administration of any labor organization, or (3) to encourage or discourage membership in any labor organization by discrimination in regard to hire or tenure of employment or any term or condition of employment.

In view of these provisions, questions have arisen as to the extent to which an employer has a statutory duty (failure to comply with which will render him liable to a charge of unfair labor practices) to permit organizational activities upon his premises. It is with these questions that the present annotation is concerned, it being sought herein to determine, from an examination of the decisions of the federal courts, whether an employer may, without violating the provisions of the federal labor relations statutes, prohibit or limit organizational activities on company premises.

[b] Summary.

The law on the questions under annotation may be summarized briefly: it is well established that, although an employer may prohibit union activities on his premises during his employees' working hours, he may not bar his employees from engaging in such activities during nonworking hours (including rest and lunch periods, whether paid for by the employer or not), except in special circumstances (as, for example, where the prohibited activities are likely to prove disruptive of employee harmony and discipline, or where the prohibition is limited to certain portions of the employer's premises at which union activity would be harmful to the employer's business or dangerous to employees).

And the employer's rights with respect to prohibition of union activities on his premises are limited still further by the settled rule that no prohibition of such activities will be upheld if it is applied discriminatorily, either against unions generally, or against one union and in favor of another.

§2. Prohibition of union activity during working hours; general rule.

A determination whether an employer must permit particular organizational activities on company property requires a working out of an adjustment between the undisputed right of self-organization assured to employees by the federal labor relations statute, and the equally undisputed right of employers to maintain discipline in their establishments. *Republic Aviation Corp.* v. *NLRB* (1945) 324 U.S. 793, 89 L.ed. 1372, 65 S.Ct. 982, 157 ALR 1081, reh den *NLRB* v. *Le Tourneau Co.* 325 U.S. 894, 89 L.ed. 2005, 65 S.Ct. 1401.

In working out this adjustment, the courts have established that, absent special circumstances, an employer is not guilty of an unfair labor practice if he promulgates and enforces a rule prohibiting union activities during working hours. *NLRB* v. *Empire Furniture Corp.* (1939, CA6th) 107 F.2d 92. . . .

In support of the rule stated above it was commented by the court in *Carter Carburetor Corp.* v. *NLRB* (1944, CA8th) 140 F.2d 714, that, if solicitation for union membership on an employer's premises during working hours gives rise to bickering, disputes, ill will, and a lack of harmony among the employees, thus affecting the employees' efficiency, it is not unreasonable to adopt such a rule as would tend to remove the causes which lowered their efficiency.

It is to be noted that the National Labor Relations Board has formulated a presumption that an employer's prohibition of union activity during working hours is valid where there is no showing that the prohibition was adopted by the employer for a discriminatory purpose. See *Republic Aviation Corp.* v. *NLRB* (1945) 324 U.S. 793, 89 L.ed. 1372, 65 S.Ct. 982, 157 ALR 1081, reh den *NLRB* v. *Le Tourneau Co.* 325 U.S. 894, 89 L.ed. 2005, 65 S.Ct. 1401 (in which the court impliedly approved Board's adoption of presumption).

§3. Prohibition of union activity during nonworking hours or during both working and nonworking hours; general rule.

[a] Generally.

Absent special circumstances, an employer is guilty of an unfair labor practice if he promulgates or enforces a rule prohibiting union activity outside of working hours, although on company property. *Republic Aviation Corp.* v. *NLRB* (1945) 324 U.S. 793, 89 L.ed. 1372, 65 S.Ct. 982, 157 ALR 1081, reh den *NLRB* v. *Le Tourneau Co.* 325 U.S. 894, 89 L.ed. 2005, 65 S.Ct. 1401; *NLRB* v. *Babcock & Wilcox Co.* (1956) 351 U.S. 105, 100 L.ed. 975, 76 S.Ct. 679; *Carter Carburetor Corp.* v. *NLRB* (1944, CA8th) 140 F.2d 714; *NLRB* v. *Glenn L. Martin-Nebraska Co.* (1944, CA8th) 141 F.2d 371; *NLRB* v. *American Pearl Button Co.* (1945, CA8th) 149 F.2d 258; *NLRB* v. *Illinois Tool Works* (1946, CA7th) 153 F.2d 811; *NLRB* v. *May Dept. Stores Co.* (1946, CA8th) 154 F.2d 533, cert den 329 U.S. 725, 91 L.ed. 627, 67 S.Ct. 72. . . .

Thus, the Supreme Court has said that an employer may place no restriction on his employees' right to discuss self-organization among themselves unless the employer can demonstrate that a restriction is necessary to maintain production or discipline. *NLRB* v. *Babcock & Wilcox Co.* (1956) 351 U.S. 105, 100 L.ed. 975, 76 S.Ct. 679.

Where it appeared that an employer's rule prohibiting solicitation of employees from membership in organizations was not limited to activities which interfered with plant efficiency (that is, to working hours or to places where work was being performed), and that, in addition, the rule was arbitrarily enforced by foreman who at the same time warned employees against joining a union, it was held that the NLRB properly found that application of the rule amounted to intimidation and coercion and constituted an unfair labor practice. *NLRB* v. *Glenn L. Martin-Nebraska Co.* (1944, CA8th) 141 F.2d 371, in which the court pointed out that under the circumstances of the case the enforcement of the rule unnecessarily interfered with and hampered the employees in their right of self-organization for collective bargaining. . . .

Enforcement of an employer's rule prohibiting union solicitation outside of working hours on company premises has been held to be an unfair labor practice, notwithstanding absence of evidence that enforcement of the rule in fact interfered with or discouraged union organization, or that the physical location of the employer's premises made solicitation away from such premises ineffective to reach prospective union members. *Republic Aviation Corp.* v. *NLRB* (1945) 324 U.S. 793, 89 L.ed.

1372, 65 S.Ct. 982, 157 ALR 1081, reh den *NLRB* v. *Le Tourneau Co.* 325 U.S. 894, 89 L.ed. 2005, 65 S.Ct. 1401.

[b] Presumption of unlawfulness of prohibition.

The National Labor Relations Board has created a presumption that a rule prohibiting union activity by an employee, on nonworking time, but on company property, is an unreasonable impediment to self-organization, and therefore discriminatory, in absence of evidence that special circumstances make the rule necessary to the maintenance of production or discipline. In *Republic Aviation Corp.* v. *NLRB* (1945) 324 U.S. 793, 89 L.ed. 1372, 65 S.Ct. 982, 157 ALR 1081, reh den *NLRB* v. *Le Tourneau Co.* 325 U.S. 894, 89 L.ed. 2005, 65 S.Ct. 1401, the United States Supreme Court found no error in the Board's adoption of this presumption. The Board's presumption was also held to be neither improper nor unreasonable in *NLRB* v. *May Dept. Stores Co.* (1946, CA8th) 154 F.2d 533, cert den 329 U.S. 725, 91 L.ed. 627, 67 S.Ct. 72.

It has been held that the NLRB's power to make a no-solicitation rule the basis of a presumption that the employer had violated the National Labor Relations Act is unaffected by the inclusion, in the 1947 amendment of the act, of a provision that Board findings are conclusive if supported by substantial evidence on the record as a whole. *NLRB* v. *La Salle Steel Co.* (1949, CA7th) 178 F.2d 829, cert den 339 U.S. 963, 94 L.ed. 1372, 70 S.Ct. 996. . . .

§4.—Exceptions to rule.

[a] Generally.

As already indicated the rule which bars' an employer from prohibiting employees from engaging, during working and nonworking time, in union activities on company premises, is subject to certain exceptions.

With respect to the special circumstances in which an employer may lawfully limit union activities on company premises, even in nonworking time, it has been held that an employer is not guilty of an unfair labor practice in forbidding the distribution on its premises of scurrilous and defamatory literature which holds the employer's officers and supervising officials up to ridicule and contempt and which has a necessary tendency to disrupt discipline in the plant. *Maryland Drydock Co.* v. *NLRB* (1950, CA4th) 183 F.2d 538, in which an employer was held not guilty of an unfair labor practice in forbidding distribution on company premises of union literature describing the company president as "Goosie," and "a vulture," and describing an association of supervisory employees as a "scab" association, the term "scab" being defined in abusive language. The court acknowledged that if the union had offered to distribute literature containing no insulting and defamatory matter and had been forbidden to do so, an inference might well be drawn of the existence of a general rule or policy forbidding the distribution of union literature, but, it was said, there was no evidence of that sort in the instant case. . . .

[b] Prohibition of union activity at particular places on employer's premises.

A rule promulgated by an employer, absolutely prohibiting union activities, at any time, on certain portions of the employer's premises, may, in some situations, be lawful. Thus, in *NLRB* v. *May Dept. Stores Co.* (1946, CA8th) 154 F.2d 533, cert den 329 U.S. 725, 91 L.ed. 627, 67 S.Ct. 72, the court stated its approval of an order issued by the Board which, in effect, permitted an employer who operated a department store to prohibit union solicitation at all times, including the employees' lunch hour, on the selling floor of the store. The court noted its agreement with the Board's reasoning that even though both the soliciting employee and the employee being solicited are on their lunch hour, solicitation, if carried on on the selling floor where customers are normally present, might conceivably be disruptive of the employer's business. . . .

§5.—What are "nonworking hours."

Since an employer may, as a general rule, lawfully prohibit union activity by employees during working hours (§2, supra), but not during nonworking hours (§3, supra), questions arise as to just what hours fall within the two classifications.

Periods of rest and lunch periods have been held to be the employees' own time, and a no-solicitation rule promulgated by an employer may not be applied during such periods, absent special circumstances. *NLRB* v. *May Dept. Stores Co.* (1946, CA8th) 154 F.2d 533, cert den 329 U.S. 725, 91 L.ed. 627, 67 S.Ct. 72.

Similarly, viewing an employer's discharge of employees for their activities in soliciting union members on company property, and during lunch and rest periods, as unfair labor practices, the court in *Olin Industries, Inc.* v. *NLRB* (1951, CA5th) 191 F.2d 613, reh den 192 F.2d 799, cert den 343 U.S. 919, 96 L.ed. 1332, 72 S.Ct. 676, reh den 343, U.S. 970, 96 L.ed. 1365, 72 S.Ct. 1055, rejected the argument that, since the discharged employees were paid during their lunch and rest periods, such periods actually constituted company time and were subject to company rules prohibiting solicitation. The court stated its approval of the Board's approach to the problem of solicitation on company property on the basis of the distinction between actual working and nonworking time, rather than on the basis of the immaterial distinction between paid and unpaid time. If the distinction were drawn between the paid and unpaid time, the court said, the right of employees to organize collectively might be seriously impaired, since a premium would be placed on attempts by employers to allocate wages or salaries and company time over the entire work week, so as to prohibit employees from discussing union activities or soliciting union membership at practically any convenient time. . . .

§6. Prohibition of union activities by nonemployees; denial of access to company property.

Does the rule which bars an employer from prohibiting his employees from engaging in union activities, on the employer's premises, in nonworking hours, also bar him from prohibiting such activities by nonemployees during those hours? In other words, may an employer deny union representatives access to his property where the organizers seek to engage in union activities in the employees' nonworking time? This is the question to be dealt with at this point.

The United States Supreme Court has ruled that an employer may validly post his property against nonemployee distribution of union literature if reasonable efforts by the union through other available channels of communication will enable it to reach the employees with its message and if employer's notice or order does not discriminate against the union by allowing other distribution. *NLRB* v. *Babcock & Wilcox Co.* (1956) 351 U.S. 105, 100 L.ed. 975, 76 S.Ct. 679. But the court limited its ruling by stating that when inaccessibility of employees makes ineffective the reasonable attempt by nonemployees to communicate with them through the usual channels, the right to exclude from property must yield to the extent needed to permit communication of information on the right to organize. The holding of the court was that the Board had improperly found an employer guilty of an unfair labor practice in refusing to permit distribution of union literature by nonemployee union organizers on the employer's property where the usual method of imparting information (including mail, personal contact, and telephone) were available to the union, the various instruments of publicity were at hand, and, although the living quarters of the employees were scattered, they were within reasonable reach of the union. . . .

In *Marshall Field & Co.* v. *NLRB* (1952, CA5th) 200 F.2d 375, it was held that an employer did not act unlawfully in prohibiting nonemployees from soliciting persons employed in a department store, where such solicitation was sought to be effected in a public waiting room and washrooms in the store, during the employees' working hours, and in an employees' restaurant and cafeteria, during the employees' nonworking hours. The court said that an employer has the duty to allow organizational activities by nonemployees on the employer's premises only when the employees are uniquely handicapped in the matter of self-organization and concerted activities, and in the instant case the evidence showed no unique handicaps to self-organization. It was pointed out that the employer had a liberal time-off policy which afforded even greater opportunities for self-organization than was the case in many business and industrial establishments. . . .

Notwithstanding an employer's right to bar nonemployee union representatives from the employer's premises, this right cannot be exercised in a discriminatory manner.

Thus in *NLRB* v. *Stowe Spinning Co.* (1949) 336 U.S. 226, 93 L.ed. 638, 69 S.Ct. 541, the Supreme Court held that even though a meeting hall owned by an employer was erected on the understanding that only a certain fraternal organization might use it, and it was not connected with the employer's business operations, nor was its use open to employees because of their employment, the NLRB could properly find that the employer was guilty of an unfair labor practice in discriminating against a union by denying its organizer, who was not an employee, the right to use the hall, where the hall was the only available meeting hall in a company-owned town, was freely given to others for purposes of meetings, and it appeared that the fraternal organization had originally permitted the union organizers to use the hall, but that the employer had rescinded his permission solely because of antiunion bias, manifested also by other acts. Reed, J., joined by Vinson, Ch. J., dissented, stating that the view taken by the majority was an overextension of the statutory guarantee to employees of the right to organize and to form labor unions. The dissenters asserted that employment furnished no baisis for employee rights to the control of property of the employer for union organization when the property is not a part of the premises used by the employer in his business.

Similarly, it has been held that, although an employer may be justified in refusing the use of its quarters to nonemployees for union electioneering purposes, when the employer allows use of such quarters for electioneering purposes by a company union, it may not deny use of the quarters to another union, even where the electioneering by the latter union is to be done by nonemployees. *Westinghouse Electric & Mfg. Co.* v. *NLRB* (1940, CA2d) 112 F.2d 657, affd without op 312 U.S. 660, 85 L.ed. 1108, 61 S.Ct. 736. . . .

§7. Discriminatory prohibition of union activity.

[a] Discrimination against unions, generally.

A limitation imposed by an employer upon organizational activities on company property, even if reasonable on its face, will be held sufficient to support a finding that the employer is guilty of an unfair labor practice, if the employer, in enforcing the limitation, discriminates against a particular union. *NLRB* v. *Babcock & Wilcox Co.* (1956) 351 U.S. 105, 100 L.ed. 975, 76 S.Ct. 679.

Thus, discharge of an employee for his activities in recruiting union members during rest periods for which he was paid by his employer was held in *NLRB* v. *Botany Worsted Mills* (1939, CA3d) 106 F.2d 263, to support a Board finding that the discharge was an unfair labor practice, where, as against the employer's contention that the discharge resulted from the employee's use of company time for purposes other than the performance of the employee's work, it was shown that employees had frequently engaged in extracurricular activities during their rest periods and such activities had never been invoked by the employer as a cause for discharge. The employer's allegation that it had no knowledge of previously unpunished extracurricular activities of its employees on company time was dismissed by the court as amounting to, at best, a specious afterthought. . . .

[b] Discrimination between unions.

It is well established that an employer is guilty of an unfair labor practice if it adopts rules limiting union activity on company premises and then applies such rules in favor of one union and against another. *NLRB* v. *Waterman S. S. Corp.* (1940) 309 U.S. 206, 84 L.ed. 704, 60 S.Ct. 493, reh den 309 U.S. 696, 84 L.ed. 1036, 60 S.Ct. 611; *NLRB* v. *Link-Belt Co.* (1941) 311 U.S. 584, 85 L.ed. 368, 61 S.Ct. 358; *NLRB* v. *Wallace Mfg. Co.* (1938, CA4th) 95 F.2d 818; *Westinghouse Electric & Mfg. Co.* v. *NLRB* (1940, CA2d) 112 F.2d 657, affd without op 312 U.S. 660, 85 L.ed. 1108, 61 S.Ct. 736; *NLRB* v. *Yale & T. Mfg. Co.* (1940, CA2d) 114 F.2d 376; *South Atlantic S. S. Co.* v. *NLRB* (1941, CA5th) 116 F.2d 480, cert den 313 U.S. 582, 85 L.ed. 1538, 61 S.Ct. 1101, reh den 314 U.S. 708, 86 L.ed. 565, 62 S.Ct. 54; *NLRB* v. *Bersted Mfg. Co.* (1942, CA6th) 124 F.2d 409, reh den 128 F.2d 738; *NLRB* v. *Hudson Motor Car Co.* (1942, CA6th) 128 F.2d 528; *Carter Carburetor Corp.* v. *NLRB* (1944, CA8th) 140 F.2d 714; *NLRB* v. *Brown Co.* (1947, CA1st) 160 F.2d 449 (by implication); *NLRB* v. *Clark Bros. Co.* (1947, CA2d) 163 F.2d 373. See, however, *Stewart-Warner Corp.* v. *NLRB* (1952, CA4th) 194 F.2d 207.

Evidence showing that after the NLRB had ordered an election for the choice of a bargaining agent for seamen of certain ships, representatives of one of two rival national unions were given passes by the employer and had an opportunity to contact members of the crews, while representatives of the other unions were refused passes and denied access to the ships under any conditions, was held sufficient to support a finding of the Board that the employer had interfered with the employees' right to select a union of their own choosing. *NLRB* v. *Waterman S. S. Corp.* (1940) 309 U.S. 206, 84 L.ed. 704, 60 S.Ct. 493, reh den 309 U.S. 696, 84 L.ed. 1036, 60 S.Ct. 611. The court approved the Board's decision that if the employer was to permit any opportunity for contact with the men, a fair election required that equal opportunity be given to both unions. . . .

II. Particular union activities

§8. In general; distribution of union literature.

[a] Generally.

The general principles governing an employer's right to limit union activities on the employer's premises have been discussed in the preceding subdivisions of this annotation. To be dealt with at this point are cases involving the application of these principles to instances in which employers have sought to limit particular forms of union activity.

[b] Distribution of union literature; prohibition held unlawful.

In a number of cases an employer's attempt to bar the distribution of union literature on company premises has been held unlawful.

Thus, where employees distributed union literature or circulars on their own time on company owned and policed parking lots, adjacent to the company's fenced-in plant, in violation of a long-standing and strictly enforced rule, adopted prior to union organization activity about the premises, it was held in *Republic Aviation Corp.* v. *NLRB* (1945) 324 U.S. 793, 89 L.ed. 1372, 65 S.Ct. 982, 157 ALR 1081, reh den *NLRB* v. *Le Tourneau Co.* 325 U.S. 894, 89 L.ed. 2005, 65 S.Ct. 1401, that an order of the NLRB directing the employer to cease and desist from interference with his employees in their right to self-organization, and to rescind the rule as it concerned the situation above described, and to pay employees who had been discharged for violating the rule for their lost time, should be enforced, notwithstanding that the rule did not single out union activities as a subject of prohibition, but extended to solicitation and distribution of handbills or literature of any type, and that it had been adopted before any union organization was attempted, and was impartially enforced without union bias or discrimination. . . .

[c]—Prohibition held lawful.

In cases presenting special circumstances, it has been held lawful for an employer to bar distribution of union literature on employer premises.

Thus, where leaflets distributed by employees on company premises, before the day's work began, were certain to arouse animosity in many employees because referring to one of two rival unions as a "company union," the suspension for two weeks of the employees who had distributed the leaflets was held not to constitute an unfair labor practice. *NLRB* v. *Aintree Corp.* (1943, CA7th) 135 F.2d 395. . . .

§9. Soliciting and recruiting members.

[a] Prohibition held unlawful.

Attempts by employers to bar solicitation of union membership upon the employers' premises have frequently been struck down by the courts as violative of the federal labor relations statutes.

Thus, where it appeared that an employer had posted a notice on his bulletin board at each of two plants stating that solicitation of any kind on the premises was forbidden and violation of the rule would be cause for dismissal, and that two days later, without further warning or caution, the employer discharged by letter an employee for the stated reason that she had engaged in solicitation, the solicitation being among the employees to join a union, the NLRB's finding that the employer's rule was promulgated and enforced to discourage membership in the union was held conclusive. *NLRB* v. *Denver Tent & Awning Co.* (1943, CA10th) 138 F.2d 410, in which the court said that the Board's order was supported by substantial evidence. It was commented that, taken as a whole, the facts were open to two conclusions— one, that the promulgation of the rule or regulation and its enforcement by the discharge of the employee were in good faith for the purpose of further efficiency in the operation of the employer's business, and the other that the rule was merely a device to restrict or impede the employees in the exercise of their right of self-organization—but that the possibility of drawing either of those conclusions did not prevent the Board from drawing the latter. . . .

[b] Prohibition held lawful.

Special circumstances have, in a few cases, been held by the courts to justify, and render lawful, limitations imposed by an employer upon the solicitation of union membership on the employer's premises.

A discharge of an employee for solicitation of union members during working hours (and for the employee's abuse of fellow workers) was held in *NLRB* v. *Empire Furniture Corp.* (1939, CA6th) 107 F.2d 92, not to make the employer liable to a charge of an unfair labor practice. . . .

§10. Wearing union buttons; displaying union insignia.

[a] Prohibition held unlawful.

An employer who attempted to prohibit employees from wearing union buttons or displaying union insignia upon the employer's premises has, in some cases, been held to have acted in violation of the provisions of the federal labor relations statutes.

Evidence showing that employees who wore union badges while at work in a plant which was not organized were discharged because of their refusal to remove them was held in *Republic Aviation Corp.* v. *NLRB* (1945) 324 U.S. 793, 89 L.ed. 1372, 65 S.Ct. 982, 157 ALR 1081, reh den *NLRB* v. *Le Tourneau Co.* 325 U.S. 894, 89 L.ed. 2005, 65 S.Ct. 1401, to support an order of the NLRB based upon a finding that the discharge of the employees was an unfair labor practice, notwithstanding that, as found by the Board, the discharges were not motivated by opposition to any particular union or to unionism. As against the employer's contention that the employees wearing the badges, who were shop stewards, would, upon employer recognition of the union, be union representatives for adjustment of grievances, and that until such recognition the employer would violate its neutrality in labor matters if it permitted the display of a union button by an employee, the court refused to disturb the Board's finding that the permitted wearing of a union button did not indicate that the employer either approved or recognized the union as the representative of its employees. . . .

[b] Prohibition held lawful.

On evidence that an employer had a rule of long standing which required that its employees should not display union insignia when on duty, the rule apparently having been designed to discourage union arguments and disputes among the men on duty, and that this rule was enforced without discrimination, it was held in *NLRB* v. *El Paso Electric Co.* (1943, CA5th) 133 F.2d 168, that the employer was not guilty of contempt of court by continuing enforcement of the rule after an order of the NLRB requiring the employer to cease and desist from dominating, interfering with, or contributing support to a named or any other labor organization had been enforced by the court. . . .

§11. Holding meetings and engaging in discussion.

Evidence that one union was given the right to use the employer's buildings for its meetings, although this privilege was denied a rival union on the ground that the latter permitted outsiders—that is, persons who were not employees—to attend its meetings was held in *NLRB* v. *Wallace Mfg. Co.* (1938, CA4th) 95 F.2d 818, to support a charge of unfair labor practices based, in part, on such facts.

And an employer's refusal to permit a union organizer to use company quarters for electioneering purposes, on the ground that the organizer was a nonemployee, was held to amount to an unfair labor practice where the employer permitted a company union to use the quarters for electioneering. *Westinghouse Electric & Mfg. Co.* v. *NLRB* (1940, CA2d) 112 F.2d 657, affd without op 312 U.S. 660, 85 L.ed. 1108, 61 S.Ct. 736 (in which the court said that equal treatment of unions, in the case of an affiliated union, presupposes that officers and representatives from affiliates or from the national offices should be accorded the right of officers of a nonaffiliated union). . . .

On the other hand in *NLRB* v. *Edinburg Citrus Asso.* (1945, CA5th) 147 F.2d 353, in which enforcement of a Board order enjoining interference by an employer with his employees' right of self-organization was denied, the court pointed out that the evidence of such interference was insufficient, since most of it related to objection to union discussion during working hours and it is well settled that an employer may so object. See also *NLRB* v. *F. W. Woolworth Co.* (1954, CA6th) 214 F.2d 78, *supra,* §7[a].

§12. Collecting dues; using bulletin board; miscellaneous activities.

In the three cases which have touched upon the point, employers' attempts to bar collection of union dues on company premises have been held unlawful. See

NLRB v. *Hudson Motor Car Co.* (1942, CA6th) 128 F.2d 528, *supra*, §7[b]; *NLRB* v. *William Davies Co.* (1943, CA7th) 135 F.2d 179, cert den 320 U.S. 770, 88 L.ed. 460, 64 S.Ct. 82, *supra*, §7[a]; *Richfield Oil Corp.* v. *NLRB* (1944, CA9th) 143 F.2d 860, *supra*, §6.

An employer has been said not to be guilty of an unfair labor practice in barring a national union from using company bulletin boards for posting union notices where the right to use such boards is refused to all unions. *Westinghouse Electric & Mfg. Co.* v. *NLRB* (1940, CA2d) 112 F.2d 657, affd without op 312 U.S. 660, 85 L.ed. 1108, 61 S.Ct. 736 (dictum).

In *NLRB* v. *Montgomery Ward & Co.* (1946, CA8th) 157 F.2d 486, the court commented, in passing, and with respect to an employee who had pasted union labels on furniture in his employer's plant, thereby occasioning expense to the employer in removing the labels, that there was no contention that the employer would not have been justified in discharging the employee for such conduct. . . .

Polymers, Inc. v. *NLRB*

414 F.2d 999 (1969)

Held: The Board has the power to evaluate an election without holding a hearing and consequently decide that there was no "reasonable possibility of irregularity," a standard which they developed to apply to an election, and it is within the Board's discretion to vary their rules from situation to situation.

Opinion:

This case presents chiefly the question whether the National Labor Relations Board should have set aside a representation election because of alleged irregularities in its conduct, the Board having concluded that "desirable election standards were met and that no *reasonable* possibility of irregularity inhered in the conduct of this election." (Emphasis added.) Subordinate questions presented are whether the Board should have held a hearing on the company's objections to the election and whether the Board was justified in refusing the company's request to inspect a Board document entitled "A Guide to the Conduct of Elections." . . .

We hold that the Board did not abuse its discretion in finding, without a hearing, that the alleged irregularities in the conduct of the representation election, considered in light of all the facts and circumstances surrounding the election, did not raise a reasonable possibility of irregularity and thus did not require that the election be set aside. We also hold under the circumstances of this case that the Board was justified in refusing to produce the Guide.

Accordingly, we deny the petition of the company to set aside the order of the Board, and we enforce the Board's order. . . .

The regional director conducted an investigation into the alleged irregularities. The Board affirmed his findings. Although the Board recognized that the conduct of the election did not comport with optimal safeguards of accuracy and security, and it acknowledged that the sealing of the ballot box could have been improved upon, it concluded that "desirable election standards were met and that no *reasonable* possibility of irregularity inhered in the conduct of this election." (Emphasis added.) Enlarging upon its specification of the "reasonableness" of the possibility as a determinative factor, the Board stated:

> "We do not think, however, that the word 'possibility' could ever be construed in this context to have the connotation of 'conceivable.' The concept of reasonableness of the possibility must be imported into this test in order for it to have meaning." . . .

In the past the Board has refused to certify election results where a possibility of irregularity existed. Although the "reasonableness" standard applied in the instant election has not been articulated explicitly in previous Board decisions, its applicability is evident both from the opinions themselves and from the instances in which the Board, as here, has declined to set aside elections.

Briefly, elections have been set aside where (1) three days after a discrepancy in the number of ballots was discovered, the ballots were found, the room having been locked during the three day period; (2) the Board agent, while being transported between polling places by company and union observers, failed to seal or tape the ballot box; (3) an unsealed package of blank ballots was left unguarded for twenty minutes in a polling area; and, most recently, an unsealed ballot box remained unattended from two to five minutes.

On the other hand, election results have been certified even though (1) blank ballots were in the voting area while the Board agent was not; (2) an unsealed ballot box was in the possession of the agent and the company observer, the union observer having suddenly departed; and (3) the Board agent was temporarily absent from the polling place.

[2] This line of conflicting precedents reflects the principle that each possibility must be assessed upon its own unique facts and circumstances, under expert analysis by the Board, to determine whether to certify or set aside. A *per se* rule of possibility would impose an overwhelming burden in a representation case. If speculation on conceivable irregularities were unfettered, few election results would be certified, since ideal standards cannot always be attained. . . .

[3-5] The burden of setting aside an election is a heavy one and falls upon the party attacking it. In the instant case, the decision of the Board to certify the union was neither arbitrary nor capricious, nor did it represent a departure from the principles by which the Board had made similar determinations in the past. . . .

NLRB v. *General Drivers, Local No. 886*

Circuit Court of Appeals, Tenth Circuit, 225 F.2d 205 (1959)

Held: It is an unfair labor practice for a union to coerce employees into joining a union or into accepting certain contractual clauses, and the Board may decide the appropriate remedy in case a violation occurs. The rule with respect to union pre-election conduct is that coercion is not permitted but promises of benefits are, so in the case presented here, the conduct would probably have been permitted if the raise had been promised instead of used as coercion to force other employees to join the union.

Opinion:

MURRAH, C. J.: This is a proceeding under Section 10(e) of the Labor Management Relations Act, 61 Stat. 136, 147; 29 U.S.C. 160(e), to enforce an order of the National Labor Relations Board, based upon a finding that the respondent violated Section 8(e)(1)(A); 29 U.S.C. 158(b)(1)(A) of the Act, by coercively withholding contractual benefits from certain of the complainant's employees until about 80 percent of them signed union membership applications and dues checkoff authorizations. The order required the respondent to reimburse the employees for the dues checked off during the critical period involved here. [Dues checkoff is when an employer deducts the union member's dues from the member's paychecks.]

The ultimate findings are derived from these facts. In February, 1956, the respondent Union became the exclusive bargaining representative for the complaining company's production and maintenance employees. After a series of bargaining conferences between the Union representative and management, the parties tentatively agreed upon a contract providing for a 7¢ per hour increase. The contract thus agreed upon was drafted by the company and submitted to the Union representative on June 7, 1956, and the company thereafter stood ready to sign the same "any time." On the same date, about 40 of the company's employees met to consider the contract. There is a sharp conflict concerning the attitude of the Union representative, but the Board found from conflicting evidence that the Union representative told the assembled employees that the 7¢ increase would not become effective until the contract was signed, and that the contract would not be signed until about 80 percent of the employees signed union membership applications and checkoff dues authorizations; that the employees then voted to accept the company's proposal "on condition that it was satisfactory to the Contract Committee and to the Union." On July 20, about 62 of the 83 employees had joined the Union and· signed dues checkoff authorization.

From this the Board concluded that the employees' action in joining the Union and executing the dues checkoff authorizations was not voluntary, but the direct result of respondent's coercive conduct; and that it was reasonably calculated to restrain and coerce the employees in the exercise of their right under Section 7 of the Act to refrain from joining or assisting the respondent Union.

Having concluded that the execution of the checkoff authorizations was the "direct result of respondent's coercive conduct," the Board thought the appropriate remedy was reimbursement of the dues. It did not believe subjective evidence necessary to warrant the order.

"The relation of remedy to policy is peculiarly a matter of administrative competence." *Phelps Dodge Corp.* v. *NLRB*, 313 U.S. 177, 194; *NLRB* v. *Seven-Up*, 344 U.S. 344. It is the primary responsibility of the Board to fashion an appropriate remedy for an unfair labor practice in order to effectuate the purposes of the Act, and we should not interfere with the designed remedy unless we can say from the whole record that it is "oppressive and therefore not calculated to effect a policy of the Act." *NLRB* v. *Seven-Up, supra; Virginia Electric Co.* v. *NLRB*, 319 U.S. 533.

The reimbursement of initiation fees and dues as an appropriate remedy cannot be doubted. *NLRB* v. *Local 404*, etc. 205 F.2d 104. And, this is so even though the employees who were coerced to pay the dues may have received some value therefor in the form of Union services. . . .

U.S. Court of Appeals Second Circuit (New York), 519 F.2d 721 (1975)

Held: If there is no union security agreement in effect, then the employer may not require employees to join a labor organization.

Opinion:

PER CURIAM: Petitioner Colonie Hill, Ltd., seeks to review and set aside a final order of the NLRB holding (1) that it violated §8(a)(1) and (2) of the National Labor Relations Act, 29 U.S.C. §158(a)(1) and (2) by requiring its employees to join a union when no valid union security agreement was in force, and (2) that it violated §8(a)(1), (2), and (3) of the Act, 29 U.S.C. §185(a)(1), (2), and (3) by discriminatorily discharging and refusing to rehire employee Squicciarini for his refusal to join the favored union. We conclude that the Board's order should be enforced.

Early in 1972, petitioner Colonie Hill, Ltd., opened a business in Hauppauge, New York. On March 4, 1972, the company and Local 100, Service Employees International Union, AFL-CIO (Local 100) entered into a three-year collective-bargaining agreement which included union security and dues checkoff provisions. On August 31, 1972, unfair labor practice charges were filed against both petitioner and Local 100 for coercing employees to join the local. When the General Counsel issued a complaint against both, a settlement agreement was entered into. In it the petitioner agreed not to recognize Local 100 as bargaining representative "unless and until said labor organization shall have been certified by the . . . Board . . . ," and not to "give any force or effect" to the collective-bargaining agreement with Local 100, "or to any modification, extension, renewal or supplement thereto. . . ."

On December 14, 1972, a representation election was held under Board auspices, and on December 26, 1972, Local 100 was certified as the exclusive representative of all employees in a bargaining unit consisting of service and maintenance employees. Thus, as of December 26, 1972, the petitioner could properly look to Local 100 as the legitimate representative of the unit employees. However, since by the terms of the settlement agreement, the March 4, 1972 contract had been abrogated and with it the union security and dues checkoff provisions, the company was not then free to condition employment on union membership or to deduct dues. Nevertheless substantial evidence suggests that during the early months of 1973 petitioner exerted pressure on its employees to join Local 100. In June it discharged Squicciarini, a long-time Local 100 opponent who refused to sign a Local 100 card.

In July 1973, petitioner and Local 100 entered into a new collective-bargaining agreement which contained both union security and dues checkoff provisions. There is no challenge to the validity of this agreement. This petition deals with the period between the December 26, 1972 certification, and the execution of the July 1973 agreement.

An employer violates §8(a)(1) and (2) of the Act if he requires that employees join a labor organization in the absence of a valid union security agreement. *I.L.G.W.U. (Bernard Altman)* v. *NLRB*, 366 U.S. 731, 48 LRRM 2251 (1961). However, petitioner contends that the effect of the settlement agreement is that upon the union's certification by the Board the March 4, 1972 collective-bargaining agreement became operative. We agree with the Board that the overall effect of the test of this settlement agreement is otherwise. Alternatively, petitioner contends that upon certification it entered into a new oral agreement with Local 100 which provided that an agreement on the old terms would continue until a new written contract came into effect. The Board's holding is that the settlement agreement precluded any such oral revival of the

March 4, 1972 agreement. We agree that according to its terms this was the intended effect of the settlement agreement, and that any mental reservations or unexpressed terms cannot vary its express provisions.

7. Union Security

General. Once the union has been elected, its officers obviously would like to do everything possible to guarantee its continued existence. The best guarantee would be to require that only union members be hired, and that if one did not maintain his dues-paying status, then he would be fired. Congress feared that these provisions would not be for the good of the employees or employers, so they restricted the conduct of the unions and employers. One of the reasons for the restriction on the employers is the fear that the union could exert sufficient influence over them so as to force them to do an action that on the surface would appear to be a voluntary act. Notice the different arrangements tried in an effort to reach the best guarantee possible in light of the regulations.

Section 8(a)(3). Section 8(a)(3) makes it an employer unfair labor practice to discriminate "in regard to hire . . . to encourage or discourage membership in any labor organization . . . ," with the proviso that the employer can agree to require as a condition of employment that one join the union within thirty days. The employer cannot treat the employee as if he were not a member of the union if the employer has reasonable grounds for believing that the employee's union membership was denied or terminated for reasons other than nonpayment of dues or initiation fees.

Section 8(b)(2). Section 8(b)(2) makes it a union unfair labor practice to force an employer to violate Section 8(a)(3) or to discriminate against an employee who has been denied union membership for reasons other than failure to pay dues and initiation fees. Notice that an employee can do many things, but he had better pay his union dues.

Section 14(b). Section 14(b) allows states to prohibit union-shop agreements. A union-shop agreement is an agreement between the employer and the union where the employer agrees to require union membership as a condition for continued employment. If Congress had spoken on the issue, it would have preempted the states, but while Congress did speak, it specifically left the decision to the states. Section 14(b) is enabling legislation in that if the states want to control union shops, they are able to, but if the states take no action, then the federal standards will apply. This section has caused a great deal of union activity and lobbying in an effort to convince the Congress to permit union shops by modifying 14(b)—the popular label for which is "the right to work" provision.

Closed Shop. The closed shop is one where the employer obligates himself to hire and retain in employment only union members. The closed shop is not permitted under federal law.

Union Shop. A union shop provision permits the hiring of a nonunion member but within a specified time he must join the union or be discharged. The difference between a union and an agency shop is that in the union shop one must become a member of the union and hence become subject to the union imposing fines for contract violations, whereas in the agency shop a non-member, who still must pay dues, is not subject to the union imposing fines.

The union shop is permitted under federal law so if the states do not execute their powers to prevent the union shop, as granted by Section 14(b), then they are permitted in that state.

There is some question concerning the constitutionality of requiring some-one to join a union in order to hold a given job, but so far this requirement has not been declared unconstitutional.

Agency Shop. An agency shop is one in which all employees—nonmembers as well as members of the union—must pay union dues as a condition of em-ployment. Whether or not one has an agency shop is within the permissive area of bargaining, and so if the union wants to bargain about it, the employer must. The Supreme Court has held that the agency shop is not prohibited by Section 8(b)(3). *NLRB* v. *General Motors*, 373 U.S. 734, 1963. Under 14(b) the states are permitted to make their "right to work laws" broad enough so as to prohibit the agency shop and almost every state with these laws has included the agency shop.

Hiring Hall. A union hiring hall is a headquarters, usually maintained by the union, from which are supplied the employees for an employer. The obvious danger is that only union members will be sent to the employer and thus by agreeing to the hiring halls the employer has violated Section 8(a)(3) by en-couraging union membership. Hiring halls are often used in conjunction with other union security devices. Hiring-hall provisions are permissible even if the employer is required to do all his recruiting through the union, but they are not permissible under 8(a)(3) if only union members will be referred for the jobs. Thus the courts will look to the actual referral practices, rather than the provisions of the agreement, to ascertain whether a nonunion person can be referred for a job by the hall.

Employer Domination. Section 8(a)(2) prohibits both employer domina-tion or interference with the formation or administration of labor organizations, and the contribution of financial or other support to such organizations. It is felt that if a company has too intimate a connection with a particular union, even a lack of proof of control is not sufficient as the influence may be unspoken. When the management and a union work closely together, such as when the only facility of a company is organized, the test becomes difficult to apply. It is a violation for management to aid a particular union in almost any matter, with the rationale being that this could be inhibiting another union's organization attempts. An antiunion campaign against one union that could result in a company union being formed is a violation. *NLRB* v. *Daylight Grocery*, 345 F.2d 239, 1965.

In an attempt to reach a set of rules which would permit the parties to be somewhat friendly and cooperative without fear of a violation, the Court of Appeals drew a distinction between support (illegal) and cooperation (lawful). *NLRB* v. *Post Publishing Co.*, 311 F.2d 565, 1962.

The domination by an employer is not difficult to prove if the union's rules permit management's control over the union. The absence of any written, specific rules for the union is also proof of domination. *Rehig-Pacific Co.*, 99 NLRB 163, 1952.

Featherbedding. "Featherbedding" is dealt with in Section 8(b)(6) of the NLRA, which also provides a definition for the term. It is an unfair labor practice to cause an employer to pay "any money or other thing of value, in the nature of an exaction, for services which are not performed or not to be performed." Note the exact language of what is prohibited. The courts have held this applies to services not to be performed but not to services that are useless or of no value to the employer (*American Newspaper Publishers Ass'n.* v. *NLRB*, 345 U.S. 100, 1953) and also not to hiring two people for the same job, with one to perform and one to watch. The transportation, printing, longshoremen, and entertainment industries are some of the leading ones where the unions have agreements that take advantage of the interpretation of Section 8(b)(6).

National Labor Relations Board v. *General Motors Corporation*

373 U.S. 734, 10 L.ed.2d 670, 83 S.Ct. 1453 (1963)

Held: An employer must bargain over whether or not an agency shop is part of his contract with the union.

        The court held that so long as the state's laws do not prohibit agency shops, union membership may be required by contract so long as the only condition of membership is payment of union dues and the members need not be active in the union.

Opinion:

    . . . Under the second proviso to §8(a)(3), the burdens of membership upon which employment may be conditioned are expressly limited to the payment of initiation fees and monthly dues. It is permissible to condition employment upon membership, but membership, insofar as it has significance to employment rights, may in turn be conditioned only upon payment of fees and dues. "Membership" as a condition of employment is whittled down to its financial core. This Court has said as much before in *Radio Officers' Union, etc.* v. *NLRB*, 347 U.S. 17, 41, 98 L.ed. 455, 477, 74 S.Ct. 323, 41 ALR2d 621:

    "This legislative history clearly indicates that Congress intended to prevent utilization of union security agreements for any purpose other than to compel payment of union dues and fees. Thus Congress recognized the validity of unions' concern about 'free riders,' i.e., employees who receive the benefits of union representation but are unwilling to contribute their fair share of financial support to such union, and gave unions the power to contract to meet that problem while withholding from unions the power to cause the discharge of employees for any other reason. . . ."

    We are therefore confident that the proposal made by the union here conditioned employment upon the practical equivalent of union "membership," as Congress used that term in the proviso to §8(a)(3). The proposal for requiring the payment of dues and fees imposes no burdens not imposed by a permissible union shop contract and compels the performance of only those duties of membership which are enforceable by discharge under a union shop arrangement. If an employee in a union shop unit refuses to respect any union-imposed obligations other than the duty to pay dues and fees, and membership in the union is therefore denied or terminated, the condition of "membership" for §8(a)(3) purposes is nevertheless satisfied and the employee may not be discharged for nonmembership even though he is not a formal member. Of course, if the union chooses to extend membership even though the employee will meet only the minimum financial burden, and refuses to support or "join" the union in any other affirmative way, the employee may have to become a "member" under a union shop contract, in the sense that the union may be able to place him on its rolls. The agency shop arrangement proposed here removes that choice from the union and places the option of membership in the employee while still requiring the same monetary support as does the union shop. Such a difference between the union and agency shop may be of great importance in some contexts, but for present purposes it is more formal than real. To the extent that it has any significance at all it serves, rather than violates, the desire of Congress to reduce the evils of compulsory unionism while allowing financial support for the bargaining agent.

    In short, the employer categorically refused to bargain with the union over a proposal for an agreement within the proviso to §8(a)(3) and as such lawful for the purposes of this case. By the same token, §7, and derivatively §8(a)(1), cannot be deemed to forbid the employer to enter such agreements, since it too is expressly limited by the §8(a)(3) proviso. We hold that the employer was not excused from his duty to bargain over the proposal on the theory that his acceding to it would necessarily involve him in an unfair labor practice. Whether a different result obtains in States which have declared such arrangements unlawful is an issue still to be resolved in *Retail Clerks International Asso.* v. *Schermerhorn*, 373 U.S. 746, 10 L.ed.2d 678, 83 S.Ct. 1461, and one which is of no relevance here because Indiana law does not forbid the present contract proposal. In the context of this case, then, the employer cannot justify his refusal to bargain. He violated §8(a)(5), and the Board properly ordered him to return to the bargaining table.

Reversed and remanded.

345 U.S. 100, 73 S.Ct. 552 (1953)

Held: Featherbedding does not occur if the employees perform work, even if the employer is not interested in having the work performed, but occurs only when the employees are paid but not doing anything.

Opinion:

The question here is whether a labor organization engages in an unfair labor practice, within the meaning of Sec. 8(b)(6) of the National Labor Relations Act, as amended by the Labor Management Relations Act, 1947, when it insists that newspaper publishers pay printers for reproducing advertising matter for which the publishers ordinarily have no use. For the reasons hereafter stated, we hold that it does not.

Petitioner, American Newspaper Publishers Association, is a New York corporation the membership of which includes more than 800 newspaper publishers. They represent over 90 percent of the circulation of the daily and Sunday newspapers in the United States and carry over 90 percent of the advertising published in such papers.

In November, 1947, petitioner filed with the National Labor Relations Board charges that the International Typographical Union, here called ITU, and its officers were engaging in unfair labor practices within the meaning of Sec. 8(b)(1), (2), and (6) of the National Labor Relations Act, as amended by the Labor Management Relations Act, 1947, here called the Taft-Hartley Act. . . .

Printers in newspaper composing rooms have long sought to retain the opportunity to set up in type as much as possible of whatever is printed by their respective publishers. In 1872, when printers were paid on a piecework basis, each diversion of composition was at once reflected by a loss in their income. Accordingly, ITU, which had been formed in 1852 from local typographical societies, began its long battle to retain as much typesetting work for printers as possible.

With the introduction of the linotype machine in 1890 the problem took on a new aspect. When a newspaper advertisement was set up in type, it was impressed on a cardboard matrix, or "mat." These mats were used by their makers and also were reproduced and distributed, at little or no cost, to other publishers who used them as molds for metal casting from which to print the same advertisement. This procedure bypassed all compositors except those who made up the original form. Facing the loss of work, ITU secured the agreement of newspapers to permit their respective compositors, at convenient times, to set up duplicate forms for all local advertisements in precisely the same manner as though the mat had not been used. For this reproduction work the printers received their regular pay. The doing of this "made work" came to be known in the trade as "setting bogus." It was a wasteful procedure. Nevertheless, it has become a recognized idiosyncrasy of the trade and a customary feature of the wage structure and work schedule of newspaper printers. . . .

On rare occasions the reproduced compositions are used to print the advertisement when rerun, but, ordinarily, they are promptly consigned to the "hell box" and melted down. . . .

However desirable the elimination of all industrial featherbedding practices may have appeared to Congress, the legislative history of the Taft-Hartley Act, 29 U.S.C.A. Sec. 141 et seq., demonstrates that when the legislation was put in final form Congress decided to limit the practice but little by law.

The Act limits its condemnation to instances where a labor organization or its agents exact pay from an employer in return for services not performed or not to be performed. Thus, where work is done by an employee, with the employer's consent, a labor organization's demand that the employee be compensated for time spent in doing the disputed work does not become an unfair labor practice. The transaction simply does not fall within the kind of featherbedding defined in the statute. In the absence of proof to the contrary, the employee's compensation reflects his entire relationship with his employer. . . .

Accordingly, the judgment of the Court of Appeals sustaining dismissal of the complaint, insofar as it was based upon Sec. 8(b)(6), is affirmed.

8. Collective Bargaining

Negotiating the Agreement. The National Labor Relations Act declares it to be the policy of the United States to "encourage" collective bargaining by protecting the rights of workers in negotiating the terms and conditions of their employment. Section 8(a)(5) makes it an unfair labor practice for the employer to refuse to bargain with the representatives of his employees and Section 10(c) gives the National Labor Relations Board the power to issue an order, enforceable in court, that requires the employer to bargain.

The Labor Management Relations Act (1947) provides unions with the duty to bargain (Section 8(b)(3)) and provides the Labor Board with the same power to issue an order as is described above.

To bargain collectively, the employer and the employee representative must meet at reasonable times and confer in good faith (*NLRB* v. *Montgomery Ward Co.*, 133 F.2d 675 (1943)) with respect to wages, hours, and other terms and conditions of employment, or the negotiation of an agreement, or of any question arising thereunder. The parties must execute a written contract incorporating any agreement reached if requested by either party. (Section 8(d)).

There is no obligation to agree to a proposal or to make a concession, but merely to bargain as briefly outlined in the preceding paragraph and as will be presented in detail in the following material.

Who Will Bargain

THE INDIVIDUAL CONTRACT. Individual contracts between the employees and management are not permitted once the union has been certified. The feeling is that the individual employee may be pressured into a private contract. If the individual's contract were worse than the one negotiated by the union, then the individual would be hurt. If the individual's contract were superior to that of the union, then the union's position would be weakened. Also, the individuals could use the union's contract as a minimum base from which to negotiate their individual increases. So once a union has been selected by a majority of employees in the bargaining unit, it has exclusive authority to represent all employees in the unit on matters which are properly the subject of collective bargaining. One may terminate an agency relationship, but the union is not simply the agent of the individual but something more, so a member may not pull out of the union and negotiate his own agreement. Once the union's contract is signed, the individual may not ask that the contract be waived. *J. I. Case Co.* v. *NLRB*, 321 U.S. 332 (1944).

MULTI-EMPLOYER BARGAINING. Sometimes it may be advantageous for the parties if the union negotiates with more than one employer simultaneously. Usually, the circumstances favoring this are numerous employers of small work forces, such as the garment industries, or employees who change employers frequently, such as the construction industry. One can readily see why in these cases the multi-employer bargaining technique may be desired by the union, but the union may request but not insist on this. Also, either party may withdraw from this type of bargaining if the timing is appropriate, i.e., before negotiations begin. *Publishers Ass'n.* v. *NLRB*, 364 F.2d 293 (1966), cert. denied 385 U.S. 971 (1966). See Chapter 12 for further discussion.

TWO UNIONS. If two unions both insist on representing the same unit of employees, then obviously a problem exists. The problem is covered by section 10(k) of the Act, which in essence gives the Board the power to resolve this issue. For example, a conflict may arise between a craft union and a general union or between two craft unions, such as metal workers and carpenters both claiming the right to hang metal doors.

SUPERVISORS. Employers have no duty to recognize or bargain with a union whose membership is restricted to supervisors (Section 14(a)). However, a supervisors' union is protected by the NLRA provisions if it admits rank-and-file employees to membership, and seasonal supervisors who also perform rank-and-file work may be included in a nonsupervisory unit. Also, while an employer may not be compelled to bargain with a supervisors-only union, he still may voluntarily bargain with such a union.

SUCCESSOR-EMPLOYER UNDER 8(a)(5). The successor-employer is not bound by the terms of its predecessor's labor contract unless it assumes, expressly or tacitly, that obligation. The new owner need not retain the incumbent employees through "continuity" of business nor is it necessary to rehire any employees, as the new owner may choose his own work force so long as his decision is not based on union affiliation. *NLRB* v. *Foodway of El Paso*, 496, F.2d 117 (5th Cir. 1974).

If the new owner elects to retain most of the employees then he still is not bound by the old contract but he may not institute terms and conditions different from those provided in his predecessor's contract without first bargaining with the employee's representative. *Overnite Transportation Co.* v. *NLRB*, 372 F.2d 765, cert. denied 389 U.S. 838 (1967). *NLRB* v. *Burns International Secur. Servs.*, 406 U.S. 272 (1972).

The Board has held that a successor-employer may establish initial terms for employment (different from those of the old contract) if before commencing operations he "announces new terms prior to or simultaneously with his invitation to the previous work force to accept employment under those terms." *Spruce Up Corp.*, 2 NLRB No. 19, 85 L.R.R.M. 1426 (1974).

Subsequent cases on the question of whether the successor-employer plans to retain the incumbents (and hence be bound by the old contract) have turned on whether the offer of employment was related to new terms and therefore contingent upon their acceptance, or whether the successor had committed itself to continue its predecessor's terms or had misled the incumbents into thinking it would. *Collinge Enterprises, Inc.*, 210 NLRB No. 8, 86 L.R.R.M. 1086 (1974).

The duty of the successor-employer to bargain with the incumbent union does not commence until the employer has hired its full complement of employees, since until then it may not be clear whether the union continues to represent a majority. Once the obligation to bargain has commenced, the initial terms unilaterally set or the terms of a predecessor's collective contract that were kept in effect may not be changed without bargaining.

SUCCESSOR-EMPLOYER UNDER 301 LMRA. The Supreme Court held that the survivor of a corporate merger which hired all the employees represented by the union was required to arbitrate its obligations towards these employees, with the key being the "substantial continuity of identity." *John Wiley & Sons* v. *Livingston*, 376 U.S. 543 (1964). A union tried to use this case to force an employer (who hired only nine of fifty-three incumbent employees) to arbitrate its obligation to employ all of the predecessor's employees. The Supreme Court distinguished *Wiley* and held that the result sought here would conflict with the successor-employer's freedom to hire its own work force, and the policies set out in the *Burns* case could not be ignored simply because the suit arose under Section 301 (duty to arbitrate) and not under an unfair labor practice context. *Howard Johnson Co.* v. *Detroit Local Joint Executive Bd.*, 417 U.S. 249 (1974).

Note that in *Wiley* the employer's right to hire as he pleased was not involved as he had already made that decision.

If the company replaces its predecessor but there is no sale of assets, the continuity of identity depends entirely on the work force and 35 percent of the predecessor's work force joining the new company is not sufficient to compel arbitration concerning the remainder of the predecessor's work force that did not join the new company. *Boeing Co.* v. *Machinists*, 504 F.2d 305 (5th Cir. 1974).

GOOD FAITH. Reaching an agreement is not compulsory but negotiations with an open mind and demonstrating an honest attempt to reach an agreement are necessary. Thus, there have been numerous cases defining the procedure that should be employed, including the subjects to be included in the bargaining, but no cases that specifically say an agreement must be reached. However, lack of an agreement may tend to support an allegation that the party did not bargain properly.

Notice that the duty to bargain is difficult to precisely define. The specific requirements have arisen case by case and virtually all the cases deal with the employer's duty. A union typically would be willing to bargain but they may insist on a set of demands that management feels are unreasonable. One reason for the case-by-case generation of principles is that management, when attempting to demonstrate "good faith," is always answering a specific set of union allegations; i.e., there must be a claim of bad faith which management tries to refute by showing good faith.

The employer's duty to bargain continues until an agreement is reached, a genuine impasse arises, or the union ceases to negotiate on its own accord. The employer must offer counterproposals, but these need not contain concessions to the demands of the union.

Lack of Good Faith. It is easier to give examples of lack of good faith than to give examples of good faith. Lack of good faith can be differentiated into basically three categories:

1. per se violations;
2. lack of good faith via tactics;
3. bargaining subjects.

It is worthwhile to consider the above in more detail.

PER SE VIOLATIONS. To label something a "per se" violation means that all that is necessary to establish a violation is to show that the given conduct occurred; i.e., there need not be an entire mode of conduct proved but simply that the labeled conduct occurred, and from this the bad faith will be inferred. *NLRB* v. *Truitt*, 351 U.S. 149 (1956).

During negotiations, an employer's attempt at unilateral action is at his own risk. The theory is that any action by an employer may inhibit the employees in their choice of whether or not to organize. Threats should obviously be prohibited and sometimes so should an increase in employee benefits. Congress did not want to deny an increase in benefits to employees but at the same time they felt that a unilateral offer of benefits may be a management tactic to undermine the union. To be safe, if management wants to increase benefits, they should do so before or after negotiations.

An impasse is reached when parties cannot agree on a vital subject. If an impasse is reached, the employer may offer anything that does not exceed its previous best offer, for this would be considered to have the effect of undermining the union by demonstrating that the employees can achieve greater gains without the union than they can achieve with the union. Deciding what is the best offer can be a very complex issue, for suppose that from offer No. 1 to offer No. 2 management raises wages by 10%, decreases the fringe benefits 5%, and reduces the work week from 40 to 35 hours, which then is the better offer? Now confuse this by adding 10 or 20 more combinations of terms, and would the reader, if an interested party, be willing to concede that the last offer is necessarily the best? *Crompton Highland Mills*, 337 U.S. 213 (1949).

There is a duty to furnish to the union all relevant and necessary data, which may include economic data if the employer intends to rely on it himself, and it is an 8(a)(5) violation if one does not furnish it in reasonable form. The terms "relevant" and "necessary" are liberally construed in favor of the union and may include the salaries of competitors if available. *General Electric*, 81 LRRM 2303 (1972).

A refusal to execute the contract is an 8(a)(5) or an 8(b)(3), depending on whether it is the union or management that refuses. If the members agree to the terms, then the union must sign the contract. *H. J. Heinz*, 311 U.S. 514 (1941).

The subject matter of the contract may be classified into three broad categories: mandatory, permissive, and illegal subjects. *Borg Warner*, 356 U.S. 342 (1958). These will be covered in detail in the topic area of Bargaining Subjects (in this chapter), so it is sufficient to state here that it is a per se violation not to bargain over a mandatory subject.

LACK OF GOOD FAITH VIA TACTICS. There are certain actions that are not so blatant as to be labeled per se violations of the duty to bargain but are still serious enough to be labeled violations. Such conduct as bargaining room tactics and conduct outside the negotiations may be sufficient to establish a lack of good faith, and usually this charge is more difficult to prove than a per se violation because it is not so blatant.

Where one particular aspect of conduct may not be sufficient to show bad faith, the total circumstances, including but not limited to past history, efforts to bypass the union in negotiations, lack of efforts towards reaching a settlement, may demonstrate a lack of good faith.

An example of this would be if an employer shifts his position every time an agreement seems to have been reached, then he may be held to be using bad faith. *Gopher Aviation, Inc.*, 160 NLRB No. 130 (1966).

"Boulwareism," named after its founder, is a technique where one makes what he considers his best offer and then in essence refuses to bargain any further. Its founder decided that the bargaining sessions, especially where one had to deal with many unions, were requiring too much time and too many resources, so he adopted a process that was "scientific." The company did a great deal of research and came in the first day of negotiations with a firm, fair offer and told the unions to "take it or leave it." However appealing the concept may be to management, the courts said "no" and held that even though some of the individual actions may be valid, one should never say "take it or leave it." The theory requires bargaining, and no matter how well supported by facts one's position may be, he still must bargain. *General Electric Co. (Electrical Workers, IUE)*, 418 F.2d 736, cert. denied (1970).

BARGAINING SUBJECTS. Bargaining subjects may be classified as mandatory, permissive, or illegal. The mandatory bargaining subjects are wages, hours, and other conditions of employment, and these are considered so crucial that it is an unfair labor practice not to bargain over them. The requirement is that the parties bargain over the mandatory subjects, so while they need not reach an agreement, if one party tries to bargain about a mandatory subject then the other party must respond. The aim of classifying topics as mandatory is to prevent one party from satisfying the bargaining requirement while discussing only trivial matters. Proof that either party is not using good faith with respect to mandatory topics is a per se violation, which means that based solely on this proof an unfair labor practice charge may be issued to an employer (8(a)(5)) or a union (8(b)(3)).

If the parties bargain properly but do not reach an agreement with respect to mandatory subjects, than an "impasse" may exist, which means that the bargaining process is not bringing the parties closer to an agreement. In the event of an impasse, the parties may pause in the bargaining and legally use conduct, such as lockouts, which may not be permitted without the impasse. Some examples of mandatory subjects are union security, arbitration clauses, wages, health and pension plans, and bonuses.

Job security is a mandatory subject and is an issue when an employer decides to subcontract work outside of the operation as opposed to having it performed by the employees of the operation. It is permissible to go out of business entirely, but if one wishes to continue the same general business, he must bargain about whether to subcontract the work currently being done by his operation. The parties do not need to reach an agreement, but they need to at least bargain, unless the work has traditionally been subcontracted, in which case no bargaining is necessary and the employer may continue to subcontract for the work. The parties sometimes disagree as to whether or not the work has previously been done within the company, and this dispute is resolved by the facts of the particular situation. *Fibreboard Paper*, 379 U.S. 203 (1964).

Permissive bargaining subjects are those subjects that may be the subject of collective bargaining only if the employer and the union mutually consent to include them in the topics of bargaining. Permissive subjects are not such that the law prohibits bargaining over them but they are not given the same significance as mandatory subjects, so either the employer or the union may refuse to bargain over these subjects and it is not an unfair labor practice. If the parties commence bargaining but fail to reach an agreement with respect to these subjects, an "impasse" cannot be held to have occurred and the parties must continue to bargain in good faith over the mandatory subjects.

Some examples of permissive subjects are defining the bargaining unit, or requiring the establishment of performance bonds as a guarantee that a particular party will perform under the contract, or any other subject that is not a mandatory or illegal subject for collective bargaining. *Arlington Asphalt*, 49 LRRM 1831 (1962).

An employer and a union are prohibited from permitting illegal bargaining subjects to become the subject of collective bargaining or to reach an agreement that provides for these subjects to occur. If either party tries to pressure the other party into pursuing these subjects and the pressure tactics result in the subjects being mutually pursued, then both parties are held to have committed an illegal act even though one party was pressured into his actions. Consequently, if one party tries to pursue an illegal subject it is the duty of the other party to resist the efforts, and obviously there can be no impasse with respect to these subjects.

Some examples of illegal subjects would be providing for a closed shop or racial discrimination or a hot cargo agreement that is not permitted under the labor laws.

Restructuring the Bargaining Relationship. The Board may not fashion the terms of the contract between an employer and a union (*H. K. Porter*, 379 U.S. 99, 1970), but once an agreement is reached the Board may order execution and implementation of the agreement. *Strong Roofing*, 393 U.S. 357 (1969).

Once a contract is reached, neither party may terminate or modify it without following a set of notice and time requirements as outlined in Sections 8(d) and 8(d)(4) of the Act. These sections provide that the contract is in force for its length or sixty days, whichever occurs later, so the contract is always good for its entirety.

The contract represents the agreement of the parties, so if an item is built into the contract there is no duty to renegotiate it, but if the item is not in the contract and it was not fully discussed during the contract negotiations, then there is a continuing duty to negotiate that item if the item is a mandatory subject of bargaining. This is not a right that can be dissolved by agreement, and failure to honor it can be an 8(a)(5) violation for an employer or an 8(b)(3) violation for a union.

If a subject is classified as a permissive or illegal subject or if the parties have fully discussed the subject during contract negotiations and decided not to include it in the contract, then there is no continuing duty to renegotiate the subject.

The parties usually provide in the contract for the procedure that is to be used in the event that a dispute arises with respect to the interpretation of the contract, and that procedure is usually arbitration. In order for an arbitration provision to be effective, the parties must provide that in the event of a dispute involving the contract, the dispute will be submitted to binding arbitration.

There exists a set of rules and cases by which arbitrators are supposed to reach their decisions, so if a party anticipates that an arbitrator will hold contrary to his argument, he may raise the question of whether the issue should be decided by arbitration or whether a court should decide it. However, it is the policy of the courts to favor arbitration, so the courts have held that the arbitrator may decide whether or not a given issue should be arbitrated, and if he decides that it should be arbitrated then he may commence with the arbitration. This is an important concept because the result is that most disputes are settled by arbitration, which is a quicker, less formal method of resolving disputes than is the court system.

National Labor Relations Board v. *Gissel Packing Co., Inc., et al.*
Food Store Employees Union, Local No. 347, Amalgamated Meat Cutters and Butcher Workmen of North America, AFL-CIO v. *Gissel Packing Co. Inc. (1969)*
Sinclair Company v. *National Labor Relations Board*

395 U.S. 575, 23 L.ed.2d 547, 89 S.Ct. 1918

Held: In some circumstances, the Board may, because of an employer's unfair labor practices connected with an election, either not hold an election or discard the results of an election and order the employer to bargain on the basis of authorization cards, but an election is still the preferred method for a union to establish itself as the representative of the employees.

Opinion:

In four separate proceedings involving unfair labor practice charges filed against employers by unions, the National Labor Relations Board found that the employers had violated §8(a)(5) of the National Labor Relations Act in refusing to recognize the unions, which had sought recognition on the basis of unambiguous authorization cards signed by a majority of the employees, and that the employers had also committed unfair labor practices in violation of §8(a)(1) of the Act in using coercion and threats of reprisals to their employees during the union organization campaigns, and in violation of §8(a)(3) in two of the cases by discharging union adherents. In two of the cases, a representation election had been held and resulted in victory for the employers. In each of the cases the relief ordered by the Board included an order directing the employers to bargain with the unions on the basis of authorization card majorities. In one of the cases (No. 585), the Board ruled against the employer's contention that its statements to the employees to dissuade them from joining the union constituted protected free speech, and the United States Court of Appeals for the First Circuit sustained the Board's findings on appeal and enforced the Board's order in full, including the bargaining order (397 F.2d 157). In the other cases (Nos. 573 and 691), which were consolidated after separate decisions on appeal, the Court of Appeals for the Fourth Circuit sustained the Board's findings as to the employers' §§8(a)(1) and (3) violations, but rejected the findings that the employers' refusal to bargain violated §8(a)(5), and declined enforcement of the Board's bargaining orders on the grounds of the inherent unreliability of authorization cards and the absence of such extensive and pervasive unfair labor practices by the employers as to render bargaining orders the only available remedy (398 F.2d 336; 398 F.2d 337; 398 F.2d 339).

On certiorari, the Supreme Court of the United States affirmed the judgment of the Court of Appeals for the First Circuit in case No. 585, and reversed the judgments of the Court of Appeals for the Fourth Circuit in cases Nos. 573 and 691 insofar as they declined enforcement of the Board's bargaining orders, and remanded the cases to the Court of Appeals with directions to remand to the Board for further proceedings. In an opinion by Warren, Ch. J., expressing the unanimous view of the court, it was held that (1) unambiguous union authorization cards—that is, cards stating on their face that the signer authorized the union to represent the employee for collective bargaining purposes and not to seek an election—if obtained from a majority of employees without misrepresentation or coercion, were reliable enough generally to provide a valid alternate route to majority status, where a fair National Labor Relations Board election probably could not be held, or where an election that had been held was set aside, because of election interference by an employer's unfair labor practices; (2) with regard to alleged irregularities in the solicitation of unambiguous authorization cards, the proper course was to apply the National Labor Relations Board's customary standards whereby the cards were to be counted unless the solicitor's statements amounted under the circumstances to an assurance that the cards would be used only for an election, or for no other purpose than an election, and to rule that there was no majority if the standards had not been satisfied; (3) a bargaining order was an appropriate and authorized remedy for an employer's rejection of a union authorization card majority, validly obtained, and the employer's refusal to bargain in violation of §8(a)(5), where the employer at the same time had committed independent unfair labor practices that tended to undermine the union's majority and make a fair election or rerun an unlikely possibility; (4) in such cases, the Board was not restricted to issuing bargaining orders only in exceptional cases marked by pervasive unfair labor practices, but could also issue bargaining orders in less extraordinary cases marked by less pervasive practices that still had the tendency to undermine majority strength and impede the election processes, there being also a category of minor or less extensive unfair labor practices which, because of their minimal impact on the election machinery, would not sustain a bargaining order; (5) the policies reflected in the amendment of §9(c) of the National Labor Relations Act, allowing an employer to petition the Board for an election after he has been requested to recognize an individual or a union, fully supported the Board's administration of the Act whereby an employer, when confronted by a recognition demand based on possession of cards allegedly signed by a majority of his employees, need not grant recognition immediately but could, unless he had knowledge independently of the cards that the union had a majority, decline the union's request and insist on an election, which election would be withheld or set aside by the Board if the employer committed independent and substantial unfair labor practices disruptive of election conditions; (6) with regard to the assertion of the constitutional right to free speech by one of the employers, his statements to the employees to the effect that the company was in a precarious financial condition and unionization would probably lead to a strike resulting in a plant shutdown, with the employees facing great difficulty in finding employment elsewhere, were properly held by the Board to constitute an election-voiding unfair labor practice, where the record supported a finding that the statements were not cast as a prediction of demonstrable economic consequences, but rather as a threat of retaliatory action; and (7) the cases reviewed by the Court of Appeals for the Fourth Circuit should be remanded to the Board for proper findings, since the Board, under its practice at the time, had phrased its findings in terms of the employers' good- or bad-faith doubts as to the unions' majority status in refusing to bargain, and had not made a finding that a bargaining order would have been necessary in the absence of an unlawful refusal to bargain because of other unfair labor practices committed by the employers, or a finding that even though traditional remedies might have been able to insure a fair election or rerun, there was insufficient indication that an election would definitely be a more reliable test of the employees' desires than the card count taken before the unfair labor practices occurred. . . .

The first issue facing us is whether a union can establish a bargaining obligation by means other than a Board election and whether the validity of alternate routes to majority status, such as cards, was affected by the 1947 Taft-Hartley amendments. The most commonly traveled route for a union to obtain recognition as the exclusive bargaining representative of an unorganized group of employees is through the Board's election and certification procedures under §9(c) of the Act (29 U.S.C. §159(c)); it is also, from the Board's point of view, the preferred route. A union is not limited to a Board election, however, for, in addition to §9, the present Act provides in §8(a)(5) (29 U.S.C. §158(a)(5)), as did the Wagner Act in §8(5), that "[i]t shall be an unfair labor practice for an employer . . . to refuse to bargain collectively with the representatives of his employees, subject to the provisions of section 9(a)." Since

§9(a), in both the Wagner Act and the present Act, refers to the representative as the one "designated or selected" by a majority of the employees without specifying precisely how that representative is to be chosen, it was early recognized that an employer had a duty to bargain whenever the union representative presented "convincing evidence of majority support." Almost from the inception of the Act, then, it was recognized that a union did not have to be certified as the winner of a Board election to invoke a bargaining obligation; it could establish majority status by other means under the unfair labor practice provision of §8(a)(5)—by showing convincing support, for instance, by a union-called strike or strike vote, or, as here, by possession of cards signed by a majority of the employees authorizing the union to represent them for collective bargaining purposes.

We have consistently accepted this interpretation of the Wagner Act and the present Act, particularly as to the use of authorization cards. See, e.g., *NLRB* v. *Bradford Dyeing Assn.*, 310 U.S. 318, 339-340, 84 L.ed. 1226, 1240, 1241, 60 S.Ct. 918 (1940); *Franks Bros. Co.* v. *NLRB*, 321 U.S. 702, 88 L.ed. 1020, 64 S.Ct. 817 (1944); *United Mine Workers* v. *Arkansas Flooring Co.*, 351 U.S. 62, 100 L.ed. 941, 76 S.Ct. 559 (1956). Thus, in *United Mine Workers, supra*, we noted that a "Board election is not the only method by which an employer may satisfy itself as to the union's majority status," 351 U.S. at 72, n.8, 100 L.ed. at 949, since §9(a), "which deals expressly with employee representation, says nothing as to how the employees' representative shall be chosen," 351 U.S. at 71, 100 L.ed. at 949. We therefore pointed out in that case, where the union had obtained signed authorization cards from a majority of the employees, that "[i]n the absence of any bona fide dispute as to the existence of the required majority of eligible employees, the employer's denial of recognition of the union would have violated §8(a)(5) of the Act." 351 U.S. at 69, 100 L.ed. at 947. We see no reason to reject this approach to bargaining obligations now. . . .

The employers argue as a reason for rejecting the use of the cards that they are faced with a Hobson's choice under current Board rules and will almost inevitably come out the loser. They contend that if they do not make an immediate, personal investigation into possible solicitation irregularities to determine whether in fact the union represents an uncoerced majority, they will have unlawfully refused to bargain for failure to have a good faith doubt of the union's majority; and if they do make such an investigation, their efforts at polling and interrogation will constitute an unfair labor practice in violation of §8(a)(1) and they will again be ordered to bargain. As we have pointed out, however, an employer is not obligated to accept a card check as proof of majority status, under the Board's current practice, and he is not required to justify his insistence on an election by making his own investigation of employee sentiment and showing affirmative reasons for doubting the majority status. See *Aaron Brothers*, 158 NLRB 1077, 1078. If he does make an investigation, the Board's recent cases indicate that reasonable polling in this regard will not always be termed violative of §8(a)(1) if conducted in accordance with the requirements set out in *Struksnes Construction Co.* 165 NLRB No. 102, 65 LRRM 1385 (1967). And even if an employer's limited interrogation is found violative of the Act, it might not be serious enough to call for a bargaining order. . . .

Brooks v. *National Labor Relations Board*

348 U.S. 96, 99 L.ed. 125, 75 S.Ct. 176 (1954)

Held: An employer's duty to bargain is not affected by the fact that shortly after the
election in which the union was certified, the union lost its majority without
any illegal action by the employer. The union still has the right to negotiate
for the employees.

Opinion:

The National Labor Relations Board conducted a representation election in
petitioner's Chrysler-Plymouth agency on April 12, 1951. District Lodge No. 727,
International Association of Machinists, won by a vote of eight to five, and the Labor
Board certified it as the exclusive bargaining representative on April 20. A week after
the election and the day before the certification petitioner received a handwritten
letter signed by nine of the 13 employees in the bargaining unit stating: "We, the
undersigned majority of the employees . . . are not in favor of being represented by
Union Local No. 727 as a bargaining agent."

Relying on this letter and the decision of the Court of Appeals for the Sixth
Circuit in *NLRB* v. *Vulcan Forging Co.* 188 F.2d 927, petitioner refused to bargain
with the union. The Labor Board found, 98 NLRB 976, that petitioner had thereby
committed an unfair labor practice in violation of §§8(a)(1) and 8(a)(5) of the
amended National Labor Relations Act, 61 Stat. 140, 141, 29 U.S.C. §§158(a)(1),
(a)(5), and the Court of Appeals for the Ninth Circuit enforced the Board's order
to bargain, 204 F.2d 899. In view of the conflict between the Circuits, we granted
certiorari, 347 U.S. 916, 98 L.ed. 1071, 74 S.Ct. 517.

The issue before us is the duty of an employer toward a duly certified bargaining
agent if, shortly after the election which resulted in the certification, the union has
lost, without the employer's fault, a majority of the employees from its membership. . . .

Petitioner contends that whenever an employer is presented with evidence that
his employees have deserted their certified union, he may forthwith refuse to bargain.
In effect, he seeks to vindicate the rights of his employees to select their bargaining
representative. If the employees are dissatisfied with their chosen union, they may
submit their own grievance to the Board. If an employer has doubts about his duty
to continue bargaining, it is his responsibility to petition the Board for relief, while
continuing to bargain in good faith at least until the Board has given some indication
that his claim has merit. Although the Board may, if the facts warrant, revoke a
certification or agree not to pursue a charge of an unfair labor practice, these are
matters for the Board; they do not justify employer self-help or judicial intervention.
The underlying purpose of this statute is industrial peace. To allow employers to rely
on employees' rights in refusing to bargain with the formally designated union is not
conducive to that end, it is inimical to it. Congress has devised a formal mode for
selection and rejection of bargaining agents and has fixed the spacing of elections,
with a view of furthering industrial stability and with due regard to administrative
prudence.

We find wanting the arguments against these controlling considerations. In
placing a nonconsenting minority under the bargaining responsibility of an agency
selected by a majority of the workers, Congress has discarded common-law doctrines
of agency. It is contended that since a bargaining agency may be ascertained by
methods less formal than a supervised election, informal repudiation should also
be sanctioned where decertification by another election is precluded. This is to make
situations that are different appear the same. Finally, it is not within the power of
this Court to require the Board, as is suggested, to relieve a small employer, like

the one involved in this case, of the duty that may be exacted from an enterprise with many employees.

To be sure, what we have said has special pertinence only to the period during which a second election is impossible. But the Board's view that the one-year period should run from the date of certification rather than the date of election seems within the allowable area of the Board's discretion in carrying out congressional policy. See *Phelps Dodge Corp.* v. *NLRB*, 313 U.S. 177, 192-197, 85 L.ed. 1271, 1282-1284, 61 S.Ct. 845, 133 ALR 1217; *NLRB* v. *Seven-Up Bottling Co.* 344 U.S. 344, 97 L.ed. 377, 73 S.Ct. 287. Otherwise, encouragement would be given to management or a rival union to delay certification by spurious objections to the conduct of an election and thereby diminish the duration of the duty to bargain. Furthermore, the Board has ruled that one year after certification the employer can ask for an election or, if he has fair doubts about the union's continuing majority, he may refuse to bargain further with it. This, too, is a matter appropriately determined by the Board's administrative authority.

We conclude that the judgment of the Court of Appeals enforcing the Board's order must be

Affirmed.

Allied Chemical & Alkali Workers of America, Local Union No. 1 v.
    Pittsburgh Plate Glass Company, Chemical Division et al.
National Labor Relations Board v. *Pittsburgh Plate Glass Company,*
    Chemical Division et al.

404 U.S. 157, 30 L.ed.2d 341, 92 S.Ct. 383

Held: Retired employees are not "employees" within the meaning of the NLRA as
amended so an employer need not bargain over their ongoing benefits. Retirees
cannot be joined in a bargaining unit with active employees and their benefits
are a mandatory subject of collective bargaining.

    If a party makes a unilateral mid-term modification in a permissive
subject then the appropriate remedy is not an unfair labor practice charge but
rather is an action for breach of contract.

Opinion:

    Section 9(a) of the Labor Relations Act accords representative status only to
the labor organization selected or designated by the majority of employees in a "unit
appropriate" "for the purposes of collective bargaining." Section 9(b) goes on to
direct the Labor Board to "decide in each case whether, in order to assure to employees the fullest freedom in exercising the rights guaranteed by this subchapter, the
unit appropriate for the purposes of collective bargaining shall be the employer unit,
craft unit, plant unit, or subdivision thereof. . . ." 49 Stat. 453, as amended, 29 U.S.C.
§159(b). We have always recognized that, in making these determinations, the Board
is accorded broad discretion. See *NLRB* v. *Hearst Publications,* 322 U.S. at 132-135,
88 L.ed. at 1185, 1186; *Pittsburgh Glass Co.* v. *NLRB,* 313 U.S. 146, 85 L.ed. 1251,
61 S.Ct. 908 (1941). Moreover, the Board's findings of fact, if supported by substantial evidence, are conclusive. National Labor Relations Act, §10(e), 49 Stat. 454,
as amended, 29 U.S.C. §160(e). But the Board's powers in respect of unit determinations are not without limits, and if its decision "oversteps the law," *Packard Co.* v.
NLRB, 330 U.S. at 491, 91 L.ed. at 1050, it must be reversed.

    In this case, in addition to holding that pensioners are not "employees" within
the meaning of the collective-bargaining obligations of the Act, we hold that they
were not and could not be "employees" included in the bargaining unit. The unit
determined by the Board to be appropriate was composed of "employees of the
Employer's plant . . . working on hourly rates, including group leaders who work on
hourly rates of pay. . . ." Apart from whether retirees could be considered "employees"
within this language, they obviously were not employees "working" or "who work"
on hourly rates of pay. Although those terms may include persons on temporary or
limited absence from work, such as employees on military duty, it would utterly destroy
the function of language to read them as embracing those whose work has ceased
with no expectation of return.

    In any event, retirees could not properly be joined with the active employees in
the unit that the Union represents. "As a standard, the Board must comply . . . with
the requirement that the unit selected must be one to effectuate the policy of the
act, the policy of efficient collective bargaining." *Pittsburgh Glass Co.* v. *NLRB, supra,*
at 165, 85 L.ed. at 1265. The Board must also exercise care that the rights of employees under §7 of the Act "to self-organization . . . [and] to bargain collectively
through representatives of their own choosing" are duly respected. In line with these
standards, the Board regards as its primary concern in resolving unit issues "to group
together only employees who have substantial mutual interests in wages, hours, and
other conditions of employment." 15 NLRB Ann. Rep. 39 (1950). Such a mutuality
of interest serves to assure the coherence among employees necessary for efficient

collective bargaining and at the same time to prevent a functionally distinct minority group of employees from being submerged in an overly large unit. See *Kalamazoo Paper Box Corp.*, 136 NLRB 134, 137 (1962). . . .

The Board found that bargaining over pensioners' rights has become an established industrial practice. But industrial practice cannot alter the conclusions that retirees are neither "employees" nor bargaining unit members. The parties dispute whether a practice of bargaining over pensioners' benefits exists and, if so, whether it reflects the views of labor and management that the subject is not merely a convenient but a mandatory topic of negotiation. But even if industry commonly regards retirees' benefits as a statutory subject of bargaining, that would at most, as we suggested in *Fibreboard Corp.* v. *NLRB*, 379 U.S. 203, 211, 13 L.ed.2d 233, 238, 85 S.Ct. 398, 6 ALR3d 1130 (1964), reflect the interests of employers and employees in the subject matter as well as its amenability to the collective-bargaining process; it would not be determinative. Common practice cannot change the law and make into bargaining unit "employees" those who are not.

Even if pensioners are not bargaining unit "employees," are their benefits, nonetheless, a mandatory subject of collective bargaining as "terms and conditions of employment" of the active employees who remain in the unit? The Board held, alternatively, that they are, on the ground that they "vitally" affect the "terms and conditions of employment" of active employees principally by influencing the value of both their current and future benefits. 177 NLRB, at 915. The Board explained: "It is not uncommon to group active and retired employees under a single health insurance contract with the result that . . . it is the size and experience of the entire group which may determine insurance rates." Ibid. Consequently, active employees may "benefit from the membership of retired employees in the group whose participation enlarges its size and might thereby lower costs per participant." . . .

We recognize that "classification of bargaining subjects as 'terms [and] conditions of employment' is a matter concerning which the Board has special expertise." *Meat Cutters* v. *Jewel Tea*, 381 U.S. 676, 685-686, 14 L.ed.2d 640, 646, 647, 85 S.Ct. 1596 (1965). The Board's holding in this cause, however, depends on the application of law to facts, and the legal standard to be applied is ultimately for the courts to decide and enforce. We think that in holding the "terms and conditions of employment" of active employees to be *vitally* affected by pensioners' benefits, the Board here simply neglected to give the adverb its ordinary meaning. Cf. *NLRB* v. *Brown*, 380 U.S. 278, 292, 13 L.ed.2d 839, 849, 85 S.Ct. 980 (1965).

The question remains whether the Company committed an unfair labor practice by offering retirees an exchange for their withdrawal from the already negotiated health insurance plan. After defining "to bargain collectively" as meeting and conferring "with respect to wages, hours, and other terms and conditions of employment," §8(d) of the Act goes on to provide in relevant part that "where there is in effect a collective-bargaining contract covering employees in an industry affecting commerce, the duty to bargain collectively shall also mean that no party to such contract shall terminate or modify such contract" except upon (1) timely notice to the other party, (2) an offer to meet and confer "for the purpose of negotiating a new contract, or a contract containing the proposed modifications," (3) timely notice to the Federal Mediation and Conciliation Service and comparable state or territorial agencies of the existence of a "dispute," and (4) continuation "in full force and effect [of] . . . all the terms and conditions of the existing contract . . . until [its] expiration date. . . ."

The structure and language of §8(d) point to a more specialized purpose than merely promoting general contract compliance. The conditions for a modification or termination set out in paragraphs (1) through (4) plainly are designed to regulate modifications and terminations so as to facilitate agreement in place of economic warfare. Thus, the party desiring to make a modification or termination is required to serve a written notice on the other party, offer to meet and confer, notify mediation and conciliation agencies if necessary, and meanwhile maintain contract relations. Accordingly, we think we accurately described the relevant aim of §8(d) when we said in *Mastro Plastics Corp.* v. *NLRB, supra,* at 284, 100 L.ed. at 321, that the provision "seeks to bring about the termination and modification of collective-bargaining agreements without interrupting the flow of commerce or the production of goods. . . ."

If that is correct, the distinction that we draw between mandatory and permissive terms of bargaining fits the statutory purpose. By once bargaining and agreeing on a permissive subject, the parties, naturally, do not make the subject a mandatory topic of future bargaining. When a proposed modification is to a permissive term, therefore, the purpose of facilitating accord on the proposal is not at all in point, since the parties are not required under the statute to bargain with respect to it. The irrelevance of the purpose is demonstrated by the irrelevance of the procedures themselves of §8(d). Paragraph (2), for example, requires an offer "to meet and confer with the other party for the purpose of negotiating a new contract or a contract containing the proposed modifications." But such an offer is meaningless if a party is statutorily free to refuse to negotiate on the proposed change to the permissive term. The notification to mediation and conciliation services referred to in paragraph (3) would be equally meaningless, if required at all. We think it would be no less beside the point to read paragraph (4) of §8(d) as requiring continued adherence to permissive as well as mandatory terms. The remedy for a unilateral mid-term modification to a permissive term lies in an action for breach of contract, see n. 20, *supra,* not in an unfair-labor-practice proceeding.

As a unilateral mid-term modification of a permissive term such as retirees' benefits does not, therefore, violate §8(d), the judgment of the Court of Appeals is
Affirmed.

National Labor Relations Board v. *Benne Katz et al.*

369 U.S. 736, 8 L.ed.2d 230, 82 S.Ct. 1107 (1962)

Held: It is an unfair labor practice if during negotiations and before an impasse, an
employer unilaterally grants numerous merit increases and announces a new
system of automatic wage increases. Any unilateral action during negotiations
that is not an "annual" event, will be suspected of being evidence of bad faith
bargaining.

Opinion:
The duty to "bargain collectively" enjoined by §8(a)(5) is defined by §8(d)
as the duty to "meet . . . and confer in good faith with respect to wages, hours, and
other terms and conditions of employment." Clearly, the duty thus defined may be
violated without a general failure of subjective good faith; for there is no occasion to
consider the issue of good faith if a party has refused even to negotiate *in fact*—"to
meet . . . and confer"—about any of the mandatory subjects. A refusal to negotiate
in fact as to any subject which is within §8(d), and about which the union seeks to
negotiate, violates §8(a)(5) though the employer has every desire to reach agreement
with the union upon an over-all collective agreement and earnestly and in all good
faith bargains to that end. We hold that an employer's unilateral change in conditions
of employment under negotiation is similarly a violation of §8(a)(5), for it is a
circumvention of the duty to negotiate which frustrates the objectives of §8(a)(5)
much as does a flat refusal.
The unilateral actions of the respondent illustrate the policy and practical
considerations which support our conclusion. . . .
At the April 4, 1957, meeting the employers offered, and the union rejected, a
three-year contract with an immediate across-the-board increase of $7.50 per week, to
be followed at the end of the first year and again at the end of the second by further
increases of $5 for employees earning less than $90 at those times. Shortly thereafter,
without having advised or consulted with the union, the company announced a new
system of automatic wage increases whereby there would be an increase of $5 every
three months up to $74.99 per week; an increase of $5 every six months between $75
and $90 per week; and a merit review every six months for employees earning over
$90 per week. It is clear at a glance that the automatic wage increase system which
was instituted unilaterally was considerably more generous than that which had
shortly theretofore been offered to and rejected by the union. Such action conclusively
manifested bad faith in the negotiations, *NLRB* v. *Crompton-Highland Mills, Inc.*, 337
U.S. 217, 93 L.ed. 1320, 69 S.Ct. 960, and so would have violated §8(a)(5) even
on the Court of Appeals' interpretation, though no additional evidence of bad faith
appeared. An employer is not required to lead with his best offer; he is free to bargain.
But even after an impasse is reached he has no license to grant wage increases greater
than any he has ever offered the union at the bargaining table, for such action is
necessarily inconsistent with a sincere desire to conclude an agreement with the union.
The respondents' third unilateral action related to merit increases, which are also
a subject of mandatory bargaining. *NLRB* v. *J. H. Allison & Co.* (CA6) 165 F.2d
766, 3 ALR2d 990. The matter of merit increases had been raised at three of the
conferences during 1956 but no final understanding had been reached. In January
1957, the company, without notice to the union, granted merit increases to 20 employees out of the approximately 50 in the unit, the increases ranging between $2
and $10. This action too must be viewed as tantamount to an outright refusal to
negotiate on that subject, and therefore as a violation of §8(a)(5), unless the fact
that the January raises were in line with the company's long-standing practice of

granting quarterly or semiannual merit reviews—in effect, were a mere continuation of the status quo—differentiates them from the wage increases and the changes in the sick-leave plan. We do not think it does. Whatever might be the case as to so-called "merit raises" which are in fact simply automatic increases to which the employer has already committed himself, the raises here in question were in no sense automatic, but were informed by a large measure of discretion. There simply is no way in such case for a union to know whether or not there has been a substantial departure from past practice, and therefore the union may properly insist that the company negotiate as to the procedures and criteria for determining such increases.

It is apparent from what we have said why we see nothing in *Insurance Agents* contrary to the Board's decision. The union in that case had not in any way whatever foreclosed discussion of any issue, by unilateral actions or otherwise. The conduct complained of consisted of partial-strike tactics designed to put pressure on the employer to come to terms with the union negotiators. We held that Congress had not, in §8(b)(3), the counterpart of §8(a)(5), empowered the Board to pass judgment on the legitimacy of any particular economic weapon used in support of genuine negotiations. But the Board *is* authorized to order the cessation of behavior which is in effect a refusal to negotiate, or which directly obstructs or inhibits the actual process of discussion, or which reflects a cast of mind against reaching agreement. Unilateral action by an employer without prior discussion with the union does amount to a refusal to negotiate about the affected conditions of employment under negotiation, and must of necessity obstruct bargaining, contrary to the congressional policy. It will often disclose an unwillingness to agree with the union. It will rarely be justified by any reason of substance. It follows that the Board may hold such unilateral action to be an unfair labor practice in violation of §8(a)(5), without also finding the employer guilty of over-all subjective bad faith. While we do not foreclose the possibility that there might be circumstances which the Board could or should accept as excusing or justifying unilateral action, no such case is presented here.

The judgment of the Court of Appeals is reversed and the case is remanded with direction to the court to enforce the Board's order.

It is so ordered.

9. Countervailing Power

In the event that unions can't or won't obtain their demands by collective bargaining, there are other actions often employed by them. Because these actions—picketing, strikes, and boycotts—are not forms of collective bargaining but are commenced when the process fails and because in order to be effective they inflict harm on the employer, these actions are the subject of considerable regulations.

Constitutional Protection. The general argument advanced in favor of picketing and strikes is that the First Amendment guarantees the right to free speech, and to freedom of the press and assembly, and these applied to the states via the Fourteenth Amendment combine to guarantee the right to picket or strike. Other arguments advanced in favor of guaranteeing the right to picket or strike involve the Fifth Amendment (no deprivation of life, liberty, or property without due process of law) and the Thirteenth Amendment (prohibiting slavery and involuntary servitude). Viewing the importance to labor of being able to enforce their demands with these tools, and the language of the Amendments, one might imagine the emotional, lengthy briefs filed by both sides on the issues of picketing and strikes.

Concerning strikes, there have been no cases that hold one has the constitutional right to strike. The only available case on the constitutionality of striking discussed it in the very limited situation presented and held that the right did not exist. The holding was so narrow that no general principles can be derived from it. *Dorchy* v. *Kansas*, 272 U.S. 306, 1926

Concerning picketing, there is constitutional protection if the picketing is done in a peaceful manner and for a lawful purpose. *Thornhill* v. *Alabama*, 310 U.S. 88 (1940). The peaceful manner criterion means that the entire setting must be peaceful and not just the picket line. Thus one may not have a peaceful picket line but violently stop all cars a block from the plant. The lawful purpose criterion means that one is not constitutionally protected if he pickets to achieve an objective which violates federal or state law or public policy. *International Brotherhood of Teamsters Local 695* v. *Vogt, Inc.*, 354 U.S. 384 (1957). Thus one may not picket to cause the employer to discriminate. The form of picketing may enable one to decide by statute the degree of the activity which entails the loss of constitutional protection. The two-part test, peaceful manner and lawful means, when considered in light of statutes and particular facts usually leads to:

1. Primary picketing by one's own employees is usually permitted.
2. Picketing by strangers is usually regulated or not permitted.
3. Secondary picketing, which is picketing by a union with whom the employer does not have a dispute is rarely permitted.

Remember that the constitutional protection is only one part of the story, and the statutory regulations are usually what resolve the cases.

Property Rights

The Courts have tried to balance the various arguments based on the constitutional Amendments that are offered to support the right to picket with the right for one to quietly enjoy his property. With respect to the rights of a third party who is not involved in the labor dispute, the location of the picketing usually determines whether he may cause the picketing to be stopped, with the general rules being that the union may picket in a public place but may not picket on the property of said third party. However, the modern trend of having many businesses located on a large tract of land, privately owned but open to the public, has forced the courts to determine whether the rules applicable to public or private property should be applied. This application of the First Amendment, separate from statutory grounds, has usually involved shopping centers but would also seem appropriate for most large private buildings.

The Supreme Court, in an early case, *Marsh* v. *Alabama*, 326 U.S. 501 (1946), held in favor of permitting the union to enter another's property to picket, but this case was unusual in that the employees, who were the object of this recognitional picketing, lived in a privately owned "company town" and literally never left the town, so there really was no alternative way for the union to reach the employees.

The Court applied the rationale of the *Marsh* case to a large, privately owned shopping center and by reasoning that the shopping center was the functional equivalent of the business area of a municipality, the Court concluded that the pickets could not be barred from exercising their First Amendment rights within the shopping center. *Amalgamated Food Employees Union* v. *Logan Valley Plaza*, 391 U.S. 308 (1968).

In 1972, the Supreme Court limited the First Amendment protection, as defined in the *Logan Valley* case, to shopping centers by holding that the parking lot of a store was not sufficiently "dedicated to a public use" and thus prohibited solicitation. *Central Hardware Co.* v. *NLRB*, 407 U.S. 539 (1972).

In 1976, the Court again confronted the same situation it had faced in the *Logan Valley* case, only this time they held that in cases involving picketing in privately owned shopping centers, "The constitutional guarantee of free expression has no part to play . . ." and thus the First Amendment does not protect pickets in a privately owned shopping center and the arrest of the strikers had not violated their constitutional rights. Holding that there was no constitutional issue, the Court found that there were only Taft-Hartley Act questions which should be decided by the National Labor Relations Board and not the Supreme Court. *Hudgens* v. *NLRB*, 420 U.S. 971, 44 LW 4282 (1976).

Statutory Regulation

The NLRA, as amended by the Taft-Hartley and Landrum-Griffin Acts, is the primary source of regulations for strikes, boycotts, or picketing. There is the constitutional overlay, as previously discussed, and other Acts such as the Norris-LaGuardia and Sherman Antitrust Acts, but the leading source is certainly the NLRA.

In the NLRA, Sections 7 and 13 provide the right to strike and picket, as 7 grants the right to "engage in concerted activity" and 13 grants the right to strike subject to qualification. Section 2(3) provides that strikers retain their "employee" status if certain criteria are met, as will be discussed in detail later. So these give the right to strike, while Section 8(b) limits the right by delineating what is an employee unfair labor practice. These sections, together with the other provisions of the NLRA and other statutes and the constitutional standards, all as construed by the courts, form the body of law governing the employees' key means of objecting to an act or assertion by management: the strike, boycott, or picket. *Boys Mkt., Inc.* v. *Retail Clerk Local 770*, 398 U.S. 235 (1970).

Note that if the Constitution prohibits an action then a statute cannot permit it; if the Constitution classifies the action as "a right" then a statute cannot prohibit it; and if the Constitution neither prohibits an action nor classifies it as a right then the legislature may pass a statute that permits, prohibits, or regulates the action. This is why constitutional protection is important.

Thornhill v. Alabama

310 U.S. 87, 84 L.ed. 1093 (1940)

Held: Peaceful picketing may be considered a form of speech, and as such it enjoys the constitutional protection accorded free speech, although there are some instances, such as secondary actions, when picketing may be severely regulated or prohibited.

Opinion:

The freedom of speech and of the press guaranteed by the Constitution embraces at the least the liberty to discuss publicly and truthfully all matters of public concern without previous restraint or fear of subsequent punishment. The exigencies of the colonial period and the efforts to secure freedom from the oppressive administration developed a broadened conception of these liberties as adequate to supply the public need for information and education with respect to the significant issues of the times. The Continental Congress in its letter sent to the Inhabitants of Quebec (October 26, 1774) referred to the "five great rights" and said: "The last right we shall mention, regards the freedom of the press. The importance of this consists, besides the advancement of truth, science, morality, and arts in general, in its diffusion of liberal sentiments on the administration of Government, its ready communication of thoughts between subjects, and its consequential promotion of union among them, whereby oppressive officers are shamed or intimidated, into more honourable and just modes of conducting affairs." *Journal of the Continental Congress*, 1904 ed., vol. 1, pp. 104, 108. Freedom of discussion, if it would fulfill its historic function in this nation, must embrace all issues about which information is needed or appropriate to enable the members of society to cope with the exigencies of their period.

In the circumstances of our times the dissemination of information concerning the facts of a labor dispute must be regarded as within that area of free discussion that is guaranteed by the Constitution. *Hague v. Committee for Industrial Organization*, 307 U.S. 496, 83 L.ed. 1423, 59 S.Ct. 954; *Schneider v. State (Town of Irvington)*, 308 U.S. 147, 155, 162, 163, ante, 155, 161, 165, 166, 60 S.Ct. 146. See *Senn v. Tile Layers Protective Union*, 301 U.S. 468, 478, 81 L.ed. 1229, 1236, 57 S.Ct. 857. It is recognized now that satisfactory hours and wages and working conditions in industry and a bargaining position which makes these possible have an importance which is not less than the interests of those in the business or industry directly concerned. The health of the present generation and of those as yet unborn may depend on these matters, and the practices in a single factory may have economic repercussions upon a whole region and affect widespread systems of marketing. The merest glance at State and Federal legislation on the subject demonstrates the force of the argument that labor relations are not matters of mere local or private concern. Free discussion concerning the conditions in industry and the causes of labor disputes appears to us indispensable to the effective and intelligent use of the processes of popular government to shape the destiny of modern industrial society. The issues raised by regulations, such as are challenged here, infringing upon the right of employees effectively to inform the public of the facts of a labor dispute are part of this larger problem. We concur in the observation of Mr. Justice Brandeis, speaking for the Court in *Senn's Case* (301 U.S. at 478, 81 L.ed. 1236, 57 S.Ct. 857): "Members of a union might, without special statutory authorization by a state, make known the facts of a labor dispute, for freedom of speech is guaranteed by the Federal Constitution."

It is true that the rights of employers and employees to conduct their economic affairs and to compete with others for a share in the products of industry are subject to modification or qualification in the interests of the society in which they exist.

98

This is but an instance of the power of the State to set the limits of permissible contest open to industrial combatants. See Mr. Justice Brandeis in *Duplex Printing Press Co.* v. *Deering,* 254 U.S. 443, at 488, 65 L.ed. 349, 365, 41 S.Ct. 172, 16 ALR 196. It does not follow that the State in dealing with the evils arising from industrial disputes may impair the effective exercise of the right to discuss freely industrial relations which are matters of public concern. A contrary conclusion could be used to support abridgment of freedom of speech and of the press concerning almost every matter of importance to society. . . .

The State urges that the purpose of the challenged statute is the protection of the community from the violence and breaches of the peace, which, it asserts, are the concomitants of picketing. The power and the duty of the State to take adequate steps to preserve the peace and to protect the privacy, the lives, and the property of its residents cannot be doubted. But no clear and present danger of destruction of life or property, or invasion of the right of privacy, or breach of the peace can be thought to be inherent in the activities of every person who approaches the premises of an employer and publicizes the facts of a labor dispute involving the latter. We are not now concerned with picketing en masse or otherwise conducted which might occasion such imminent and aggravated danger to these interests as to justify a statute narrowly drawn to cover the precise situation giving rise to the danger. Compare *American Steel Foundaries* v. *Tri-City Central Trades Council,* 257 U.S. 184, 205, 66 L.ed. 189, 197, 42 S.Ct. 92, 27 ALR 360. Section 3448 in question here does not aim specifically at serious encroachments on these interests and does not evidence any such care in balancing these interests against the interest of the community and that of the individual in freedom of discussion on matters of public concern.

It is not enough to say that §3448 is limited or restricted in its application to such activity as takes place at the scene of the labor dispute. "[The] streets are natural and proper places for the dissemination of information and ·opinion; and one is not to have the exercise of his liberty of expression in appropriate places abridged on the plea that it may be exercised in some other place." *Schneider* v. *State (Town of Irvington),* 308 U.S. 147, 161, 163, ante, 155, 164, 165, 60 S.Ct. 146; *Hague* v. *Committee for Industrial Organization,* 307 U.S. 496, 515, 516, 83 L.ed. 1423, 1436, 1437, 59 S.Ct. 954. The danger of breach of the peace or serious invasion of rights of property or privacy at the scene of a labor dispute is not sufficiently imminent in all cases to warrant the legislature in determining that such place is not appropriate for the range of activities outlawed by §3448.

Reversed.

10. Picketing

The term *picketing* is not defined in the NLRA, so the determination has been made by the courts—generally, picketing occurs where a dispute arises and union members gather at a job site to enforce their demands by applying pressure on the employer. Usually, a confrontation between employees of the picketed employer and those purportedly engaged in picketing must take place.

General. Public policy is directed towards peaceful harmony and freedom of speech and actions. Thus, when employees picket, an activity which is a combination of speech and actions, a balance is sought between the rights of the employer and the rights of the employees. Violence is to be avoided by both parties. At common law, conduct was judged by an "ends-means" test that required both the end sought and the means employed to be lawful. An example of unlawful ends would be an unlawful restraint of trade and an example of unlawful means would be the "human fence" technique, where members join hands to prevent anyone from crossing their line.

Section 8(b)(1) of the NLRA places a general restriction upon a union's activities, similar to that placed upon an employer's activities by Section 8(a)(1). Under 8(b)(1)(A), a union's restraint or coercion of employees in the exercise of their Section 7 rights, including the right to refrain from concerted activities, is prohibited. A proviso preserves the union's power to prescribe its own rules relating to the acquisition or retention of membership.

Section 8(b)(7) prohibits a labor organization that is not currently certified as the employees' representative from picketing or threatening to picket with the object of obtaining recognition by the employer (recognitional picketing) or acceptance by his employees as their representative (organizational picketing). The object of picketing is ascertained from the surrounding facts, including the message on the picket signs and any communications between the union and the employer. See Chapter 13, Secondary Activities, for coverage of Section 8(b)(4).

Section 8(b)(1). To establish a Section 8(b)(1) violation, an employer (through the General Counsel) must show union activity restraining or coercing employees in the exercise of their Section 7 rights, unprotected by the proviso.

The intent was to protect employees against coercive union conduct, including violence and economic duress, during a union's organization drive. Union action is required, so an individual who is not a union agent cannot violate the statute. Section 8(b)(1)(A) prohibits both mass picketing that deters employees from entering or leaving a plant, and picketing accompanied by threats or violence. Obstructing plant entrances with the intent of prohibiting nonstrikers from entering or leaving has been held to be unlawful, even if the attempt is unsuccessful.

The courts had limited the prohibitions against unions to cases involving violence, so Congress passed 8(b)(7). That section eliminated the need for violence before picketing could be regulated and also eliminated the difference between organizational and recognitional picketing by prohibiting picketing for either of these.

Organizational and Recognitional Picketing. Congress felt it was unfair for a union to picket an employer to force him or his employees to organize or recognize a union, as there are protected procedures for employees to accomplish these ends if desired. Also, an employer or union cannot force an organization on the employees if the employees do not want it, so there is no need for picketing for organizational or recognitional purposes.

SECTION 8(b)(7). Section 8(b)(7) limits organizational and recognitional picketing by any union not "currently certified as representative" of the employees within the place picketed. This section is aimed primarily at picketing by a minority, unrecognized union to obtain members or force the employer to recognize it, but it also applies to an uncertified union representing a majority of employees.

Picketing (or the threat thereof) by an unrecognized union is prohibited in three situations, all of which deal with when "an object" of the picketing is to force the employer to recognize the union or to induce the employees to choose the union as their representative.

a. First, picketing is prohibited where the employer has already lawfully recognized a union and the representation question cannot presently be raised. For example, picketing where contract-bar rules prevent another election is prohibited under this subsection.
b. Second, picketing is prohibited where there has been an election within the preceding twelve months.
c. Third, picketing, after a reasonable time has elapsed (30 days maximum) without the union having filed a petition for representation, is unlawful. A proviso to this third limitation, however, sanctions picketing to "truthfully advise the public" (including consumers) of the employer's non-union status.

THE POLICY FOR 8(b)(7). The policy behind Section 8(b)(7) is a corollary to the federal policy of ensuring employees a free choice in the selection or rejection of a bargaining representative. The policy is to encourage the parties to use the Board's election machinery, instead of the pressures of picketing, as the method for settling representation questions. Picketing is recognized as a legitimate organizational weapon until the employees have expressed their wishes in an NLRB election. Once an election has been conducted, there can be no picketing for at least twelve months. Thus if the union wins, its majority status is protected for at least a year, and if the union loses, the employees' rejection of it is protected from the economic pressures of picketing for the same period.

Picketing which does not have an organizational or recognitional purpose, such as "standards picketing" (picketing to mitigate the competition to union shops created by substandard conditions and wages in nonunion shops), falls outside the prohibitions of Section 8(b)(7). Any organizational pressure generated by "standards picketing" is at most indirect, since the employer always has the option of meeting the union standards without recognizing the union. Picketing to protest unfair labor practices, or to secure reinstatement of discharged employees or strikers, does not come within Section 8(b)(7), as the employer can accede to the union's demands without bargaining. Remember that picketing that is not prohibited by 8(b)(7), which pertains to organizational or recognitional picketing, may be prohibited under another section or policy.

THE PUBLICITY PROVISO (SECTION 8(b)(7)(c)). Picketing to "truthfully advise the public" (including consumers) of the employer's nonunion status is permitted by the proviso to Section 8(b)(7)(c). Thus the union's purpose in picketing must be analyzed. The union may appeal to the unorganized public as individuals, and ask them not to deal with the company (publicity picketing to effect a consumer boycott), so long as the communications element dominates the picketing.

The proviso does not sanction "signal picketing" (calls to other unions for concerted economic action), so if the result is to halt pickups, deliveries, or services of the employees of a neutral employer, then this picketing is prohibited. Signal picketing is prohibited because it exerts unwanted pressure on both the employer and the employees. The employer has his business disrupted and the employees have undo pressure placed on their freedom of choice concerning whether or not to be represented.

To determine whether the picketing is for the purpose of truthfully advising the public of the employer's nonunion status, the courts look only at the union's *immediate* purpose—even though the publicity picketing is usually accompanied by an ultimate, but unvoiced, recognitional objective. Thus, if the court finds that recognition is the immediate object of the picketing, it is illegal. But where "informing the public" is an immediate object, the picketing will be permitted even though its ultimate object is success through recognition by the employer. *Local 3, IBEW* v. *NLRB*, 317 F.2d 193 (1963); *Smithley* v. *NLRB*, 327 F.2d 351 (1964).

Picketing for various other objectives (e.g., standards picketing) can no longer be presumed to necessarily encompass recognitional or organizational purposes. Rather, such picketing raises a factual issue as to whether the protest is an artifice to conceal a present organizational or recognitional object.

The NLRB and the courts have interpreted the proviso as requiring a substantial stoppage before the picketing loses the protection of the proviso. A mere scattering of refusals to cross the picket line is not enough. Test: whether the picketing *actually* had an impact on the employer's business. *Barker Bros.* v. *NLRB*, 328 F.2d 431 (C.A. 9), (1964).

Election Procedure under 8(b)(7). A more expeditious election procedure exists where the union is picketing than in the ordinary representation case. The statute requires the NLRB to dispense with the hearing and showing of interest requirements and hold the election. If the union wins, it is no longer violating Section 8(b)(7) because it is recognized; if it loses, it can no longer picket because an election has been held within the preceding twelve months.

Either the employer or the union can petition for an election, once a reasonable time has elapsed. It becomes a matter of union strategy whether to use picketing in connection with an organization drive since it may trigger off the election before the union has obtained majority status. Filing within the statutory period legalizes subsequent picketing until there is a valid election in which the union is defeated.

11. Strikes

General. A strike is a concerted suspension of work. The definition given by Congress is quite broad:

> "The term 'strike' includes any strike or other concerted stoppage of work by employees (including a stoppage by reason of the expiration of a collective bargaining agreement) and any concerted slowdown or other concerted interruption of operations by employees." (NLRA §501)

Thus, the strike is a powerful weapon for labor, and just having the weapon is sometimes sufficient for labor to achieve its aim without ever having to actually call a strike.

Section 2(3) of the NLRA provides that strikers retain their employee status and are entitled to protection under the Act so long as the labor dispute is current. This, coupled with Section 13, which provides that "nothing in this Act, except as specifically provided for herein, shall be construed so as either to interfere with or impede or diminish in any way the right to strike . . . ," spells out the basic right to strike. However, in certain circumstances the employer may terminate the important employee status of the individuals and hence eliminate some of their protection under the Act. The circumstances are dependent upon designating the strike as an unfair labor practice strike or an economic strike, with the designation emanating from whatever the disagreement was that caused the strike. See Chapter 13 for coverage of secondary strikes.

Unfair labor practices are practices that have been specified as such by either Congress or the courts when they construe the congressional Acts.

Economic Strikes. An employer may hire strike replacements in order to continue operations if the employees are striking for economic reasons. Once the strike is terminated, there becomes a problem in that there can be two workers for the same position—the original one who was on strike and the replacement (sometimes called a "scab" by the union).

The employer has no duty to discharge the replacement workers, but he also may not discharge the original employees who have been on strike. The result is that the replacement workers can stay but the strikers are entitled to reinstatement upon application if their particular position has not been filled (which oftentimes it will not be because a skeleton crew has been used until the strike ends). Even if the positions have been filled, the strikers are entitled

104

to preferential treatment if a vacancy occurs later, if they are still interested and have not found other equivalent employment.

It is an unfair labor practice to refuse to reinstate an employee whose job is available.

Even though the employers need not reinstate the striking employees, he may not discriminate against them, such as by granting an instantaneous 20 years of experience to the replacements to enrich their rights with respect to seniority.

Unfair Labor Practices Strikes. If the strike is for an unfair labor practice, then at the end of the strike the employees have a right to their jobs back, even if this means dismissing the replacement employees. A strike that was initially over economic issues may later offer the strikers the protection guaranteed in an unfair labor practice situation if the employer prolongs the strike via an unfair practice. If the investigation of the entire circumstances shows that the charge was not justified on its face, then the strikers are not protected. An example of this would be where slowdowns and walkouts were conducted to force recognition of a union which had been erroneously certified after winning an election that should have been barred because there had been another election in the preceding 12 months. *NLRB* v. *Blades Mfg. Co.*, 344 F.2d 998 (1965).

Illegal Conduct and Illegal Strikes. Regardless of the reason for the strike, certain types of employee conduct during the strike will be held to give the employer an option of whether or not to discharge the employees involved. Violence is one of these types of conduct. The occurrence of violence can lead to cause for discharge of the employees involved, even if the strike is for an unfair labor practice, but the violent acts of others may not be imputed to those who took no part in the actions. *NLRB* v. *Cambria Clay Products Co.*, 215 F.2d 48 (1954).

The employer and nonstriking employees have the right to continue to work, so strikers who threaten or harass other employees by picketing may be discharged, as may those who seize an employer's building or property. *NLRB* v. *Fansteel Metallurgical Corp.*, 306 U.S. 240 (1939).

The employer has the right to expect the union and its members to follow their leadership and agreements, so wildcat strikers who do not have the union's sanction and strikers who violate an agreement may be discharged. However, disobeying a state court injunction is not reason for discharge but any accompanying acts, such as violence occurring, may lead to reason for discharge.

Strikers' Right to Reinstatement

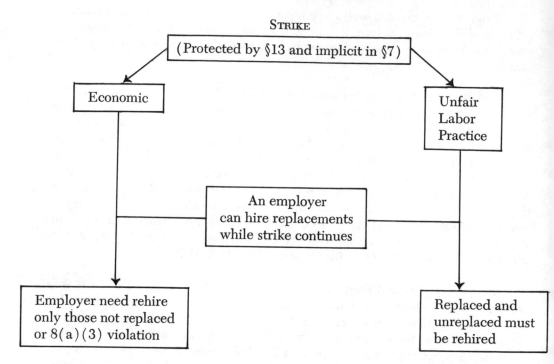

Strikers: Not protected if slowdowns, quickie strikes,* disloyalty.** Protected if refuse to cross picket lines. Can give up via a contract the right to strike for economic reasons but cannot contract away the right to strike for an unfair labor practice violation.

---

* Quickie strikes: Work stoppages called without advance notice and usually not authorized by the national union.

** Disloyalty: The strikers not loyal to their employer, such as assist a competitor.

The Boys Markets, Inc. v. *Retail Clerks Union, Local 770*

398 U.S. 235, 26 L.ed.2d 199, 90 S.Ct. 1583 (1970)

Held: If the employer and the union have a contract with a clause that prohibits strikes and provides for binding arbitration, and if the union goes on strike anyway, then an employer may obtain an injunction to stop the strike even if the Norris-LaGuardia Act might usually prohibit the injunction, as the key is the union's violation of the contract.

Opinion:

Although an employer and a union had made a collective-bargaining agreement which contained a no-strike clause and a provision for binding arbitration, the union later called a strike rather than submitting a grievance dispute to arbitration. The employer obtained from a state court a temporary restraining order forbidding continuation of the strike, and after the union removed the case to the United States District Court for the Central District of California, the District Court granted the employer's request for injunctive relief against the strike. The Court of Appeals for the Ninth Circuit reversed (416 F.2d 368), holding that under the Supreme Court's decision in *Sinclair Refining Co.* v. *Atkinson* (1962), 370 U.S. 195, 8 L.ed.2d 440, 82 S.Ct. 1328, injunctive relief from the District Court was precluded by the anti-injunction provisions of the Norris-LaGuardia Act.

On certiorari, the United States Supreme Court reversed the judgment of the Court of Appeals and remanded the case with directions to affirm the District Court's order. In an opinion by Brennan, J., expressing the views of five members of the court, the *Sinclair Case* was overruled, and it was held that the anti-injunction provisions of the Norris-LaGuardia Act did not preclude a Federal District Court from enjoining a strike in breach of a no-strike obligation under a collective-bargaining agreement containing provisions, enforceable under §301(a) of the Labor Management Relations Act, for binding arbitration of the grievance dispute concerning which the strike was called.

In this case we re-examine the holding of *Sinclair Refining Co.* v. *Atkinson*, 370 U.S. 195, 8 L.ed.2d 440, 82 S.Ct. 1328 (1962), that the anti-injunction provisions of the Norris-LaGuardia Act preclude a federal district court from enjoining a strike in breach of a no-strike obligation under a collective-bargaining agreement, even though that agreement contains provisions, enforceable under §301(a) of the Labor Management Relations Act, 1947, for binding arbitration of the grievance dispute concerning which the strike was called. The Court of Appeals for the Ninth Circuit considering itself bound by *Sinclair*, reversed the grant by the District Court for the Central District of California of petitioner's prayer for injunctive relief. 416 F.2d 368 (1969). We granted certiorari. 396 U.S. 1000, 24 L.ed.2d 492, 90 S.Ct. 572 (1970). Having concluded that *Sinclair* was erroneously decided and that subsequent events have undermined its continuing validity, we overrule that decision and reverse the judgment of the Court of Appeals. . . .

Our holding in the present case is a narrow one. We do not undermine the vitality of the Norris-LaGuardia Act. We deal only with the situation in which a collective-bargaining contract contains a mandatory grievance adjustment or arbitration procedure. Nor does it follow from what we have said that injunctive relief is appropriate as a matter of course in every case of a strike over an arbitrable grievance. The dissenting opinion in *Sinclair* suggested the following principles for the guidance of the district courts in determining whether to grant injunctive relief—principles that we now adopt:

"A District Court entertaining an action under §301 may not grant injunctive relief against concerted activity unless and until it decides that the case is one in which an injunction would be appropriate despite the Norris-LaGuardia Act. When a strike is sought to be enjoined because it is over a grievance which both parties are contractually bound to arbitrate, the District Court may issue no injunctive order until it first holds that the contract *does* have that effect; and the employer should be ordered to arbitrate, as a condition of his obtaining an injunction against the strike. Beyond this, the District Court must, of course, consider whether issuance of an injunction would be warranted under ordinary principles of equity—whether breaches are occurring and will continue, or have been threatened and will be committed; whether they have caused or will cause irreparable injury to the employer; and whether the employer will suffer more from the denial of an injunction than will the union from its issuance." 370 U.S. at 228, 8 L.ed.2d at 460. (Emphasis in original.)

In the present case there is no dispute that the grievance in question was subject to adjustment and arbitration under the collective-bargaining agreement and that the petitioner was ready to proceed with arbitration at the time an injunction against the strike was sought and obtained. The District Court also concluded that, by reason of respondent's violations of its no-strike obligation, petitioner "has suffered irreparable injury and will continue to suffer irreparable injury." Since we now overrule *Sinclair*, the holding of the Court of Appeals in reliance on *Sinclair* must be reversed. Accordingly, we reverse the judgment of the Court of Appeals and remand the case with directions to enter a judgment affirming the order of the District Court.

It is so ordered.

International Union, United Automobile, Aircraft and Agricultural Implement Workers of America Local 833 v. NLRB

Kohler Company, Intervenor. Court of Appeals, D.C. Circuit (Jan. 26, 1962)
300 F.2d 699 (1962), cert. denied 825 S.Ct. 1258

Held: An employee may be fired for participating in a strike that is not a protected activity by the labor laws, but if the employer had previously committed an unprotected act, then the employees may not be fired for their actions.

Opinion:

In No. 15961 the Union challenges the Board's refusal to reinstate seventy-seven employees discharged for misconduct. It alleges that the Board failed to balance that misconduct against the Company's unfair labor practices. This balancing, it contends, is required by the statutory command that the Board's remedy "effectuate the policies of the (Act). . . ." *National Labor Relations Board v. Thayer Co.*, 213 F.2d 748 (1st Cir.), cert. denied, 348 U.S. 883 (1954). The Union also contends that the Board should have found that Kohler failed, both in form and substance, to bargain in good faith in the unsuccessful negotiations which culminated in the 1954 strike and that the walkout was therefore an unfair labor practice strike from its inception on April 5, 1954. In the absence of such a finding, the Board ordered reinstatement only of employees whose jobs were filled after June 1, 1954. Had it found that Kohler's unfair labor practices caused the walkout on April 5, it might have ordered reinstatement of all strikers replaced by nonstrikers at any time during the dispute. Moreover, if the *Thayer* doctrine is valid, the Board should have balanced Kohler's unfair labor practices against the discharged strikers' misconduct whether it occurred either before or after June 1, 1954.

We first set forth the facts revelant to the Union's request that the Board be directed to reconsider its decision not to reinstate seventy-seven strikers discharged for misconduct. Their misconduct occurred in connection with three series of incidents.

First, forty-four discharges were based on participation in "belly-to-back" mass picketing ranging from presence on the picket line to a physical assault upon a nonstriker. The Board found that from April 5 through May 28 this picketing prevented any person who did not have a Union pass from entering Kohler's plants. The second series of incidents involved demonstrations by large, jeering crowds outside the homes of nonstrikers during the month of August, 1954. Some strikers who actively participated in the demonstrations and others who were merely present in the crowds were discharged. The third series of incidents took place near Kohler's employment office in December 1954 and January 1955 when a group of Union pickets hindered applicants from entering by blocking, pushing, and shoving some of them and by forcing others to walk around the pickets. Kohler discharged the participants. The last two series of incidents accounted for twenty-one discharges. The remaining twelve dischargees were members of the Union's strike committee which the Board found instigated some of the misconduct.

Thayer holds that where an employer who has committed unfair labor practices discharges employees for unprotected acts of misconduct, the Board must consider both the seriousness of the employer's unlawful acts and the seriousness of the employees' misconduct in determining whether reinstatement would effectuate the policies of the Act. Those policies inevitably come into conflict when both labor and management are at fault. To hold that employee "misconduct" automatically precludes compulsory reinstatement ignores two considerations which we think important. First, the employer's antecedent unfair labor practices may have been so blatant that they provoked employees to resort to unprotected action. Second, reinstatement is the only sanction which prevents an employer from benefiting from his unfair labor practices through discharges which may weaken or destroy a union. *In re H. N. Thayer Co.*, 115 NLRB 1591, 1605-06 (1956) (dissenting opinion). But sanctions other than discharge —criminal prosecutions, civil suits, union unfair labor practice proceedings and the possibility of discharge—are available to prevent or remedy certain employee misconduct. *Berkshire Knitting Mills*, 139 F.2d 134 (3d Cir. 1943), cert. denied, 322 U.S. 747 (1944). Hence automatic denial of reinstatement prevents the Board from protecting the rights of employees, but may not be essential to the protection of legitimate interests of employers and the public. We conclude that the teaching of the *Thayer* case is sound and must be followed in order to assure the Board's compliance with the statutory command that its remedial orders effectuate the policies of the Act.

The record indicates that the Board disregarded the *Thayer* doctrine. Despite exceptions taken by both the Union and the general counsel to the trial examiner's express refusal to follow *Thayer*, the Board's decision refers neither to the doctrine nor to the considerations it requires. On the contrary, the Board held that strikers who did not themselves obstruct applicants but were present at the employment office picketing could not be reinstated because they were engaged in unprotected activity. That approach to formulating the remedy for an employer's antecedent unfair labor practice was specifically disapproved by *Thayer*. In ordering the Board to reconsider its determination not to reinstate certain employees who had engaged in unprotected acts of misconduct, the *Thayer* court reasoned that where the issue is simply whether a discharge was an attempt to coerce employees in the exercise of their rights under §7, a finding that an employee was fired for participation in unprotected activity ends the inquiry; but where there has been an antecedent employer unfair labor practice, a finding that employees have engaged in unprotected activity is only the first step in determining whether reinstatement is appropriate. We think that view of the Board's remedial powers is correct. See *National Labor Relations Board* v. *Thayer Co., supra.*

388 U.S. 26, 87 S.Ct. 1792, 18 L.ed.2d 1027 (1967)

Held: An employer may not use benefits to discriminate between employees on the basis of who is or is not on strike. There are two standards for evaluating the employer's conduct, which are:

(1) If the conduct is inherently destructive of important employee rights, then it is an unfair practice even if there is no antiunion motivation and the conduct was motivated by business considerations.

(2) If the adverse effect of the discriminatory conduct on employee rights is slight, then a business justification may be a sufficient defense for the employer.

Opinion:

The issue here is whether, in the absence of proof of an antiunion motivation, an employer may be held to have violated §§8(a)(3) and (1) of the National Labor Relations Act when he refused to pay striking employees vacation benefits accrued under a terminated collective-bargaining agreement while he announced an intention to pay such benefits to striker replacements, returning strikers, and nonstrikers who had been at work on a certain date during the strike.

The respondent company and the union entered into a collective-bargaining agreement which was effective by its terms until March 31, 1963. The agreement contained a commitment by the company to pay vacation benefits to employees who met certain enumerated qualifications. In essence, the company agreed to pay specified vacation benefits to employees who, during the preceding year, had worked at least 1,525 hours. It was also provided that, in the case of a "lay-off, termination or quitting," employees who had served more than 60 days during the year would be entitled to pro rata shares of their vacation benefits. Benefits were to be paid on the Friday nearest July 1 of each year. . . .

The refusal to pay vacation benefits to strikers, coupled with the payments to nonstrikers, formed the bases of an unfair labor practice complaint filed with the Board while the strike was still in progress. Violations of §§8(a)(3) and (1) were charged. A hearing was held before a trial examiner who found that the company's action in regard to vacation pay constituted a discrimination in terms and conditions of employment which would discourage union membership, as well as an unlawful interference with protected activity. He held that the company had violated §§8(a)(3) and (1) and recommended that it be ordered to cease and desist from its unfair labor practice and to pay the accrued vacation benefits to strikers. The Board, after reviewing the record, adopted the Trial Examiner's conclusions and remedy. . . .

[T]he Court of Appeals held that, although discrimination between striking and nonstriking employees had been proved, the Board's conclusion that the company had committed an unfair labor practice was not well-founded inasmuch as there had been no affirmative showing of an unlawful motivation to discourage union membership or to interfere with the exercise of protected rights. Despite the fact that the company itself had not introduced evidence of a legitimate business purpose underlying its discriminatory action, the Court of Appeals speculated that it might have been motivated by a desire "(1) to reduce expenses; (2) to encourage longer tenure among present employees; or (3) to discourage leaves immediately before vacation periods." Believing that the possibility of the existence of such motives was sufficient to overcome the inference of an improper motive which flowed from the conduct itself, the court denied enforcement of the order. 363 F.2d 130 (1966). We granted certiorari

111

to determine whether the treatment of the motivation issue by the Court of Appeals was consistent with recent decisions of this Court. 385 U.S. 1000 (1967).

The unfair labor practice charged here is grounded primarily in §8(a)(3) which requires specifically that the Board find a discrimination and a resulting discouragement of union membership. *American Ship Building Co.* v. *NLRB*, 380 U.S. 300, 311 (1965). There is little question but that the result of the company's refusal to pay vacation benefits to strikers was discrimination in its simplest form. Compare *Republic Aviation Corp.* v. *NLRB*, 324 U.S. 793 (1945), with *Teamsters Union* v. *NLRB*, 365 U.S. 667 (1961). Some employees who met the conditions specified in the expired collective bargaining agreement were paid accrued vacation benefits in the amounts set forth in that agreement, while other employees who also met the conditions but who had engaged in protected concerted activity were denied such benefits. Similarly, there can be no doubt but that the discrimination was capable of discouraging membership in a labor organization within the meaning of the statute. Discouraging membership in a labor organization "includes discouraging participation in concerted activities . . . such as a legitimate strike." *Erie Resistor Corp.* v. *NLRB*, 373 U.S. 221, 233 (1963). The act of paying accrued benefits to one group of employees while announcing the extinction of the same benefits for another group of employees who are distinguishable only by their participation in protected concerted activity surely may have a discouraging effect on either present or future concerted activity.

But inquiry under §8(a)(3) does not usually stop at this point. The statutory language "discrimination . . . to . . . discourage" means that the finding of a violation normally turns on whether the discriminatory conduct was motivated by an antiunion purpose. *American Ship Building Co.* v. *NLRB*, 380 U.S. 300 (1965). It was upon the motivation element that the Court of Appeals based its decision not to grant enforcement, and it is to that element which we now turn. In three recent opinions we considered employer motivation in the context of asserted §8(a)(3) violations. *American Ship Building Co.* v. *NLRB*, *supra*; *NLRB* v. *Brown*, 380 U.S. 278 (1965); and *Erie Resistor Corp.* v. *NLRB*, *supra*. We noted in *Erie Resistor*, *supra* at 227, that proof of an antiunion motivation may make unlawful certain employer conduct which would in other circumstances be lawful. Some conduct, however, is so "inherently destructive of employee interests" that it may be deemed proscribed without need for proof of an underlying improper motive. *NLRB* v. *Brown*, *supra* at 287; *American Ship Building Co.* v. *NLRB*, *supra* at 311. That is, some conduct carries with it "unavoidable consequences which the employer not only foresaw but which he must have intended" and thus bears "its own indicia of intent." *Erie Resistor Corp.* v. *NLRB*, *supra* at 228, 231. If the conduct in question falls within this "inherently destructive" category, the employer has the burden of explaining away, justifying or characterizing "his actions as something different than they appear on their face," and if he fails, "an unfair labor practice charge is made out." *Id.* at 228. And even if the employer does come forward with counterexplanations for his conduct in this situation, the Board may nevertheless draw an inference of improper motive from the conduct itself and exercise its duty to strike the proper balance between the asserted business justifications and the invasion of employee rights in light of the Act and its policy. *Id.* at 229. On the other hand, when "the resulting harm to employee rights is . . . comparatively slight, and a substantial and legitimate business end is served, the employer's conduct is prima facie lawful," and an affirmative showing of improper motivation must be made. *NLRB* v. *Brown*, *supra* at 289; *American Ship Building Co.* v. *NLRB*, *supra* at 311-313.

From this review of our recent decisions, several principles of controlling importance here can be distilled. First, if it can reasonably be concluded that the employer's discriminatory conduct was "inherently destructive" of important employee rights, no proof of an antiunion motivation is needed and the Board can find an unfair labor practice even if the employer introduces evidence that the conduct was motivated by business considerations. Second, if the adverse effect of the discriminatory conduct on employee rights is "comparatively slight," an antiunion motivation must be proved to sustain the charge *if* the employer has come forward with evidence of legitimate and substantial business justifications for the conduct. Thus, in either situation, once it has been proved that the employer engaged in discriminatory conduct which could have adversely affected employee rights to *some* extent, the burden is upon the employer to establish that it was motivated by legitimate objectives since proof of motivation is most accessible to him.

Applying the principles to this case then, it is not necessary for us to decide the degree to which the challenged conduct might have affected employee rights. As the Court of Appeals correctly noted, the company came forward with no evidence of legitimate motives for its discriminatory conduct. 363 F.2d at 134. The company simply did not meet the burden of proof, and the Court of Appeals misconstrued the function of judicial review when it proceeded nonetheless to speculate upon what *might have* motivated the company. Since discriminatory conduct carrying a potential for adverse effect upon employee rights was proved and no evidence of a proper motivation appeared in the record, the Board's conclusions were supported by substantial evidence, *Universal Camera Corp.* v. *NLRB*, 340 U.S. 474 (1951), and should have been sustained.

The judgment of the Court of Appeals is reversed and the case is remanded with directions to enforce the Board's order.

United Mine Workers of America et al. v. *Patton et al.*

United States Court of Appeals, Fourth Circuit. 211 F.2d 742 (1954)

Held: The union is bound by the acts of its agents, which is a general law of agency,
so if a representative of the union calls a strike, then even if the union officers
did not officially call the strike the union is still liable for any damages that
might arise as a result of the acts of its representative in calling the strike.

Opinion:

The chief argument of defendants in support of their motion for directed verdict
is that there is no evidence that they authorized or ratified the strikes upon which
plaintiffs rely for recovery. It is true that there is no evidence of any resolution of
either the United Mine Workers or District 28 authorizing or ratifying the strikes.
There is evidence, however, that the strikes were called by the Field Representative
of the United Mine Workers, who was employed by District 28, and that he was
engaged in the organization work that was being carried on by the international union
through District 28, which was a mere division of the international union. Members
of the union are members of local and district unions as well as the international;
and of the $4 monthly dues paid by them, $2 goes to the international union, $1 to
the local union and $1 to the district organization. It is clear that in carrying on
organizational work the field representative is engaged in the business of both the
international union and the district and that both are responsible for acts done by him
within the scope and course of his employment. *Stockwell* v. *United States*, 13 Wall.
531, 545-548, 20 L.ed. 491; *Hindman* v. *First Nat. Bk. of Louisville*, 6 Cir., 112 F.
931, 57 L.R.A. 108; *Oman* v. *United States*, 10 Cir., 179 F.2d 738. . . . The relationship between the international union and the district organization was pointed
out by the Supreme Court of Appeals of Virginia in *United Const. Workers* v.
Laburnum Const. Corp., 194 Va. 872, 75 S.E.2d 694, 703-704, where the court said:

> "United Mine Workers of America is a labor organization with approxi-
> mately 650,000 members who are primarily engaged in mining and processing
> coal at the mines. District 50 United Mine Workers of America has a member-
> ship of 112,000 which is largely made up of workers who convert coal into
> chemical constituents, such as dyes, drugs, plastics, etc. A part of its charter
> fees, initiation fees and dues is paid to the United Mine Workers of America.
> According to defendants' brief, 'Its members are part of UMWA, but retain their
> identity, membership rights and privileges at all times as members of District 50.'
> In other words, District 50 is an arm or branch of the United Mine Workers of
> America. . . .
>
> "Thus, while the defendants' brief insists that 'members of District 50,
> UCW and UMWA are not members of one organization,' a fair deduction from
> the record is that District 50 is a component part of United Mine Workers of
> America, *or at least its agent* in organizing workers in businesses other than that
> of mining coal." (Italics supplied.)

Section 301(b) of the Labor Management Relations Act, 29 U.S.C.A. §185(b)
expressly provides:

> "(b) Any labor organization which represents employees in an industry
> affecting commerce as defined in this chapter and any employer whose activities
> affect commerce as defined in this chapter shall be bound by the acts of its
> agents. . . ."

114

12. Lockouts

A lockout is the withholding of employment by an employer from his employees for the purpose of resisting demands or to gain a concession from the employees. The purpose of the action differentiates it from a layoff or shutdown (for other reasons), and the lockout is sometimes considered to be analagous to the employer as the strike is to the union.

The balancing of interests is between the union's power to decide if and when to strike versus the employer's right to have some control over how and when his work will be conducted.

In the statutes there are no specific prohibitions to lockouts but unions typically assert that lockouts violate Sections 8(a)(1), which is the general charge of violating Section 7 rights, and of violating Section 8(a)(3), which is discrimination to encourage or discourage union membership.

If these violations concerning the purpose of the lockout can be proven, then the lockout is not permitted. In practice, it is extremely rare to have a lockout without first there having been a strike or threat of a strike, and so where there is a binding arbitration clause in the union's contract there are literally no lockouts.

Permissible Lockouts

UNUSUAL CIRCUMSTANCES. Historically, an employer could lock out his employees at any time, but today the purpose is the deciding factor on whether or not this is permitted.

In the event of unusual economic circumstances, where the union is planning to pick a time to strike when the employer is particularly vulnerable to suffering great economic harm, the employer may lock out his employees in anticipation of this strike. For example, the employer might be expecting a large shipment of fresh fruit which will spoil if not processed quickly; if the union threatens to strike as soon as the shipment arrives, then the employer may lock out the employees before the shipment arrives and either cancel the shipment or use some other means of preventing this large loss. *Buffalo Linen*, 353 U.S. 87 (1957).

The Supreme Court has held that the right to strike does not carry with it the right to select the time and may economically injure the union. When there is a legitimate business end served, and the resulting harm to employees

115

is slight, then the employer's conduct is presumed lawful and his conduct must be shown to be discriminating against the union to be unlawful. *NLRB* v. *Brown*, 380 U.S. 278, 85 S.Ct. (1965).

IMPASSE. If a bargaining impasse has been reached then an employer may lock out his employees if his motivation is to resist union bargaining demands. *American Ship Building* v. *NLRB*, 380 U.S. 300, 85 S.Ct. 955 (1965).

A pre-impasse lockout is not necessarily unlawful, with consideration given to the length of negotiations and the seasonal nature of the business. *Darling & Co.*, 171 NLRB 95 (1968).

MULTI-EMPLOYER UNITS. In recent years the biggest problems involving lockouts have been where the union strikes one employer of a multi-employer bargaining unit and the other employers lock their employees out so as to prevent the union from accomplishing its demands by selecting one employer to shut down and thus conducting a "whip-saw" strike. A whip-saw strike is when the employers have a multi-employer bargaining pact and the union cannot or will not obtain its demands by bargaining, so it calls a strike against one employer, which injures him economically, and supports the strikers by contributions from the union members who are employees of the non-struck employers and hence are still drawing wages.

The aim of the union is to put tremendous pressure on the struck employer because his competitors, who are usually the other members of the employer bargaining pact, are still open for business and might capture some of his customers who will not return to him even after the strike is over. If the union wins its demands, it could repeat this procedure on each employer until all the employers have agreed to their demands and thus circumvent the collective-bargaining process.

The employers may not combat this union technique by temporarily withdrawing from the multi-employer bargaining unit, for the decision must contemplate a sincere abandonment, with relative permanency, of the unit and the embracement of a different course of bargaining on an individual-employer basis. The element of good faith is a necessary requirement to withdraw and adequate notice must be given to all parties. *Retail Associates, Inc.*, 120 NLRB 388 (1958).

Where actual bargaining negotiations based on the existing multi-employer unit have begun, a party may not abandon the unit without consent of the other members of the unit. *Sheridan Creations, Inc.*, 357 F.2d 245 (1966).

The party may withdraw if the union has given consent, express or implied, and consent may be held to have been given if the union agrees to bargain with an individual employer after reaching an agreement with the multi-employer unit. *Atlas Sheet Metal Works, Inc.*, 148 NLRB 27 (1964).

Thus, absent the union's consent, the employers may not leave the multi-employer unit once bargaining has begun, so to combat the whip-saw strike the employers sometimes lock out their employees.

The employers may, after locking out their employees, hire temporary replacements in order to continue their business, but it has not been decided whether permanent replacements may be hired. *NLRB* v. *Brown, supra*.

Thus, if the union commences a whip-saw strike then the other employers can lock out their employees and hire temporary replacements. *Intercollegiate Press*, 84 LRRM 2582 (1973).

UNLAWFUL LOCKOUTS. Lockouts are unlawful if the employer is evading his duty, as imposed by law, to bargain in good faith, or is discriminating either in favor of or against a particular union, such as a lockout to favor union A over union B. *Wire Products*, 84 LRRM 2038 (1973).

TERMINATION OF BUSINESS. Perhaps the ultimate lockout is to lock the employees out and never to reopen. One manufacturer decided to buy another mill for his textile chain and as soon as he purchased it, the mill voted for a union. The manufacturer closed his mill, alleged economic reasons, and never reopened it. A lawsuit evolved that went to higher courts several different times for several different reasons, and one of the results was a holding that one can terminate his business at any time for any reason. There is the caveat that a manufacturer cannot close down a single plant and shift the work to another of his plants if his motivation is to avoid a union, and if he does so this is labeled a "runaway shop" and is not permissible.

A "runaway shop" is where an operation is transferred to another location in order to destroy the effectiveness of the union, and this action is held to be a violation of the duty to bargain. *Textile Workers Union* v. *Darlington Manufacturing Company*, 85 S.Ct. 994 (1965).

American Ship Building Company v. National Labor Relations Board

380 U.S. 300, 13 L.ed.2d 855, 85 S.Ct. 955 (1965)

Held: An employer does not violate §8(a)(1) or 8(a)(3) when, after a bargaining impasse has been reached, he temporarily shuts down his plant and lays off his employees for the sole purpose of bringing economic pressure to bear to support his legitimate bargaining position. Thus, in certain conditions, the lockout may be used as a bargaining device.

Opinion:

An operator of four Great Lakes shipyards reached a bargaining impasse with unions representing his employees, and when the parties separated after the expiration of the existing contract, the operator, being apprehensive of a work stoppage when circumstances gave the unions increased strike leverage, completely shut down one shipyard, laid off all but two employees at another shipyard, and gradually laid off employees at a third shipyard. The National Labor Relations Board concluded that the layoffs violated §8(a)(1) and (3) of the amended National Labor Relations Act. (142 NLRB 1362). The United States Court of Appeals for the District of Columbia enforced the Board's order. (118 App. D.C. 78, 331 F.2d 839.)

On certiorari, the Supreme Court of the United States reversed. In an opinion by Stewart, J., expressing the views of six members of the Court, it was held that an employer does not violate §8(a)(1) or (3) where, after a bargaining impasse has been reached, he temporarily shuts down his plant and lays off his employees for the sole purpose of bringing economic pressure to bear in support of his legitimate bargaining position.

White, J., concurring in the result, stated that the facts did not show a bargaining lockout, but merely a layoff for lack of work because the operator's customers feared a strike, and that the legality of a bargaining lockout is determined by balancing conflicting legitimate interests.

Goldberg, J., joined by Warren, Ch. J., concurring in the result, stated that the employer's fear of a strike was reasonable and therefore the lockout was justified, but that, absent antiunion animus, in a §8(a)(1) or (3) case the legality of an employer's conduct requires balancing conflicting legitimate interests.

[1] In analyzing the status of the bargaining lockout under §§8(a)(1) and (3) of the National Labor Relations Act, it is important that the practice with which we are here concerned be distinguished from other forms of temporary separation from employment. No one would deny that an employer is free to shut down his enterprise temporarily for reasons of renovation or lack of profitable work unrelated to his collective-bargaining situation. Similarly, we put to one side cases where the Board has concluded on the basis of substantial evidence that the employer has used a lockout as a means to injure a labor organization or to evade his duty to bargain collectively. *Hopwood Retinning Co.*, 4 NLRB 922; *Scott Paper Box Co.*, 81 NLRB 535. What we are here concerned with is the use of a temporary layoff of employees solely as a means to bring economic pressure to bear in support of the employer's bargaining position, after an impasse has been reached. This is the only issue before us, and all that we decide.

[2] To establish that this practice is a violation of §8(a)(1), it must be shown that the employer has interfered with, restrained, or coerced employees in the exercise of some right protected by §7 of the Act. The Board's position is premised on the view that the lockout interferes with two of the rights guaranteed by §7: the right to bargain collectively and the right to strike. In the Board's view, the use of the

lockout "punishes" employees for the presentation of and adherence to demands made by their bargaining representatives and so coerces them in the exercise of their right to bargain collectively. It is important to note that there is here no allegation that the employer used the lockout in the service of designs inimical to the process of collective bargaining. There was no evidence and no finding that the employer was hostile to its employees' banding together for collective bargaining or that the lockout was designed to discipline them for doing so. It is therefore inaccurate to say that the employer's intention was to destroy or frustrate the process of collective bargaining. What can be said is that it intended to resist the demands made of it in the negotiations and to secure modification of these demands. We cannot see that this intention is in any way inconsistent with the employees' rights to bargain collectively.

[3] Moreover, there is no indication, either as a general matter or in this specific case, that the lockout will necessarily destroy the unions' capacity for effective and responsible representation. The unions here involved have vigorously represented the employees since 1952, and there is nothing to show that their ability to do so has been impaired by the lockout. Nor is the lockout one of those acts which are demonstrably so destructive of collective bargaining that the Board need not inquire into employer motivation, as might be the case, for example, if an employer permanently discharged his unionized staff and replaced them with employees known to be possessed of a violent antiunion animus. Cf. *Labor Board* v. *Erie Resistor Corp.*, 373 U.S. 221, 10 L.ed.2d 308, 83 S.Ct. 1139, 94 ALR2d 1147. The lockout may well dissuade employees from adhering to the position which they initially adopted in the bargaining, but the right to bargain collectively does not entail any "right" to insist on one's position free from economic disadvantage. Proper analysis of the problem demands that the simple intention to support the employer's bargaining position as to compensation and the like be distinguished from a hostility to the process of collective bargaining which could suffice to render a lockout unlawful. See *Labor Board* v. *Brown*, 380 U.S. 278, 13 L.ed.2d 839, 85 S.Ct. 980.

[4, 5] The Board has taken the complementary view that the lockout interferes with the right to strike protected under §§7 and 13 of the Act in that it allows the employer to pre-empt the possibility of a strike and thus leave the union with "nothing to strike against." Insofar as this means that once employees are locked out, they are deprived of their right to call a strike against the employer because he is already shut down, the argument is wholly specious, for the work stoppage which would have been the object of the strike has in fact occurred. It is true that recognition of the lockout deprives the union of exclusive control of the timing and duration of work stoppages calculated to influence the result of collective-bargaining negotiations, but there is nothing in the statute which would imply that the right to strike "carries with it" the right exclusively to determine the timing and duration of all work stoppages. The right to strike as commonly understood is the right to cease work— nothing more. No doubt a union's bargaining power would be enhanced if it possessed not only the simple right to strike but also the power exclusively to determine when work stoppages should occur, but the Act's provisions are not indefinitely elastic, content-free forms to be shaped in whatever manner the Board might think best conforms to the proper balance of bargaining power.

Thus, we cannot see that the employer's use of a lockout solely in support of a legitimate bargaining position is in any way inconsistent with the right to bargain collectively or with the right to strike. Accordingly, we conclude that on the basis of the findings made by the Board in this case, there has been no violation of §8(a)(1).

[6-8] Section 8(a)(3) prohibits discrimination in regard to tenure or other conditions of employment to discourage union membership. Under the words of the

statute there must be both discrimination and a resulting discouragement of union membership. It has long been established that a finding of violation under this section will normally turn on the employer's motivation. See *Labor Board* v. *Brown*, 380 U.S. 278, 13 L.ed.2d 839, 85 S.Ct. 980; *Radio Officers' Union* v. *Labor Board*, 347 U.S. 17, 43, 98 L.ed. 455, 478, 74 S.Ct. 323, 41 ALR2d 621; *Labor Board* v. *Jones & Laughlin Steel Corp.*, 301 U.S. 1, 46, 81 L.ed. 893, 916, 57 S.Ct. 615, 108 ALR 1352. Thus when the employer discharges a union leader who has broken shop rules, the problem posed is to determine whether the employer has acted purely in disinterested defense of shop discipline or has sought to damage employee organization. It is likely that the discharge will naturally tend to discourage union membership in both cases, because of the loss of union leadership and the employees' suspicion of the employer's true intention. But we have consistently construed the section to leave unscathed a wide range of employer actions taken to serve legitimate business interests in some significant fashion, even though the act committed may tend to discourage union membership. See, e.g., *Labor Board* v. *Mackay Radio & Telegraph Co.*, 304 U.S. 333, 347, 82 L.ed. 1381, 1391, 58 S.Ct. 904. Such a construction of §8(a)(3) is essential if due protection is to be accorded the employer's right to manage his enterprise. See *Textile Workers* v. *Darlington Mfg. Co.*, 380 U.S. 263, 13 L.ed.2d 827, 85 S.Ct. 994. . . .

[11, 12] To find a violation of §8(a)(3), then, the Board must find that the employer acted for a proscribed purpose. Indeed, the Board itself has always recognized that certain "operative" or "economic" purposes would justify a lockout. But the Board has erred in ruling that only these purposes will remove a lockout from the ambit of §8(a)(3), for that section requires an intention to discourage union membership or otherwise discriminate against the union. There was not the slightest evidence and there was no finding that the employer was actuated by a desire to discourage membership in the union as distinguished from a desire to affect the outcome of the particular negotiations in which it was involved. We recognize that the "union membership" which is not to be discouraged refers to more than the payment of dues and that measures taken to discourage participation in protected union activities may be found to come within the proscription. *Radio Officers' Union* v. *Labor Board, supra* 347 U.S. at 39-40, 98 L.ed. 477, 41 ALR2d 621. However, there is nothing in the Act which gives employees the right to insist on their contract demands, free from the sort of economic disadvantage which frequently attends bargaining disputes. Therefore, we conclude that where the intention proven is merely to bring about a settlement of a labor dispute on favorable terms, no violation of §8(a)(3) is shown.

[13] The conclusions which we draw from analysis of §§8(a)(1) and (3) are consonant with what little of relevance can be drawn from the balance of the statute and its legislative history. In the original version of the Act, the predecessor of §8(a)(1) declared it an unfair labor practice "[t]o attempt, by interference, influence, restraint, favor, coercion, or lockout, or by any other means, to impair the right of employees guaranteed in section 4." Prominent in the criticism leveled at the bill in the Senate Committee hearings was the charge that it did not accord even-handed treatment to employers and employees because it prohibited the lockout while protecting the strike. In the face of such criticism, the Committee added a provision prohibiting employee interference with employer bargaining activities and deleted the reference to the lockout. A plausible inference to be drawn from this history is that the language was deleted to mollify those who saw in the bill an inequitable denial of resort to the lockout, and to remove any language which might give rise to fears that the lockout was being proscribed per se. It is in any event clear that the Committee was concerned

with the status of the lockout and that the bill, as reported and as finally enacted, contained no prohibition on the use of the lockout as such. . . .

[18] We are unable to find that any fair construction of the provisions relied on by the Board in this case can support its findings of an unfair labor practice. Indeed, the role assumed by the Board in this area is fundamentally inconsistent with the structure of the Act and the function of the sections relied upon. The deference owed to an expert tribunal cannot be allowed to slip into a judicial inertia which results in the unauthorized assumption by an agency of major policy decisions properly made by Congress. Accordingly, we hold that an employer violates neither §8(a)(1) nor §8(a)(3) when, after a bargaining impasse has been reached, he temporarily shuts down his plant and lays off his employees for the sole purpose of bringing economic pressure to bear in support of his legitimate bargaining position.

Reversed.

National Labor Relations Board v. *John Brown et al.*

380 U.S. 278, 13 L.ed.2d 839, 85 S.Ct. 980 (1965)

Held: If a union which has bargained with a multi-employer bargaining group
decides to strike one of the employers, the other employers may lock out their
employees who are in this union and hire temporary replacements in order
to continue business, so long as the lockout serves a legitimate business purpose
and there is no antiunion motive. Thus, the lockout may be used to protect
the members of a multi-employer bargaining group.

Opinion:

The respondents, who are members of a multi-employer bargaining group,
locked out their employees in response to a whipsaw strike against another member
of the group. They and the struck employer continued operations with temporary
replacements. The National Labor Relations Board found that the struck employer's
use of temporary replacements was lawful under *Labor Board* v. *Mackay Radio &
TeleGraph Co.*, 304 U.S. 333, 82 L.ed. 1381, 58 S.Ct. 904, but that the respondents
had violated §§8(a)(1) and (3) of the National Labor Relations Act by locking out
their regular employees and using temporary replacements to carry on business. 137
NLRB 73. The Court of Appeals for the Tenth Circuit disagreed and refused to
enforce the Board's order. 319 F.2d 7. We granted certiorari, 375 U.S. 962, 11 L.ed.2d
413, 84 S.Ct. 484. We affirm the Court of Appeals. . . .

[1, 2] It is true that the Board need not inquire into employer motivation to
support a finding of an unfair labor practice where the employer conduct is demonstrably destructive of employee rights and is not justified by the service of significant
or important business ends. See, e.g., *Labor Board* v. *Erie Resistor Corp.*, 373 U.S.
221, 10 L.ed.2d 308, 83 S.Ct. 1139, 94 ALR2d 1147; *Labor Board* v. *Burnup &
Sims, Inc.*, 379 U.S. 21, 13 L.ed.2d 1, 85 S.Ct. 171. We agree with the Court of
Appeals that, in the setting of this whipsaw strike and Food Jet's continued operations,
the respondents' lockout and their continued operations with the use of temporary
replacements, viewed separately or as a single act, do not constitute such conduct.

[3-7] We begin with the proposition that the Act does not constitute the Board
as an "arbiter of the sort of economic weapons the parties can use in seeking to gain
acceptance of their bargaining demands." *Labor Board* v. *Insurance Agents*, 361 U.S.
477, 497, 4 L.ed.2d 454, 469, 80 S.Ct. 419. In the absence of proof of unlawful
motivation, there are many economic weapons which an employer may use that either
interfere in some measure with concerted employee activities, or which are in some
degree discriminatory and discourage union membership, and yet the use of such
economic weapons does not constitute conduct that is within the prohibition of either
§8(a)(1) or §8(a)(3). See, e.g., *Labor Board* v. *Mackay Radio & Telegraph Co.*,
supra; Labor Board v. *Dalton Brick & Tile Corp.*, 301 F.2d 886, 896. Even the Board
concedes that an employer may legitimately blunt the effectiveness of an anticipated
strike by stockpiling inventories, readjusting contract schedules, or transferring work
from one plant to another, even if he thereby makes himself "virtually strike proof."
As a general matter he may completely liquidate his business without violating either
§8(a)(1) or §8(a)(3), whatever the impact of his action on concerted employee
activities. *Textile Workers* v. *Darlington Mfg. Co.*, Nos. 37 and 41, 380 U.S. 263, 13
L.ed.2d 827, 85 S.Ct. 994. Specifically, he may in various circumstances use the lockout
as a legitimate economic weapon. See, e.g., *Labor Board* v. *Truck Drivers Union*,
supra; Labor Board v. *Dalton Brick & Tile Corp., supra; Leonard* v. *Labor Board*, 205
F.2d 355; *Betts Cadillac Olds, Inc.*, 96 NLRB 268; *International Shoe Co.*, 93 NLRB

907; *Pepsi-Cola Bottling Co.*, 72 NLRB 601, 602; *Duluth Bottling Assn.*, 48 NLRB 1335; *Link-Belt Co.*, 26 NLRB 227. And in *American Ship Building Co.* v. *Labor Board*, 380 U.S. 300, 13 L.ed.2d 855, 85 S.Ct. 955, we hold that a lockout is not an unfair labor practice simply because used by an employer to bring pressure to bear in support of his bargaining position after an impasse in bargaining negotiations has been reached.

[8] In the circumstances of this case, we do not see how the continued operations of respondents and their use of temporary replacements imply hostile motivation any more than the lockout itself; nor do we see how they are inherently more destructive of employee rights. Rather, the compelling inference is that this was all part and parcel of respondents' defensive measure to preserve the multi-employer group in the face of the whipsaw strike. Since Food Jet legitimately continued business operations, it is only reasonable to regard respondents' action as evincing concern that the integrity of the employer group was threatened unless they also managed to stay open for business during the lockout. For with Food Jet open for business and respondents' stores closed, the prospect that the whipsaw strike would succeed in breaking up the employer association was not at all fanciful. The retail food industry is very competitive and repetitive patronage is highly important. Faced with the prospect of a loss of patronage to Food Jet, it is logical that respondents should have been concerned that one or more of their number might bolt the group and come to terms with the Local, thus destroying the common front essential to multi-employer bargaining. The Court of Appeals correctly pictured the respondents' dilemma in saying, "If . . . the struck employer does choose to operate with replacements and the other employers cannot replace after lockout, the economic advantage passes to the struck member, the non-struck members are deterred in exercising the defensive lockout, and the whipsaw strike . . . enjoys an almost inescapable prospect of success." 319 F.2d at 11. Clearly respondents' continued operations with the use of temporary replacements following the lockout were wholly consistent with a legitimate business purpose.

Nor are we persuaded by the Board's argument that justification for the inference of hostile motivation appears in the respondents' use of temporary employees rather than some of the regular employees. It is not common sense, we think, to say that the regular employees were "willing to work at the employers' terms." 137 NLRB, at 76. It seems probable that this "willingness" was motivated as much by their understandable desire to further the objective of the whipsaw strike—to break through the employers' united front by forcing Food Jet to accept the Local's terms—as it was by a desire to work for the employers under the existing unacceptable terms. As the Board's dissenting members put it, "These employees are willing only to receive wages while their brethren in the rest of the associationwide unit are exerting whipsaw pressure on one employer to gain benefits that will ultimately accrue to all employees in the associationwide unit, including those here locked out." 137 NLRB, at 78. Moreover, the course of action to which the Board would limit the respondents would force them into the position of aiding and abetting the success of the whipsaw strike and consequently would render "largely illusory," 137 NLRB, at 78-79, the right of lockout recognized by Buffalo Linen; the right would be meaningless if barred to nonstruck stores that find it necessary to operate because the struck store does so. . . .

[9] Nor does the record show any basis for concluding that respondents violated §8(a)(3). Under that section both discrimination and a resulting discouragement of union membership are necessary, but the added element of unlawful intent is also required. In Buffalo Linen itself the employers treated the locked-out employees less

favorably because of their union membership, and this may have tended to discourage continued membership, but we rejected the notion that the use of the lockout violated the statute. The discriminatory act is not by itself unlawful unless intended to prejudice the employees' position because of their membership in the union; some element of antiunion animus is necessary. See *Radio Officers' Union* v. *Labor Board*, 347 U.S. 17, 42-44, 98 L.ed. 455, 478, 479, 74 S.Ct. 323, 41 ALR2d 621. . . .

[21, 22] Courts must, of course, set aside Board decisions which rest on an "erroneous legal foundation." *Labor Board* v. *Wilcox Co., supra*, 351 U.S. at 112-113, 100 L.ed. 983. Congress has not given the Board untrammeled authority to catalogue which economic devices shall be deemed freighted with indicia of unlawful intent. *Labor Board* v. *Insurance Agents, supra*, 361 U.S. at 498, 4 L.ed.2d 469. In determining here that the respondents' conduct carried its own badge of improper motive, the Board's decision, for the reasons stated, misapplied the criteria governing the application of §§8(a)(1) and (3). Since the order therefore rested on an erroneous legal foundation, the Court of Appeals properly refused to enforce it.

Affirmed.

13. Secondary Activities

General. A secondary activity is an activity directed by a union against an employer with whom it does not have a dispute, where the objective is to persuade that employer to stop doing business with another employer with whom the union does have a dispute.

A boycott is a refusal by one person to deal with another person, and with respect to labor there are two types of boycotts, consumption and production.

A secondary boycott is when employees refuse to deal with a neutral employer in a labor dispute, and this refusal is usually accompanied by a demand that the neutral employer bring pressure upon the employer who is involved in the labor dispute to force this involved employer to agree to the union's demands.

An example of a secondary consumption boycott would be where the union has a dispute with its employer, Manufacturer A, so the union boycotts the store that sells Manufacturer A's product even though they have no direct dispute with the store. This is a secondary consumption boycott with respect to the store, and the union anticipates that the store owner will in turn pressure Manufacturer A to accept the union's demands.

An example of a secondary production boycott is where the union does not have a dispute with their employer, an owner of a store, but still they stop work in order to bring pressure on the nonunion drivers who deliver to the store to force these drivers to vote in the union.

Notice in both of these examples that the union directed action against a neutral employer to involve him in the hope that he would then also pressure the employer with whom the union does have a dispute.

Secondary boycotts are an unfair labor practice under the National Labor Relations Act, Section 8(b)(4), within certain conditions which will be discussed herein. The general rule is that if Union A, which deals directly with Employer A (primary), decides to try to influence Employer A by action against Employer B (a nonunion contractor who does business with Employer A), then Employer B is a secondary employer, and the activity is secondary and illegal. The activity is illegal if directed at Employer B or his employees and is illegal whether picketing, or some form of direct inducement or encouragement to B's employees to strike to force B to cease doing business with Employer A, is used to pressure Employer A into accepting Union A's demands.

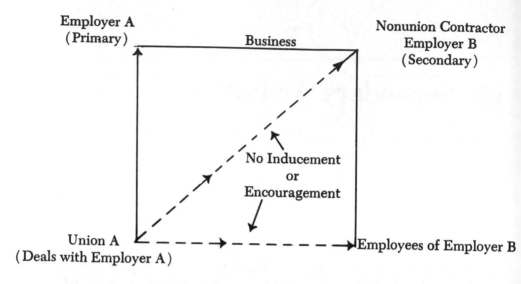

The two competing interests are the union's interest in bringing all the economic pressure possible on the employers with whom it has a dispute, and the interest of protecting "neutral employers" from someone else's labor disputes. Section 8(b)(4) is designed to eliminate some of the impact on the secondary employer. It employs an ends-means analysis where both the end sought and the means employed must be illegal before there is a violation. In Section 8(b)(4), the means are listed as numbers i and ii and include threats, and the ends are listed as A-D.

Section 8(b)(4) declares it an unfair labor practice for a labor organization or its agents to (1) induce any employee or other person in an industry affecting commerce to refuse to work or to handle goods or perform services or (2) to coerce an employer or other persons in an industry affecting commerce, where the object of such action is any of the following:

a. Forcing any employer or self-employed person to join any labor or employer organization or to enter into any hot cargo agreement prohibited by Section 8(e);[1]
b. Forcing any person to cease doing business with any other person, or forcing any other employer to recognize or bargain with an uncertified union;
c. Forcing any employer to recognize or bargain with a union in defiance of another union's certification;
d. Forcing any employer to assign work to a particular group of employees, rather than to another group, unless the assignment is required by an NLRB order or certification.

The most controversial section is 8(b)(4)(B), the "secondary boycott" ban, which also contains a proviso that exempts any primary strike or picketing. In

---

[1] A hot cargo agreement is a clause in a union contract that permits the union members to refuse to handle any goods shipped from a plant which is being struck at that time. See "Hot Cargo" section of this chapter for exceptions to 8(e), which in turn became an exception to 8(b)(4)(a).

addition, there is a proviso for the entire Section 8(b) which holds that union men may lawfully refuse to cross picket lines of other unions where the picketing employees are engaged in a strike ratified by the proper union.

Secondary Employer Defined. Initially the test of whether one was a secondary employer, and thus protected, was simply a geographic one—is the employer at a different location? This test still works in some situations, but the following paragraphs describe some of the fact problems that arose and the courts' solutions to them.

The "ally doctrine" refers to circumstances where employer B is not completely neutral but is in the same business as employer A, and in addition, A subcontracts some work to B. This subcontracting is held to be an abandoning of the required neutral position. Also, if two corporations have the same general owners, then the operations are considered integrated and not neutral towards each other. The test is one of "unity of interest"; i.e., does the person being picketed have sufficient interest to connect him to the dispute?

The neutral third party's position becomes more difficult to segregate and protect when the employers share a work site, such as a construction site. The activity sometimes referred to as "common situs picketing" is difficult to regulate because to prohibit secondary picketing would be at the same time inhibiting or eliminating the protected primary activities.

In the *Moore Dry Dock Case*, 92 NLRB 547, 1950, the union tried to force its economic demands on a ship owner, whose ship was in dry dock, by picketing the entire dock. This is sometimes called "ambulatory" picketing, which is picketing an employer whose business moves around. The Board said that this type of ambulatory and common situs picketing might be permitted, with the standard being that the pickets must get as close as possible to the targets of the picketing and therefore minimize the effect on others.

The test that evolved is referred to as the Moore Dry Dock Test and consists of:

1. The picketing must be limited to those times when the situs of the dispute was at the secondary employer's premises;
2. The primary employer must be engaged in normal business operation;
3. The picketing must be reasonably close to the primary situs; and
4. The picketing must clearly disclose that the dispute lies with the primary employer.

Later cases have held that these *Moore* standards are not conclusive but merely factors to be considered.

In one of these cases, a decision involving *General Electric Local 761, IUEW v. G.E.*, 366 U.S. 667, 1961, the Supreme Court differentiated between construction work and other activities, something which both the courts and legislatures have also done in other situations. (If one is dealing with construction work be sure to look for possible differences). In this situation the employer had provided separate gates for secondary employers (subcontractors) and the union wanted to picket the entire operation as being a primary work site. The Supreme Court said that it depends on the type of work the employees are doing whether picketing is permitted; if the work is normal, everyday work such as maintenance work, then the picketing is primary and the separate gates would not work, but if the work is construction work, then the reserved gates will prohibit picketing at other gates.

Secondary Consumer Boycotts. The 1959 Act added the following proviso to 8(b)(4):

> ". . . for the purpose of this paragraph (4) only, nothing contained in such paragraph shall be construed to prohibit publicity, *other than picketing,* for the purpose of truthfully advising the public, including consumers and members of a labor organization, that a product or products are produced by an employer with whom the labor organization has a primary dispute and are distributed by another employer, as long as such publicity does not have an effect of inducing any individual employed by any person other than the primary employer in the course of his employment to refuse to pick up, deliver, or transport any goods, or not to perform any services, at the establishment of the employer engaged in such distribution" (emphasis added).

The situations arise when the union wishes to influence employer A, with whom it has a dispute, by activities towards employer B, with whom employer A does business. A balance was sought between the right of free speech and the prohibition against hurting an innocent person (employer B). The Act prohibited secondary activity and the above proviso reinforces this restriction in its latter part but attempts to achieve a balance by permitting activities which truthfully advise the public of the dispute. This author feels that by permitting activities "other than picketing" as the proviso states, if the section is read backwards it must mean that picketing is not protected. However, the courts do not agree with this interpretation and have consistently protected picketing.

The products-produced language of the section is not limited to products but also includes services, such as advertising, and thus a union may picket a television station which advertises for the employer involved in the dispute. *Great Western Broadcasting Corp.* v. *NLRB,* 356 F.2d 434, 1966.

The products must be restricted to the particular product in dispute and cannot be aimed at the secondary employer's entire business, so if his business is a supermarket and the dispute involves bread, then the picketing must involve only bread. If the product has been merged into another product so that the entire business of the secondary employer is involved or so that the disputed product cannot be distinguished, then the picketing is not protected. *Honolulu Typographical Union No. 37* v. *NLRB,* 401 F.2d 952, 1968.

Hot Cargo. "Hot cargo" refers to items produced by an employer (say employer A) with whom the union has a disagreement, so the union tries to influence a secondary employer (say employer B) not to handle the products of employer A, or to treat the items as "too hot to handle" or as "hot cargo." Prior to the 1959 Act, it was illegal to coerce employer B not to handle the goods, but it was not illegal to contract with him not to handle the goods. The 1959 Act prohibits "hot cargo" clauses that state that a union does not have to handle cargo from an employer with whom the union is having a dispute, by stating in Section 8(e):

"It shall be an unfair labor practice for any labor organization and any employer to enter into any contract or agreement, express or implied, whereby such employer ceases or refrains or agrees to cease or refrain from handling, using, selling, transporting or otherwise dealing in any of the products of any other employer, or to cease doing business with any other person. . . ."

This section is the only place where conduct is held to be a simultaneous violation by both parties and has been construed to prohibit honoring of the clause, whether or not the agreement is voluntary. So to achieve their aims, the unions have tried two types of clauses commonly called "union signatory" and "union standards" clauses. Union signatory clauses provide that if an employer contracts out work, he will do so only to an employer who has a union. These clauses are in violation of Section 8(e) as a secondary action. Union standards clauses provide that an employer agrees to contract work only to an employer who maintains standards comparable to those of the union, and these clauses are held to be valid as a primary action to protect one's own work.

Where is the line drawn between signatory and standards clauses? The Supreme Court held that Section 8(e) must be applied in conjunction with 8(b)(4)(B), and work of the particular bargaining unit and that of union members generally must be distinguished. If the clause deals with work traditionally performed by that bargaining unit, then it does not violate 8(e) as a work preservation measure. If the clause deals with protection of work for union members generally, then it is a violation of 8(e). *National Woodwork Manufacturers Ass'n.* v. *NLRB*, 386 U.S. 612, 1967.

The NLRB has stated that it will follow a slightly different rule, referred to as the "right of control" test. Under this test, the legality of the clause is not controlling but rather the controlling element is whether the employer could control the disputed conduct. If the employer could control the conduct, then actions against him do not violate 8(e), but if he could not control the conduct, then activities against him do violate 8(e). *Plumbers Local 636 Mechanical Contractors Ass'n. of Detroit, Inc.*, 177 NLRB No. 14, 1969. For example, in a decision involving the contracting out of work, if the employer has no choice, because of technology or other restrictions, but to contract with a supplier who does not maintain standards comparable to those of the union, then activities against the employer by the union will not be permitted, but if the employer has a choice of suppliers with standards comparable to those of the union and picks a supplier without such standards, union activities against the employer may be permitted.

So, at least until the Supreme Court rules on the legality of the NLRB's approach, there are apparently two tests available.

There are two provisos to Section 8(e) that extend privileges to unions in the construction and garment industries. The proviso concerning the construction industry applies to voluntary hot cargo agreements and exempts them from the unfair labor provisions of 8(e) if the work is to be done at the construction site. There is a split of authority as to whether picketing or coercion can be used to enter into or enforce the hot cargo agreement. Note that Section 8(f) provides another exception for the construction industry by permitting a prehire agreement that designates that anyone hired must be a member of a union, unless the state involved has a law to the contrary.

The second proviso to Section 8(e) concerns the garment industry and exempts it entirely from the unfair labor charges of 8(e). Thus, hot cargo agreements are permitted and may be enforced by strikes, threats, or other coercion.

Remedies. There are special remedies for secondary activities because by definition one of the employers is innocent, so any delay in remedy would be unfair. In addition, the illegal activities can cause irreparable harm, so to insure prompt action, there is a special corrective procedure for these violations, which in some instances is also applied elsewhere. Under Section 10(1) the Board must seek an injunction for an 8(b)(4)(A), (B), or (C) violation. Under Section 10(k), the Board may use its discretion on whether to seek an injunction for an 8(b)(4)(D) violation. If it appears that irreparable harm may evolve quickly, then under Section 10(1) the Board may ask for a temporary restraining order (TRO) which is a powerful weapon as it is not required that one notify the other party of the hearing. However, these orders are effective for a very short time and are only meant to prevent harm until a hearing may be held. Section 303 of the Labor Management Relations Act provides an additional remedy, that of permitting law suits for actual harm suffered, and possibly punitive damages if violence occurred.

National Labor Relations Board v. *Business Mach. & Office A., Etc.*

228 F.2d 553 (1955)

Held: The "ally" doctrine is a doctrine whereby if one employer is struck by a union, then another employer becomes his "ally" and fulfills his contractual obligations for him, in which event the union may choose to also picket the ally. The ally is not protected by §8(b)(4)(A), which prohibits secondary activities, from the picketing if he is not an independent businessman but is "too closely allied" with the employer being struck, where "too closely allied" is a question of fact; if the first employer arranged for the work then this is too close and picketing is permitted.

Opinion:

We approve the "ally" doctrine which had its origin in a well reasoned opinion by Judge Rifkind in the Ebasco case, *Douds* v. *Metropolitan Federation of Architects, Engineers, Chemists & Technicians, Local 231,* D.C.S.D.N.Y. 1948, 75 F.Supp. 672, 676. Ebasco, a corporation engaged in the business of providing engineering services, had a close business relationship with Project, a firm providing similar services. Ebasco subcontracted some of its work to Project and when it did so Ebasco supervised the work of Project's employees and paid Project for the time spent by Project's employees on Ebasco's work plus a factor for overhead and profit. When Ebasco's employees went on strike, Ebasco transferred a greater percentage of its work to Project, including some jobs that had already been started by Ebasco's employees. When Project refused to heed the Union's requests to stop doing Ebasco's work, the Union picketed Project and induced some of Project's employees to cease work. On these facts Judge Rifkind found that Project was not "doing business" with Ebasco within the meaning of §8(b)(4)(A) and that the Union had therefore not committed an unfair labor practice under that section. He reached this result by looking to the legislative history of the Taft-Hartley Act and to the history of the secondary boycotts which it sought to outlaw. He determined that Project was not a person " 'wholly unconcerned in the disagreement between an employer and his employees' " such as §8(b)(4)(A) was designed to protect. This result has been described as a proper interpretation of the Act by its principal sponsor, Senator Taft, 95 Cong. Rec. (1949) 8709, and President Eisenhower in his January 1954 recommendations to Congress for revision of the Act included a suggestion which would make this rule explicit.

Here there was evidence of only one instance where Royal contacted an independent (Manhattan Typewriter Service, not named in the complaint) to see whether it could handle some of Royal's calls. Apart from that incident there is no evidence that Royal made any arrangement with an independent directly. It is obvious, however, that what the independents did would inevitably tend to break the strike. As Judge Rifkind pointed out in the Ebasco case: "The economic effect upon Ebasco's employees was precisely that which would flow from Ebasco's hiring strikebreakers to work on its own premises." And at 95 Cong. Rec. (1949) page 8709 Senator Taft said:

> "The spirit of the Act is not intended to protect a man who in. the last case I mentioned is cooperating with a primary employer and taking his work and doing the work which he is unable to do because of the strike."

President.Eisenhower's recommendation referred to above was to make it explicit "that concerted action against (1) an employer who is performing 'farmed-out' work for the account of another employer whose employees are on strike . . . will not be treated as a secondary boycott." Text of President's Message to Congress on Taft-Hartley Amendments, January 11, 1954. . . . Thus the picketing of the independent typewriter companies was not the kind of secondary activity which §8(b)(4)(A) of the Taft-Hartley Act was designed to outlaw. Where an employer is attempting to avoid the economic impact of a strike by securing the services of others to do his work, the striking union obviously has a great interest, and we think a proper interest, in preventing those services from being rendered. This interest is more fundamental than the interest in bringing pressure on customers of the primary employer. Nor are those who render such services completely uninvolved in the primary strike. By doing the work of the primary employer they secure benefits themselves at the same time that they aid the primary employer. The ally employer may easily extricate himself from the dispute and insulate himself from picketing by refusing to do that work. A case may arise where the ally employer is unable to determine that the work he is doing is "farmed-out." We need not decide whether the picketing of such an employer would be lawful, for that is not the situation here. The existence of the strike, the receipt of checks from Royal, and the picketing itself certainly put the independents on notice that some of the work they were doing might be work farmed-out by Royal. Wherever they worked on new Royal machines they were probably aware that such machines were covered by a Royal warranty. But in any event, before working on a Royal machine they could have inquired of the customer whether it was covered by a Royal contract and refused to work on it if it was. There is no indication that they made any effort to avoid doing Royal's work. The Union was justified in picketing them in order to induce them to make such an effort. We therefore hold that an employer is not within the protection of §8(b)(4)(A) when he knowingly does work which would otherwise be done by the striking employees of the primary employer and where this work is paid for by the primary employer pursuant to an arrangement devised and originated by him to enable him to meet his contractual obligations. The result must be the same whether or not the primary employer makes any direct arrangement with the employers providing the services.

The Customer Picketing

The picketing of Royal's customers was clearly secondary picketing with the object defined in §8(b)(4)(A). The Union conceded that its aim was to force the customers to cease doing business with Royal and with the independent repair companies. But the Taft-Hartley Act does not proscribe all secondary activity. We have held that requests and threats addressed directly to secondary employers are not illegal, *Rabouin* v. *NLRB*, 2 Cir., 1952, 195 F.2d 906, 911, 912; see *NLRB* v. *Associated Musicians of Greater New York, Local 802*, 2 Cir., 226 F.2d 900; and we have indicated that solicitation of customers of secondary employers is also lawful. See *NLRB* v. *Service Trade, Chauffeurs, Salesmen, and Helpers, Local 145, supra*, at 191 F.2d at page 68. The only thing proscribed by §8(b)(4) is inducement or encouragement of the employees of customers. . . .

The words of the statute, "to induce or encourage," do not necessarily carry with them a requirement that intent to induce or encourage be shown. It may be true that something less than a finding of specific intent to induce or encourage employees will suffice to support the Board's conclusion that §8(b)(4)(A) has been violated. If it were shown that such inducement was the inevitable result or even the "natural and probable consequence" of the picketing this would perhaps be enough. Certainly if it were shown that the employees actually ceased work, no finding of intent would be necessary. But in this case there was insufficient evidence to support any of these findings. It was not shown that the picketing had any tendency to induce the employees to strike or cease performing services. The evidence showed, on the contrary, that no employee refused to work or to use a Royal machine. . . .

Brewery & Beverage Drivers v. *NLRB*, 1955, 95 U.S. App. D.C. 117, 220 F.2d 380, is not authority contrary to our holding here. The Board's finding and the Trial Examiner's intermediate report in that case show that there were distinguishing features, such as picketing of entrances used only for deliveries and actual stopping of deliveries. 107 NLRB 2991 (1953). Since we find in this case neither intent to induce, nor effective inducement, nor even probable inducement of employees, we conclude that there is no substantial evidence to support the Board's finding of unlawful inducement and encouragement of employees in violation of §8(b)(4)(A).

Enforcement of the Board's order is therefore in all respects denied.

Connell Construction Company v. *Plumbers and Steamfitters Local Union 100*

U.S. Supreme Court (No. 73-1256) (June, 1975) Lower Ct. 483 F.2d 1154 (1973)

Held: Congress granted to the unions in the construction industry certain exemptions from the prohibitions against secondary activities that are imposed on all other unions, with the exception of the unions involved in the garment industry. In the construction industry, unions are permitted certain secondary activities on the construction site, but these activities are limited to the site and are not permitted for nonjobsite work.

Section 8(e) outlaws "hot cargo" agreements and has a proviso that gives more rights to unions in the construction industry but this proviso does not permit a union to picket in order to force a contractor to subcontract only to a union contractor.

The remedies provided by labor laws for a violation of 8(e) are not exclusive and a charge of limiting competition under the antitrust laws may be appropriate.

Opinion:

This Court has held, that §8(e) must be interpreted in light of the statutory setting and the circumstances surrounding its enactment:

> "It is a 'familiar rule, that a thing may be within the letter of the statute and yet not within the statute, because not within its spirit, nor within the intention of its makers.' *Holy Trinity Church* v. *United States*, 143 U.S. 457, 459." *National Woodwork Manufacturers Assn.* v. *NLRB*, 386 U.S. 612, 619 (1967).

Section 8(e) was part of a legislative program designed to plug technical loopholes in §8(b)(4)'s general prohibition of secondary activities. In §8(e) Congress broadly proscribed using contractual agreements to achieve the economic coercion prohibited by §8(b)(4). See *National Woodwork Manufacturers Assn.*, *supra*, at 634. The provisos exempting the construction and garment industries were added by the Conference Committee in an apparent compromise between the House Bill, which prohibited all hot-cargo agreements, and the Senate Bill, which prohibited them only in the trucking industry. Although the garment industry proviso was supported by detailed explanations in both Houses, the construction industry proviso was explained only by bare references to "the pattern of collective bargaining" in the industry. It seems, however, to have been adopted as a partial substitute for an attempt to overrule this Court's decision in *NLRB* v. *Denver Building & Construction Trades Council*, 341 U.S. 675 (1951). Discussion of "special problems" in the construction industry, applicable to both the §8(e) proviso and the attempt to overrule *Denver Building Trades*, focused on the problems of picketing a single nonunion subcontractor on a multiemployer building project, and the close relationship between contractors and subcontractors at the jobsite. Congress limited the construction industry proviso to that single situation, allowing subcontracting agreements only in relation to work done on a jobsite. In contrast to the latitude it provided in the garment industry proviso, Congress did not afford construction unions an exemption from §8(b)(4)(B) or otherwise indicate that they were free to use subcontracting agreements as a broad organizational weapon. In keeping with these limitations, the Court has interpreted the construction industry proviso as

> "a measure designed to allow agreements pertaining to certain secondary activities on the construction site because of the close community of interests there, but to ban secondary-objective agreements concerning nonjobsite work, in which

respect the construction industry is no different from any other." *National Wood-work Manufacturers Assn., supra,* at 638-639.

One of the major aims of the 1959 Act was to limit "top-down" organizing campaigns, in which unions used economic weapons to force recognition from an employer regardless of the wishes of his employees. Congress accomplished this goal by enacting §8(b)(7), which restricts primary recognitional picketing, and by further tightening §8(b)(4)(B), which prohibits the use of most secondary tactics in organizational campaigns. Construction unions are fully covered by these sections. The only special consideration given them in organizational campaigns is §8(f), which allows "prehire" agreements in the construction industry, but only under careful safeguards preserving workers' rights to decline union representation. The legislative history accompanying §8(f) also suggests that Congress may not have intended that strikes or picketing could be used to extract prehire agreements from unwilling employers.

These careful limits on the economic pressure unions may use in aid of their organizational campaigns would be undermined seriously if the proviso to §8(e) were construed to allow unions to seek subcontracting agreements, at large, from any general contractor vulnerable to picketing. Absent a clear indication that Congress intended to leave such a glaring loophole in its restrictions on "top-down" organizing, we are unwilling to read the construction industry proviso as broadly as Local 100 suggests. Instead, we think its authorization extends only to agreements in the context of collective-bargaining relationships and, in light of congressional references to the *Denver Building Trades* problem, possibly to common-situs relationships on particular jobsites as well. . . .

Congress rejected attempts to regulate secondary activities by repealing the antitrust exemptions in the Clayton and Norris-LaGuardia Acts, and created special remedies under the labor law instead. It made secondary activities unfair labor practices under §8(b)(4), and drafted special provisions for preliminary injunctions at the suit of the NLRB and for recovery of actual damages in the district courts. Sections 10(*l*), 303; 29 U.S.C. §§160(*l*), 187. But whatever significance this legislative choice has for antitrust suits based on those secondary activities prohibited by §8(b)(4), it has no relevance to the question whether Congress meant to preclude antitrust suits based on the "hot-cargo" agreements that it outlawed in 1959. There is no legislative history in the 1959 Congress suggesting that labor-law remedies for §8(e) violations were intended to be exclusive, or that Congress thought allowing antitrust remedies in cases like the present one would be inconsistent with the remedial scheme of the NLRA.

Neither the District Court nor the Court of Appeals decided whether the agreement between Local 100 and Connell, if subject to the antitrust laws, would constitute an agreement that restrains trade within the meaning of the Sherman Act. The issue was not briefed and argued fully in this Court. Accordingly, we remand for consideration whether the agreement violated the Sherman Act.

Reversed in part and remanded.

Mr. Justice Douglas, dissenting.

While I join the opinion of Mr. Justice Stewart, I write to emphasize what is, for me, the determinative feature of the case. Throughout this litigation, Connell has maintained only that Local 100 coerced it into signing the subcontracting agreement. With the complaint so drawn, I have no difficulty in concluding that the union's conduct is regulated solely by the labor laws. The question of antitrust immunity would be far different, however, if it were alleged that Local 100 had conspired with mechanical subcontractors to force nonunion subcontractors from the market by entering into exclusionary agreements with general contractors like Connell. An arrangement of that character was condemned in *Allen Bradley Co.* v. *Local 3, IBEW,* 325 U.S. 797, which held that Congress did not intend "to immunize labor unions who aid and abet manufacturers and traders in violating the Sherman Act," *id.,* at 810. Were such a conspiracy alleged, the multiemployer bargaining agreement between Local 100 and the mechanical subcontractors would unquestionably be relevant. See *United Mine Workers* v. *Pennington,* 381 U.S. 657, 673 (concurring opinion); *Meat Cutters* v. *Jewel Tea Co.,* 381 U.S. 676, 737 (dissenting opinion). But since Connell has never alleged or attempted to show any conspiracy between Local 100 and the subcontractors, I agree that Connell's remedies, if any, are provided exclusively by the labor laws.

14. The Individual and the Union

The activities of unions were somewhat regulated by the 1947 Taft-Hartley Act, but it was in 1959 that the broadest restrictions were initiated by the Labor Management Reporting and Disclosure Act (LMRDA), or the Landrum-Griffin Act. The 1950's demonstrated to Congress that some restrictions were needed on the manner in which some companies and unions dealt with individuals and with the abuse of power by union officers, so Congress passed the 1959 Act to deal with these injustices. This Act, plus other legislation, comprises the rules governing the internal conduct of unions, for there is very little relevant common law. The Civil Rights Act of 1964 is a significant influence in that it prevents discrimination by a union.

Admission to Membership. The National Labor Relations Act protects the employees' right to join or to refrain from joining labor unions, but these additional words are also in the Act (Section 8(b)(1)):

> "Provided that this paragraph shall not impair the right of a labor organization to prescribe its own rules with respect to the acquisition or retention of membership therein. . . ."

Considering this passage and the rest of the Act, the rule seems to be that a union may exclude anyone it wants to exclude so long as the result will not deprive a worker of his right to pursue gainful employment.

The law is that collective-bargaining agreements may provide for membership in a union as a condition of employment, except in "right to work" states where no such requirement can be imposed except under the Railway Labor Act, which contains no equivalent to Section 14(b) of the LMRA. The membership requirement has been interpreted by the Supreme Court to be limited to "financial core" membership; i.e., the requirement to pay an amount of money to a union which is equivalent to uniform dues and initiation fees. In *NLRB* v. *General Motors*, 373 U.S. 374, 1963, the Supreme Court included the following in their opinion:

> "Under the second proviso to §8(a)(3), the burdens of membership upon which employment may be conditioned are expressly limited to the payment of initiation fees and monthly dues. It is permissible to condition employment upon membership, but membership, insofar as it has significance to employment

137

rights, may in turn be conditioned only upon payment of fees and dues. 'Membership' as a condition of employment is whittled down to its financial core. This Court has said as much before in *Radio Officers' Union, etc.* v. *NLRB*, 347 U.S. 17, 41, 74 S.Ct. 323:

'This legislative history clearly indicates that Congress intended to prevent utilization of union security agreements for any purpose other than dues and fees. Thus Congress recognized the validity of unions' concern about 'free riders,' i.e., employees who receive the benefits of union representation but are unwilling to contribute their fair share of financial support to such union, and gave unions the power to contract to meet that problem while withholding from unions the power to cause the discharge of employees for any other reason . . .' "

Duty of Fair Representation. Section 9(a) of the LMRDA imposes a duty of fair representation on the union, while vesting the correlative right to fair representation in the employees. This right is enforceable by suit in federal or state court for an injunction or damages. Racial discrimination is one way in which the duty of fair representation may be violated. Even though there are separate laws, such as Title VII of the Civil Rights Act, to deal with racial discrimination, the courts have found it to be a violation of Section 7 (NLRA) to racially discriminate—creating a new Section 7 right, if you will. In *Local 12* v. *NLRB*, 368 F.2d 12, 1966, the Court held that "by summarily refusing to process complainant's grievances concerning back wages and segregated facilities," the Union restrained its employees' Section 7 rights.

The Bill of Rights for Union Members. The Landrum-Griffin Act (LMRDA) has been claimed to contain the "Bill of Rights for Union Members" because of the protection against the unions that it affords members.

MEMBERS' RIGHTS (TITLE I)

a. *Equal Rights* (Section 101(a)(1)). Union members are guaranteed certain specifically enumerated rights that are subject to reasonable rules and regulations imposed by the union. The balance of interests is between the union's institutional interest and the democratic rights of union members. The rights specifically granted are to vote in union elections, to nominate candidates, and to attend and participate in union meetings.

b. *Freedom of Speech and Assembly* (Section 101(a)(2)). Subject to reasonable union limitations, union members are guaranteed a right to free speech exercised in the context of union meetings, business discussions, and comments upon candidates. The limitations are basically designed to permit some order at a meeting, to forbid support of a rival union, and to forbid interference with the union's performance of its obligations.

c. *Dues, Initiation Fees, and Assessments* (Section 101(a)(3)). There are detailed procedures for conducting a special election that must be followed for increases in dues, fees, and assessments.

d. *Protection of the Right to Sue* (Section 101(a)(4)). "No union shall limit the right of any member to sue . . . provided that any member may be required to exhaust a reasonable hearing procedure (but not to exceed a four-month lapse of time) within such organization before instituting . . . proceedings." The courts have consistently interpreted this limitation as a court-imposed limitation on suit; i.e., a court can continue to apply the exhaustion of remedies for up to four months; then the doctrine can no longer be used to block a court action.

e. *Safeguards Against Improper Disciplinary Action* (Section 101(a)(5)). Certain procedural safeguards for union members have been specified, so before a member may be fined, suspended, expelled, or otherwise disciplined, he must be:

1) served with specific charges;
2) given a reasonable time to prepare his defenses; and
3) afforded a full and fair hearing.

     The procedure is similar to an informal hearing. The accused must be given a chance to present evidence and countercharges, and he must be furnished counsel (who need not be a lawyer; he may be a union member instead).

REPORTING AND DISCLOSURE PROVISIONS (TITLE II). Title II is meant to provide the availability of information concerning union activities. Section 201 requires the union to disclose certain basic information, such as: names of officers, various procedures, and fiscal condition.

Union officers are required to disclose financial transactions with the employer, and the employers are required to report certain expenditures or agreements with union officials, union employees, or managerial employees.

TRUSTEESHIPS (TITLE III). The term "trusteeship," as used in the Act, is defined as "a method of supervision or control whereby a labor organization suspends the autonomy otherwise available to a subordinate body under its constitution or bylaws." Prior to the Act, trusteeships had been used by the international unions as a means of controlling and plundering the treasuries of local unions, so Title III is meant to regulate the means for imposing and maintaining trusteeships.

Within the constitution and bylaws of the labor organization, trusteeships may be imposed only to:

1) correct corruption;
2) prevent misappropriation of assets;
3) assure performance of the union's contractual and bargaining representative duties;
4) restore democratic procedures; and/or
5) carry out "the legitimate objectives of (the) labor organization."

Reports on the trusteeships must be periodically filed with the Secretary of Labor.

UNION ELECTIONS (TITLE IV). Title IV of the LMRDA was added to provide a procedure to assure fair and frequent elections of union officers. This title deals with the frequency of union elections, procedures for conducting them, nomination and equal treatment of candidates, the right to vote, distribution of campaign literature, expenditure of union funds, and the removal of officers for misconduct.

These regulations provide for minimum standards, so a union can prescribe stricter requirements if it desires.

SAFEGUARDS FOR LABOR ORGANIZATIONS (TITLE V). Title V imposes limitations on union officials by aiding the members in ridding their organization of corrupt union officials. It places the officials in a trustee relationship with the members, so the developed law of trusts that imputes the highest duty on trustees also imputes this duty to union officials.

Besides leaving the majority of rules for the courts to prescribe in the analogy to trusts, some specific requirements were listed. Union officials are prohibited from using union funds or acquiring financial or other interests for purposes which conflict with the interest of the labor organization.

Section 501(b) permits individual union members to sue union officials for damages, an accounting, or other appropriate relief, if the union itself fails or refuses to do so. Union officials who are found to have embezzled, stolen, or otherwise willfully misappropriated union funds may be fined up to $10,000 and imprisoned up to five years. It is also illegal for unions to lend more than $2,000 to union officials or for persons convicted of certain crimes to hold union office.

National Labor Relations Board v.
  Television and Radio Broadcasting Studio Employees, Local 804

315 F.2d 398

Held: A union may be held to have committed an unfair labor practice if it requires
an excessive or a discriminatory fee for a person to become a member of the
union, and the employer may file the charge against the union.

Opinion:
The National Labor Relations Board has found that respondent violated §8(b)(5)
of the National Labor Relations Act, 29 U.S.C.A. §158(b)(5) by charging certain of
its members excessive and discriminatory initiation fees. The case is here on the
Board's petition for enforcement of its order entered pursuant to that determination.

Respondent is the collective bargaining representative of the employees who
work for the Radio and Television Division of Triangle Publications, Inc. ("company")
in the operation of a radio and television station in Philadelphia. These employees
include, among others, technicians, equipment operators, and studio and stage managers in a non-supervisory capacity. The collective bargaining agreement between
the parties for a number of years prior to the alleged unfair labor practice contained
a union security provision. During this period it was the company's practice to hire
both part-time and temporary employees in the unit covered by the contract. In
accordance with the union-shop clause they were advised that they would have to
join the union.

[1] The respondent objected to the use of part-time employees because it considered this practice a threat to the job security of regular, full-time employees. In
1957 it increased its initiation fee from $50 to $500 for all new members except those
employed in newly organized units. When the company protested, the union relented
to the extent of permitting a $50 down payment with $25 monthly payments for
each month worked until the entire fee was paid. However, in November 1960,
respondent changed the method of payment, requiring a $300 initial payment to be
followed by two consecutive monthly payments of $100. The company then filed
the unfair labor practice charge which resulted in the order now before us.

This is the first case in which a court has been called upon to construe this
particular subsection of the statute, and respondent argues that its legislative history
shows that it was never intended to apply to the facts before us. Reduced to its
essence, the argument is that §8(b)(5) was intended to proscribe the maintenance
of a closed shop by means of excessive or discriminatory initiation fees, and that this
was not the purpose of respondent, which desired the hiring of more full-time employees by the company. Conceding that one of the purposes of the statute was to
inhibit closed shop conditions, we think the argument is devoid of merit. The union's
desire for more full-time employees is beside the point for, as found by the Board,
the increase in the fee "was designed for the purpose of restraining the Employer in
the hiring of part-time employees who were not union members, or to end the practice,
thereby restricting employment to full-time union members." 135 NLRB 632 (1962).
This conduct falls squarely within that prohibited by the statute.

There is substantial evidence to support the Board's conclusion that the fee
was excessive and discriminatory under all the circumstances. In accordance with the
express mandate of the statute, the Board considered, among other relevant factors,
the initiation fees of other unions in the industry, and the wages currently paid to
employees affected. The evidence fully supports its finding that no other union in
the Philadelphia area representing technicians and crew men charged comparable fees.
One union which charged a fee of $1,000 had units in New York as well as

141

Philadelphia and covered newsreel cameramen as well as independent newsreel production. According to General Counsel's Exhibit No. 5, the fees charged by other comparable Philadelphia unions ranged from $10 to $200. In considering the wages currently paid to the employees affected, the Board noted that skilled technicians may eventually earn $200 per week, but deemed the starting salary of from $90 to $95 per week of greater significance. Since we are dealing with initiation fees which by definition are amounts paid by new union members, this analysis is obviously appropriate. These are the employees "affected" by the fee. Respondent's contention that the average weekly earnings of the company's employees exceed $200 per week is not significant, for these are the earnings of regular full-time personnel.

Among the other circumstances considered by the Board were the amount of the increase and the context in which it was effected. The fact that the fee was raised ten fold is obviously important. When this is coupled with the union's vigorous objection to the practice of hiring part-time employees, the Board's inference that the purpose of the fee was to end this practice, thereby restricting employment to full-time union members, was certainly permissible, if, indeed not ineluctable. . . .

International Bro. of Electrical Workers v. *NLRB*

487 F.2d 1113 (1972)

Held: Supervisors may be members of a union, but the union may not impose discipline for conduct that was performed by the supervisors as part of their job, which may be a critical distinction during a strike.

Opinion:
[1] Section 8(b)(1)(B) of the NLRA prohibits union coercion or restraint of an employer "in the selection of his representatives for the purposes of collective bargaining or the adjustment of grievances." This provision, of course, clearly proscribes *direct* union interference with an employer's selection of his section 8(b)(1)(B) representatives. However, as the Labor Board and several courts, including this one, have recently recognized, it also has much broader application. It prohibits *indirect* union restraint or coercion of an employer, accomplished through the imposition of discipline upon the employer's representatives for actions performed by them within the general scope of their supervisory or managerial responsibilities. Although the unions involved in the instant case have challenged this latter interpretation of section 8(b)(1)(B) as being an unwarranted extension of the express language of the statutory provision, we must reject this assertion as contrary to the legislative intent of Congress. . . .
[2] To ensure the accomplishment of the clear intention of Congress when it enacted section 8(b)(1)(B), that provision must not be interpreted in a hypertechnical manner. To construe that section as only applying to union discipline of a supervisor based upon his actions on behalf of management regarding a specific disagreement with the union over the proper interpretation of the collective-bargaining agreement or the adjustment of a particular grievance, would defeat the reasons underlying Congress' enactment of section 8(b)(1)(B). When a supervisor is disciplined by a union because of the manner in which he exercised his supervisory or managerial authority—whether or not he was applying a contract provision or adjusting a grievance—that disciplinary action necessarily impinges upon the supervisor's loyalty to his employer, thereby effectively depriving the employer of the undivided loyalty which he has the right to expect under section 8(b)(1)(B). The fact that in such a situation the union "may [seek] the substitution of attitudes rather than persons, and may [exert] its pressure upon the [employer] by indirect rather than direct means, cannot alter the ultimate fact that pressure [is] exerted . . . for the purpose of interfering with the [employer's] control over its representatives . . . [and it realistically will] have to replace its foremen or face *de facto* nonrepresentation by them." It is therefore intuitively obvious that if the principles underlying the Congressional enactment of section 8(b)(1)(B) are to be given full effect, such conduct by a union cannot be permitted, as the National Labor Relations Board has properly recognized.
[3] The fact that section 14(a) of the NLRA permits supervisors to be union members does not detract from the undivided loyalty they owe to their employer under section 8(b)(1)(B) when they are engaged in supervisory or managerial endeavors. See *Meat Cutters Union Local 81 of Amalgamated Meat Cutters and Butcher Workmen of North America* v. *NLRB*, 147 U.S. App. D.C. 375, 380-381, 458 F.2d 794, 799-800 (1972). Similarly, the fact that an employer may have consented to the compulsory union membership of his supervisors under an appropriate union-security provision does not negate his right to the full protection of section 8(b)(1)(B). See *Toledo Locals Nos. 15-P and 272 of the Lithographers and Photo-Engravers International Union*, 175 NLRB 1072, 1080 (1969), enfd., 437 F.2d 55 (6th Cir. 1971); *Local Union No. 2150, International Brotherhood of Electrical Workers*, 192 NLRB No. 16, slip op. at 5, 1971 CCH NLRB ¶23,280 (1971). . . .

United States of America v. *Edwin L. Sullivan*

498 F.2d 146

Held: Section 501 of the Landrum-Griffin Act was designed to protect union members from union corruption, so while the intent was to prevent larcenies or embezzlements, a member is also guilty if he knowingly receives monies which he should not be receiving.

Opinion:

Defendant was convicted by a jury on two counts of unlawfully and willfully embezzling, stealing, abstracting, and converting to his own use funds of the International Union of Operating Engineers, Local No. 57, of which he was an employee and minor official, in violation of 29 U.S.C. §501(c) (1970). On appeal, defendant principally contends that §501(c) could not have been properly applied to him, and further that, in any case, the evidence presented at the trial did not support his conviction.

(1) Defendant's initial claim is substantially without merit. Section 501(c) provides unambiguously that

> "Any person who embezzles, steals, or unlawfully and willfully abstracts or converts to his own use . . . any of the moneys, funds, securities, property or other assets of a labor organization of which he is an officer, or by which he is employed (is guilty of a crime)."

At the time of the illicit activities alleged in the indictment, it is undisputed that defendant was a bonded employee of the local union's business office, being responsible, in part, for the preparation of checks and the acceptance and receipt of monthly union dues. Moreover, during this period, defendant occupied the union office of Guard, though the evidence revealed that this position was largely a ceremonial one. Consequently, it seems evident that, upon consideration of defendant's status both as an employee and an officer, §501(c) would prima facie apply to proscribe his participation in the unlawful conduct described therein.

Section 501(a) states, inter alia, that "officers, agents, shop stewards and other representatives of a labor organization occupy positions of trust in relation to such organization and its members as a group." These officials are vested with a statutory fiduciary responsibility to "hold (union) money and property solely for the benefit of the organization and its members and to manage, invest, and expend the same in accordance with its constitution and bylaws." Section 501(a) is to some extent modified by §402(q) so as to include within its terms "elected officials and key administrative personnel, whether elected or appointed . . . , but . . . not . . . salaried, nonsupervisory professional staff, stenographic, and service personnel."

Preliminarily we note that even a liberal construction of this court's decision in *Colella* v. *United States*, 360 F.2d 792, 799, cert. denied, 385 U.S. 829 (1966) compels rejection of defendant's broad contention that §§402(q) and 501(a) completely circumscribe §501(c). While recognizing that "insofar as embezzlement is concerned, the existence of a fiduciary relationship is necessary" for conviction, our opinion in *Colella* emphasized that

> "[w]e are not dealing with an indictment charging simply embezzlement. Section 501(c) establishes 'a new Federal crime of embezzlement of any funds of a labor organization.' [citation omitted] The new crime can be accomplished in one of four ways: embezzling, stealing, unlawfully and willfully abstracting, and unlawfully and willfully converting." 360 F.2d at 799.

And, while suggesting that a §501(a) or §402(q) fiduciary relationship may arguably be an "essential element of the embezzlement means of committing the new federal crime," *Colella* seems to make clear that such a relationship "is not essential to the three other means."

We must note that the alleged wrongdoing on the part of defendant is somewhat unique to prosecutions under §501(c). Whereas most criminal actions brought pursuant to that section involve "affirmative" misconduct—generally in the form of either intentional falsification of union expense vouchers, see, e.g., *United States* v. *Dibrizzi*, 393 F.2d 642 (2d Cir. 1968); improper application of union funds by union management, see, e.g., *United States* v. *Boyle*, 482 F.2d 755, cert. denied, 414 U.S. 1076 (1973); *United States* v. *Silverman*, 430 F.2d 106 (2d Cir.), modified per curiam on other grounds, 439 F.2d 1198 (2d Cir. 1970), cert. denied, 402 U.S. 953 (1971); or illicit behavior approaching outright theft, see, e.g., *United States* v. *Bryant*, 430 F.2d 237 (8th Cir. 1970)—defendant here was essentially convicted of having "passively" received unauthorized salary increases and Christmas bonuses, knowing the same to have been unauthorized, and hence, illegal. However, as the Second Circuit has observed in a somewhat different context, "the reach of §501(c) is not limited to union officers who engage in stealthy larcenies or devious embezzlements," *United States* v. *Dibrizzi, supra*, 393 F.2d at 645. Considering that §501(c) was designed essentially to protect general union memberships from the corruption, however novel, of union officials and employees, see *United States* v. *Harmon*, 339 F.2d 354 (6th Cir. 1964), cert. denied, 380 U.S. 944 (1965), we do not believe that the proscriptions of that section should be read to operate solely against those who violate its terms in an active manner. In our view, the willing acceptance of misappropriated union funds by a recipient who knows that such funds are unauthorized and illegal will constitute a violation of §501(c).

The remaining contentions raised by defendant have been carefully examined and have been found to be either clearly without merit, or at most, to constitute harmless error.

Affirmed.

15. Governmental Employees

General. As a general matter, the Supreme Court of the United States stated, in the case which upheld the National Labor Relations Act, that employees have the fundamental right to organize and join a union apart from legislation. *NLRB* v. *Jones & Loughlin Steel Corp.*, 301 U.S. 1, 81 L.ed. 893 (1937). The right to engage in collective bargaining is probably an accompanying right, although often legislation is required before the right is exercised.

However, employees of federal or state governments have traditionally been afforded unique treatment, and most labor law acts, including the National Labor Relations Act, exempt these employees from their provisions. Hence, these employees must be considered separately, with the further distinction being made between state and federal employees. State employees include those employed by state agencies. The trend is for the states to take some sort of action regarding these employees, but because of the wide spectrum of programs enacted, only general statements may be presented here.

Federal employees include those employed by the various federal agencies, such as HEW, HUD, and all the rest. The number of persons employed by government at all levels is increasing tremendously, so this area will increase in importance and will probably generate a body of applicable statutes and cases. The trend seems to be towards applying the same rules as are used in the private sector.

Public and Private Sectors. One of the prime differences between the public and private sectors is the prohibition against strikes in the public sector.

Basically the U.S. is a democracy that believes in free enterprise, and it is only when certain services become so vital to everyone that they cannot be left to chance that the public bands together and performs them. Consequently, for most governmental services there is no competition. In theory, if a union negotiates too high a compensation level from a private employer, the employer must raise his prices and consumers will seek another brand or a substitute product. Granted that this does not always work in practice, as in the automobile industry where the same contract is forced on all manufacturers; so in these instances an import tariff "is required" to protect the entire industry from foreign competition. In governmental matters, there is not even the theory that consumers may switch suppliers, so the only balance against unreasonable union demands is the budget of the organization. Thus, often the negotiations appear to be unilateral (one-sided) rather than a balancing of interests. Even though the right to strike is not officially granted, it is granted unofficially as those who do strike are seldom penalized, for the penalties are negotiable. Permitting the penalties to be negotiated means that typically the agreement provides for a dismissal of all'penalties for the illegal strike. This is true even in the case of vital services such as garbage collection, so the prohibition against strikes is not a guarantee that they will not occur. The only guarantee that vital services would not be interrupted would be an automatic, nonnegotiable penalty against strikers.

State Employees. Many states have taken a position on the right of public employees to organize and join a union. The states have used constitutional amendments, legislation, judicial decision, or executive order to deal with such a variety of jobs as transit employees, teachers, port authority employees, and many more, at both the state and local levels. In the cases where this right is denied, the reason of preservation of public order is consistently mentioned, and the police or fire departments are typically involved.

Outside of the prohibition against strikes and the probable prohibition against union security clauses such as an agency or closed shop, many of the rules that apply to the private sector also apply to the public sector. Some examples of this are that both parties must bargain collectively, and the employer may not interfere with the employee's right to engage in union activity. A possible source of future litigation is the inclusion of an arbitration clause in contracts. The legislators, bound by state law, empower the agencies to hire and control governmental employees, and it may be illegal to pass this control to an arbitrator. In the limited litigation on this matter, the courts have split and ruled on the very specific facts presented and not on the broad question.

Federal Employees. Historically there has been an implicit right for federal government employees to organize, but it was not until 1962 that President Kennedy specifically recognized their right to organize with the issuance of Executive Order No. 10988. Their rights to organize and to negotiate on employment terms were given additional strength by President Nixon's Executive Order No. 11491, issued in 1969. Under 11491, the entire program of employee relations was placed under the supervision of a Federal Labor Relations Council. A high-level governmental panel was created to assist the parties in case of an impasse. The Assistant Secretary of Labor for Labor Management Relations was given the authority to decide representation questions and to settle charges of violations of the code of fair labor standards.

Executive Order 11491 states that union membership may not be imposed on employees and that employees have the right to form, join, and assist any employee organization which seeks to participate in the formulation and implementation of policies and procedures affecting their condition of employment. There are three requirements that a union must meet in order to represent federal employees, and they are:

1. The primary purpose of the union must be the improvement of working conditions.

2. The union must have been voluntarily formed.
3. The union must refrain from certain practices, as spelled out by the Order. Basically, these practices that must be avoided are strikes, overthrow of the government, discrimination, and Communist influence.

Once the union demonstrates that it represents a majority of the employees, it has the exclusive right to bargain and contract for the employees. However, recognition does not bar agencies from dealing with individual employees, veterans' organizations, or religious, social, fraternal, or other lawful associations. The head of the agency involved must approve all agreements.

The matters that are negotiable are generally personnel policies and practices and such matters affecting employment conditions as are within the discretion of the agency officials. Negotiations may not cover the mission of the agency, its budget, its organization, the assignment of personnel, the technology of performing its work, or its internal security practices. Negotiations must be held on the employees' own time and not while one is on the job.

An impasse could be particularly bothersome and injurious to third parties, so a special procedure has been enacted. The Federal Mediation and Conciliation Service provides assistance during the course of negotiations for an agreement, and if its efforts fail, then either party may request the services of the Federal Service Impasse Panel, which may recommend procedures to the parties and also settle the dispute as would an arbitrator. Once enacted, the agreement may provide for the grievance procedure, which is typically arbitration, with the restriction that the procedure must conform to the negotiated grievance procedures established by the Civil Service Commission.

Unfair labor practices for employers and employees are basically the same as in the private sector, with an important addition to the prohibited conduct of unions. Employees are specifically denied the right to strike, and the government may condition employment on employees neither striking nor asserting the right to strike.

The Order provides a complete grievance procedure for all grievances that may arise, but also recognizes that perhaps a party might ignore the procedure. If the conduct is of a serious nature, such as a strike, and this might create an irreparable injury, then injunctive relief may be granted from a court.

McLaughlin v. *Tilendis*

398 F.2d 287 (1968)

Held: The First Amendment confers the right to join a labor union but this right is subject to there being no illegal intent. Public school teachers have a right to free association, and this right may not be subject to unjustified interference. In addition, public employment may not be subject to unreasonable conditions.

The states may impose some restrictions on the unionization of public employees, but these restrictions must be reasonable and will vary from state to state.

In Illinois it is not against public policy for teachers to unionize.

Opinion:

Steele was not offered a second-year teaching contract and McLaughlin was dismissed before the end of his second year of teaching. Steele alleged that he was not rehired and McLaughlin alleged that he was dismissed because of their association with Local 1663 of the American Federation of Teachers, AFL-CIO. Neither teacher had yet achieved tenure.

In two additional Counts, Local 1663 and the parent union, through their officers and on behalf of all their members, sought an injunction requiring the defendants to cease and desist from discriminating against teachers who distribute union materials and solicit union membership. . . .

It is settled that teachers have the right of free association, and unjustified interference with teachers' associational freedom violates the Due Process clause of the Fourteenth Amendment. *Shelton* v. *Tucker*, 364 U.S. 479, 485-487, 81 S.Ct. 247, 5 L.ed.2d 231. Public employment may not be subjected to unreasonable conditions, and the assertion of First Amendment rights by teachers will usually not warrant their dismissal. *Keyishian* v. *Board of Regents*, 385 U.S. 589, 605-606, 87 S.Ct. 675, 17 L.ed.2d 629; *Garrity* v. *State of New Jersey*, 385 U.S. 493, 500, 87 S.Ct. 616, 17 L.ed.2d 562; *Pickering* v. *Board of Education*, 391 U.S. 563, 88 S.Ct. 1731, 20 L.ed.2d 811. Unless there is some illegal intent, an individual's right to form and join a union is protected by the First Amendment. *Thomas* v. *Collins*, 323 U.S. 516, 534, 65 S.Ct. 315, 89 L.ed. 430; see also *Hague* v. *CIO*, 307 U.S. 496, 512, 519, 523-524, 59 S.Ct. 594, 83 L.ed. 1423; *Griswold* v. *State of Connecticut*, 381 U.S. 479, 483, 85 S.Ct. 1678, 14 L.ed.2d 510; *Stapleton* v. *Mitchell*, 60 F.Supp. 51, 59-60, 61 (D.Kan. 1945; opinion of Circuit Judge Murrah), appeal dismissed, *Mitchell* v. *McElroy*, 326 U.S. 690, 66 S.Ct. 172, 90 L.ed. 406. As stated in *NAACP* v. *State of Alabama*, 357 U.S. 449, 460, 78 S.Ct. 1163, 1171, 2 L.ed.2d 1488:

> "It is beyond debate that freedom to engage in association for the advancement of beliefs and ideas is an inseparable aspect of the 'liberty' assured by the Due Process Clause of the Fourteenth Amendment, which embraces freedom of speech." . . .

Just this month the Supreme Court held that an Illinois teacher was protected by the First Amendment from discharge even though he wrote a partially false letter to a local newspaper in which he criticized the school board's financial policy. *Pickering* v. *Board of Education*, 391 U.S. 563, 88 S.Ct. 1731, 20 L.ed.2d 811. There is no showing on this record that plantiffs' activities impeded "[the] proper performance of [their] daily duties in the classroom." Idem, 88 S.Ct. at p. 1737. If teachers can engage in scathing and partially inaccurate public criticism of their school board, surely they can form and take part in associations to further what they consider to be their well-being.

149

The trial judge was motivated by his conclusion that more than free speech was involved here, stating:

> "The union may decide to engage in strikes, to set up machinery to bargain with the governmental employer, to provide machinery for arbitration, or may seek to establish working conditions. Overriding community interests are involved. The very ability of the governmental entity to function may be affected. The judiciary, and particularly this Court, cannot interfere with the power or discretion of the state in handling these matters."

It is possible of course that at some future time plaintiffs may engage in union-related conduct justifying their dismissal. But the Supreme Court has stated that

> "Those who join an organization but do not share its unlawful purposes and who do not participate in its unlawful activities surely pose no threat, either as citizens or as public employees." *Elfbrandt* v. *Russell*, 384 U.S. 11, 17, 86 S.Ct. 1238, 1241, 16 L.ed.2d 321.

Even if this record disclosed that the union was connected with unlawful activity, the bare fact of membership does not justify charging members with their organization's misdeeds. Idem. A contrary rule would bite more deeply into associational freedom than is necessary to achieve legitimate state interests, thereby violating the First Amendment.

Illinois has not prohibited membership in a teachers' union, and defendants do not claim that the individual plaintiffs engaged in any illegal strikes or picketing. Moreover, collective bargaining contracts between teachers' unions and school districts are not against the public policy of Illinois. *Chicago, etc., Education Association* v. *Board of Education of City of Chicago*, 76 Ill.App.2d 456, 222 N.E.2d 243 (1966). Illinois even permits the automatic deduction of union dues from the salaries of employees of local governmental agencies. Ill. Rev. Stats. 1967, Ch. 85, Sec. 472. These very defendants have not adopted any rule, regulation or resolution forbidding union membership. Accordingly, no paramount public interest of Illinois warranted the limiting of Steele's and McLaughlin's right of association. Of course, at trial defendants may show that these individuals were engaging in unlawful activities or were dismissed for other proper reasons, but on this record we hold that the complaint sufficiently states a justifiable claim under Section 1983. There is nothing anomalous in protecting teachers' rights to join unions. Other employees have long been similarly protected by the National Labor Relations Act. See *National Labor Relations Board* v. *Jones & Laughlin*, 301 U.S. 1, 33, 57 S.Ct. 615, 81 L.ed.2d 893. . . .

United Federation of Postal Clerks v. Blount

325 F.Supp. 879 (1971)

Held: Executive Order 11491 recognized the right of federal employees to join labor organizations but did not grant to them the right to strike. The withholding of the right to strike is justified and does not interfere with the right to organize, select representatives, or engage in collective bargaining.

Opinion:

At common law no employee whether public or private, had a constitutional right to strike in concert with his fellow workers. Indeed, such collective action on the part of employees was often held to be a conspiracy. When the right of private employees to strike finally received full protection, it was by statute, Section 7 of the National Labor Relations 'Act, which "took this conspiracy weapon away from the employer in employment relations which affect interstate commerce" and guaranteed to employees in the private sector the right to engage in concerted activities for the purpose of collective bargaining. See discussion in *International Union, UAWA, AF of L Local 232* v. *Wisconsin Employment Relations Board*, 336 U.S. 245, 257-259, 69 S.Ct. 516, 93 L.ed. 651 (1948). It seems clear that public employees stand on no stronger footing in this regard than private employees and that in the absence of a statute, they too do not possess the right to strike. The Supreme Court has spoken approvingly of such a restriction, see *Amell* v. *United States*, 384 U.S. 158, 161, 86 S.Ct. 1384, 16 L.ed.2d 445 (1965), and at least one federal district court has invoked the provisions of a predecessor statute, 5 U.S.C. §118p-r, to enjoin a strike by government employees. *Tennessee Valley Authority* v. *Local Union No. 110 of Sheet Metal Workers*, 233 F.Supp. 997 (D.C.W.D. Ky. 1962). Likewise, scores of state cases have held that state employees do not have a right to engage in concerted work stoppages, in the absence of legislative authorization. See, e.g., *Los Angeles Metropolitan Transit Authority* v. *Brotherhood of R.R. Trainmen*, 54 Cal. 684, 8 Cal. Rptr. 1, 355 P.2d 905 (1960); *Board of Education, etc.* v. *Redding*, 32 Ill.2d 567, 207 N.E.2d 427 (1965); *Alcoa, City of,* v. *International Brotherhood of Electrical Workers*, 203 Tenn. 13, 308 S.W.2d 476 (1957). It is fair to conclude that, irrespective of the reasons given, there is a unanimity of opinion in the part of courts and legislatures that government employees do not have the right to strike. See Moberly, "The Strike and Its Alternative in Public Employment," *University of Wisconsin Law Review* (1966), pp. 549-550, 554.

Congress has consistently treated public employees as being in a different category than private employees. The National Labor Relations Act of 1937 and the Labor Management Relations Act of 1947 (Taft-Hartley) both defined "employer" as not including any governmental or political subdivisions, and thereby indirectly withheld the protections of §7 from governmental employees. Congress originally enacted the no-strike provision separately from other restrictions on employee activity, i.e., such as those struck down in *Stewart* v. *Washington* and *NALC* v. *Blount, supra,* by attaching riders to appropriations bills which prohibited strikes by government employees. See for example the Third Urgent Deficiency Appropriation Act of 1946, which provided that no part of the appropriation could be used to pay the salary of anyone who engaged in a strike against the Government. Section 305 of the Taft-Hartley Act made it unlawful for a federal employee to participate in a strike, providing immediate discharge and forfeiture of civil service status for infractions. Section 305 was repealed in 1955 by Public Law 330, and re-enacted in 5 U.S.C. §118p-r, the predecessor to the present statute.

Given the fact that there is no constitutional right to strike, it is not irrational or arbitrary for the Government to condition employment on a promise not to with-hold labor collectively, and to prohibit strikes by those in public employment, whether because of the prerogatives of the sovereign, some sense of higher obligation associated with public service, to assure the continuing functioning of the Government without interruption, to protect public health and safety or for other reasons. Although plaintiff argues that the provisions in question are unconstitutionally broad in covering all Government employees regardless of the type or importance of the work they do, we hold that it makes no difference whether the jobs performed by certain public employees are regarded as "essential" or "non-essential," or whether similar jobs are performed by workers in private industry who do have the right to strike protected by statute. Nor is it relevant that some positions in private industry are arguably more affected with a public interest than are some positions in the Government service. While the Fifth Amendment contains no Equal Protection Clause similar to the one found in the Fourteenth Amendment, concepts of Equal Protection do inhere in Fifth Amendment Principles of Due Process. *Bolling* v. *Sharpe*, 347 U.S. 497, 74 S.Ct. 693, 98 L.ed. 884 (1954). The Equal Protection Clause, however, does not forbid all discrimination. Where fundamental rights are not involved, a particular classification does not violate the Equal Protection Clause if it is not "arbitrary" or "irrational," i.e., "if any state of facts reasonably may be conceived to justify it." *McGowan* v. *Maryland*, 366 U.S. 420, 426, 81 S.Ct. 1101, 1105, 6 L.ed.2d 393 (1961). Compare *Kramer* v. *Union Free School District*, 395 U.S. 621, 627-628, 89 S.Ct. 1886, 23 L.ed.2d 583 (1969). Since the right to strike cannot be considered a "fundamental" right, it is the test enunciated in *McGowan* which must be employed in this case. Thus, there is latitude for distinctions rooted in reason and practice, especially where the difficulty of drafting a no-strike statute which distinguishes among types and classes of employees is obvious.

Furthermore, it should be pointed out that the fact that public employees may not strike does not interfere with their rights which are fundamental and constitutionally protected. The right to organize collectively and to select representatives for the purposes of engaging in collective bargaining is such a fundamental right. *Thomas* v. *Collins*, 323 U.S. 516, 65 S.Ct. 315, 89 L.ed. 430 (1945); *NLRB* v. *Jones & Laughlin*, 301 U.S. 1, 33, 57 S.Ct. 615, 81 L.ed. 893 (1937); *Hague* v. *CIO*, 307 U.S. 496, 59 S.Ct. 954, 83 L.ed. 1423 (1939). But, as the Supreme Court noted in *International Union, etc., Local 232* v. *Wisconsin Employment Relations Board, supra*, "The right to strike, because of its more serious impact upon the public interest, is more vulnerable to regulation than the right to organize and select representatives for lawful purposes of collective bargaining which this Court has characterized as a 'fundamental right' and which, as the Court has pointed out, was recognized as such in its decisions long before it was given protection by the National Labor Relations Act." 336 U.S. at 259, 69 S.Ct. at 524.

Executive Order 11491 recognizes the right of federal employees to join labor organizations for the purpose of dealing with grievances, but that Order clearly and expressly defines strikes, work stoppages and slow-downs as unfair labor practices. As discussed above, that Order is the culmination of a long-standing policy. There certainly is no compelling reason to imply the existence of the right to strike from the right to associate and bargain collectively. In the private sphere, the strike is used to equalize bargaining power, but this has universally been held not to be appropriate when its object and purpose can only be to influence the essentially political decisions of Government in the allocation of its resources. Congress has an obligation to ensure that the machinery of the Federal Government continues to function at all times without interference. Prohibition of strikes by its employees is a reasonable implementation of that obligation. . . .

Text of Labor Management Relations Act, 1947, as Amended by Public Laws 86–257, 1959,* and 93–360, 1974**

[Public Law 101—80th Congress]

AN ACT

To amend the National Labor Relations Act, to provide additional facilities for the mediation of labor disputes affecting commerce, to equalize legal responsibilities of labor organizations and employers, and for other purposes.

Be it enacted by the Senate and House of Representatives of the United States of America in Congress assembled,

SHORT TITLE AND DECLARATION OF POLICY

SECTION 1. (a) This Act may be cited as the "Labor Management Relations Act, 1947."

(b) Industrial strife which interferes with the normal flow of commerce and with the full production of articles and commodities for commerce, can be avoided or substantially minimized if employers, employees, and labor organizations each recognize under law one another's legitimate rights in their relations with each other, and above all recognize under law that neither party has any right in its relations with any other to engage in acts or practices which jeopardize the public health, safety, or interest.

It is the purpose and policy of this Act, in order to promote the full flow of commerce, to prescribe the legitimate rights of both employees and employers in their relations affecting commerce, to provide orderly and peaceful procedures for preventing the interference by either with the legitimate rights of the other, to protect the rights of individual employees in their relations with labor organizations whose activities affect commerce, to define and proscribe practices on the part of labor and management which affect commerce and are inimical to the general welfare, and to protect the rights of the public in connection with labor disputes affecting commerce.

TITLE I—AMENDMENT OF NATIONAL LABOR RELATIONS ACT

SEC. 101. The National Labor Relations Act is hereby amended to read as follows:

FINDINGS AND POLICIES

SECTION 1. The denial by some employers of the right of employees to organize and the refusal by some employers to accept the procedure of collective bargaining

---

*Sec. 201(d) and (e) of the Labor-Management Reporting and Disclosure Act of 1959 which repealed Sec. 9(f), (g), and (h) of the Labor Management Relations Act, 1947, and Sec. 505 amending Sec. 302(a), (b), and (c) of the Labor Management Relations Act, 1947, took effect upon enactment of Public Law 86–257, Sept. 14, 1959. As to the other amendments of the Labor Management Relations Act, 1947, Sec. 707 of the Labor-Management Reporting and Disclosure Act provides:

The amendments made by this title shall take effect sixty days after the date of the enactment of this Act and no provision of this title shall be deemed to make an unfair labor practice, any act which is performed prior to such effective date which did not constitute an unfair labor practice prior thereto.

**The amendments to Secs. 2(2) and (14), 8(d) and (g), 19, and 213 became effective on the 30th day (Aug. 25, 1974) after its date of enactment, July 26, 1974.

lead to strikes and other forms of industrial strife or unrest, which have the intent or the necessary effect of burdening or obstructing commerce by (a) impairing the efficiency, safety, or operation of the instrumentalities of commerce; (b) occurring in the current of commerce; (c) materially affecting, restraining, or controlling the flow of raw materials or manufactured or processed goods from or into the channels of commerce, or the prices of such materials or goods in commerce; or (d) causing diminution of employment and wages in such volume as substantially to impair or disrupt the market for goods flowing from or into the channels of commerce.

The inequality of bargaining power between employees who do not possess full freedom of association or actual liberty of contract, and employers who are organized in the corporate or other forms of ownership association substantially burdens and affects the flow of commerce, and tends to aggravate recurrent business depressions, by depressing wage rates and the purchasing power of wage earners in industry and by preventing the stabilization of competitive wage rates and working conditions within and between industries.

Experience has proved that protection by law of the right of employees to organize and bargain collectively safeguards commerce from injury, impairment, or interruption, and promotes the flow of commerce by removing certain recognized sources of industrial strife and unrest, by encouraging practices fundamental to the friendly adjustment of industrial disputes arising out of differences as to wages, hours, or other working conditions, and by restoring equality of bargaining power between employers and employees.

Experience has further demonstrated that certain practices by some labor organizations, their officers, and members have the intent or the necessary effect of burdening or obstructing commerce by preventing the free flow of goods in such commerce through strikes and other forms of industrial unrest or through concerted activities which impair the interest of the public in the free flow of such commerce. The elimination of such practices is a necessary condition to the assurance of the rights herein guaranteed.

It is hereby declared to be the policy of the United States to eliminate the causes of certain substantial obstructions to the free flow of commerce and to mitigate and eliminate these obstructions when they have occurred by encouraging the practice and procedure of collective bargaining and by protecting the exercise by workers of full freedom of association, self-organization, and designation of representatives of their own choosing, for the purpose of negotiating the terms and conditions of their employment or other mutual aid or protection.

DEFINITIONS

SEC. 2. When used in this Act—

(1) The term "person" includes one or more individuals, labor organizations, partnerships, associations, corporations, legal representatives, trustees, trustees in bankruptcy, or receivers.

(2) The term "employer" includes any person acting as an agent of an employer, directly or indirectly, but shall not include the United States or any wholly owned Government corporation, or any Federal Reserve Bank, or any State or political subdivision thereof,* or any person subject to the Railway Labor Act, as amended from time to time, or any labor organization (other than when acting as an employer), or anyone acting in the capacity of officer or agent of such labor organization.

---

* Pursuant to Public Law 93–360, 93d Cong., S. 3203, 88 Stat. 395, Sec. 2(2) is amended by deleting the phrase "or any corporation or association operating a hospital, if no part of the net earnings inures to the benefit of any private shareholder or individual,".

(3) The term "employee" shall include any employee, and shall not be limited to the employees of a particular employer, unless the Act explicitly states otherwise, and shall include any individual whose work has ceased as a consequence of, or in connection with, any current labor dispute or because of any unfair labor practice, and who has not obtained any other regular and substantially equivalent employment, but shall not include any individual employed as an agricultural laborer, or in the domestic service of any family or person at his home, or any individual employed by his parent or spouse, or any individual having the status of an independent contractor, or any individual employed as a supervisor, or any individual employed by an employer subject to the Railway Labor Act, as amended from time to time, or by any other person who is not an employer as herein defined.

(4) The term "representatives" includes any individual or labor organization.

(5) The term "labor organization" means any organization of any kind, or any agency or employee representation committee or plan, in which employees participate and which exists for the purpose, in whole or in part, of dealing with employers concerning grievances, labor disputes, wages, rates of pay, hours of employment, or conditions of work.

(6) The term "commerce" means trade, traffic, commerce, transportation, or communication among the several States, or between the District of Columbia or any Territory of the United States and any State or other Territory, or between any foreign country and any State, Territory, or the District of Columbia, or within the District of Columbia or any Territory, or between points in the same State but through any other State or any Territory or the District of Columbia or any foreign country.

(7) The term "affecting commerce" means in commerce, or burdening or obstructing commerce or the free flow of commerce, or having led or tending to lead to a labor dispute burdening or obstructing commerce or the free flow of commerce.

(8) The term "unfair labor practice" means any unfair labor practice listed in section 8.

(9) The term "labor dispute" includes any controversy concerning terms, tenure or conditions of employment, or concerning the association or representation of persons in negotiating, fixing, maintaining, changing, or seeking to arrange terms or conditions of employment, regardless of whether the disputants stand in the proximate relation of employer and employee.

(10) The term "National Labor Relations Board" means the National Labor Relations Board provided for in section 3 of this Act.

(11) The term "supervisor" means any individual having authority, in the interest of the employer, to hire, transfer, suspend, lay off, recall, promote, discharge, assign, reward, or discipline other employees, or responsibly to direct them, or to adjust their grievances, or effectively to recommend such action, if in connection with the foregoing the exercise of such authority is not of a merely routine or clerical nature, but requires the use of independent judgment.

(12) The term "professional employee" means—

(a) any employee engaged in work (i) predominantly intellectual and varied in character as opposed to routine mental, manual, mechanical, or physical work; (ii) involving the consistent exercise of discretion and judgment in its performance; (iii) of such a character that the output produced or the result accomplished cannot be standardized in relation to a given period of time; (iv) requiring knowledge of an advanced type in a field of science or learning customarily acquired by a prolonged course of specialized intellectual instruction and study in an institution of higher learning or a hospital, as distinguished from a general academic education or from an apprenticeship or from training in the performance of routine mental, manual, or physical processes; or

(b) any employee, who (i) has completed the courses of specialized intellectual instruction and study described in clause (iv) of paragraph (a), and (ii) is performing related work under the supervision of a professional person to qualify himself to become a professional employee as defined in paragraph (a).

(13) In determining whether any person is acting as an "agent" of another person so as to make such other person responsible for his acts, the question of whether the specific acts performed were actually authorized or subsequently ratified shall not be controlling.

(14) The term "health care institution" shall include any hospital, convalescent hospital, health maintenance organization, health clinic, nursing home, extended care facility, or other institution devoted to the care of sick, infirm, or aged person.*

NATIONAL LABOR RELATIONS BOARD

SEC. 3. (a) The National Labor Relations Board (hereinafter called the "Board") created by this Act prior to its amendment by the Labor Management Relations Act, 1947, is hereby continued as an agency of the United States, except that the Board shall consist of five instead of three members, appointed by the President by and with the advice and consent of the Senate. Of the two additional members so provided for, one shall be appointed for a term of five years and the other for a term of two years. Their successors, and the successors of the other members, shall be appointed for terms of five years each, excepting that any individual chosen to fill a vacancy shall be appointed only for the unexpired term of the member whom he shall succeed. The President shall designate one member to serve as Chairman of the Board. Any member of the Board may be removed by the President, upon notice and hearing, for neglect of duty or malfeasance in office, but for no other cause.

(b) The Board is authorized to delegate to any group of three of more members any or all of the powers which it may itself exercise. The Board is also authorized to delegate to its regional directors its powers under section 9 to determine the unit appropriate for the purpose of collective bargaining, to investigate and provide for hearings, and determine whether a question of representation exists, and to direct an election or take a secret ballot under subsection (c) or (e) of section 9 and certify the results thereof, except that upon the filing of a request therefor with the Board by any interested person, the Board may review any action of a regional director delegated to him under this paragraph, but such a review shall not, unless specifically ordered by the Board, operate as a stay of any action taken by the regional director. A vacancy in the Board shall not impair the right of the remaining members to exercise all of the powers of the Board, and three members of the Board shall, at all times, constitute a quorum of the Board, except that two members shall constitute a quorum of any group designated pursuant to the first sentence hereof. The Board shall have an official seal which shall be judicially noticed.

(c) The Board shall at the close of each fiscal year make a report in writing to Congress and to the President stating in detail the cases it has heard, the decisions it has rendered,** and an account of all moneys it has disbursed.

---

* Pursuant to Public Law 93–360, 93d Cong., S. 3203, 88 Stat. 395, Sec. 2 is amended by adding subsection (14).

** Pursuant to Public Law 93–608, 93d Cong., H.R. 14718, 88 Stat. 1972, approved Jan. 2, 1975, Sec. 3(c) is amended by deleting the phrase "the names, salaries, and duties of all employees and officers in the employ or under the supervision of the Board,".

(d) There shall be a General Counsel of the Board who shall be appointed by the President, by and with the advice and consent of the Senate, for a term of four years. The General Counsel of the Board shall exercise general supervision over all attorneys employed by the Board (other than trial examiners and legal assistants to Board members) and over the officers and employees in the regional offices. He shall have final authority, on behalf of the Board, in respect of the investigation of charges and issuance of complaints under section 10, and in respect of the prosecution of such complaints before the Board, and shall have such other duties as the Board may prescribe or as may be provided by law. In case of a vacancy in the office of the General Counsel the President is authorized to designate the officer or employee who shall act as General Counsel during such vacancy, but no person or persons so designated shall so act (1) for more than forty days when the Congress is in session unless a nomination to fill such vacancy shall have been submitted to the Senate, or (2) after the adjournment *sine die* of the session of the Senate in which such nomination was submitted.

SEC. 4. (a) Each member of the Board and the General Counsel of the Board shall receive a salary of $12,000* a year, shall be eligible for reappointment, and shall not engage in any other business, vocation, or employment. The Board shall appoint an executive secretary, and such attorneys, examiners, and regional directors, and such other employees as it may from time to time find necessary for the proper performance of its duties. The Board may not employ any attorneys for the purpose of reviewing transcripts of hearings or preparing drafts of opinions except that any attorney employed for assignment as a legal assistant to any Board member may for such Board member review such transcripts and prepare such drafts. No trial examiner's report shall be reviewed, either before or after its publication, by any person other than a member of the Board or his legal assistant, and no trial examiner shall advise or consult with the Board with respect to exceptions taken to his findings, rulings, or recommendations. The Board may establish or utilize such regional, local, or other agencies, and utilize such voluntary and uncompensated services, as may from time to time be needed. Attorneys appointed under this section may, at the direction of the Board, appear for and represent the Board in any case in court. Nothing in this Act shall be construed to authorize the Board to appoint individuals for the purpose of conciliation or mediation, or for economic analysis.

(b) All of the expenses of the Board, including all necessary traveling and subsistence expenses outside the District of Columbia incurred by the members or employees of the Board under its orders, shall be allowed and paid on the presentation of itemized vouchers therefor approved by the Board or by any individual it designates for that purpose.

SEC. 5. The principal office of the Board shall be in the District of Columbia, but it may meet and exercise any or all of its powers at any other place. The Board may, by one or more of its members or by such agents or agencies as it may designate, prosecute any inquiry necessary to its functions in any part of the United States. A member who participates in such an inquiry shall not be disqualified from subsequently participating in a decision of the Board in the same case.

SEC. 6. The Board shall have authority from time to time to make, amend, and rescind, in the manner prescribed by the Administrative Procedure Act, such rules and regulations as may be necessary to carry out the provisions of this Act.

---

*Pursuant to Public Law 90-206, 90th Cong., 81 Stat. 644, approved Dec. 16, 1967, and in accordance with Sec. 225(f)(ii) thereof, effective in 1969, the salary of the Chairman of the Board shall be $40,000 per year and the salaries of the General Counsel and each Board member shall be $38,000 per year.

RIGHTS OF EMPLOYEES

SEC. 7.   Employees shall have the right to self-organization, to form, join, or assist labor organizations, to bargain collectively through representatives of their own choosing, and to engage in other concerted activities for the purpose of collective bargaining or other mutual aid or protection, and shall also have the right to refrain from any or all of such activities except to the extent that such right may be affected by an agreement requiring membership in a labor organization as a condition of employment as authorized in section 8(a)(3).

UNFAIR LABOR PRACTICES

SEC. 8.   (a) It shall be an unfair labor practice for an employer—

(1) to interfere with, restrain, or coerce employees in the exercise of the rights guaranteed in section 7;

(2) to dominate or interfere with the formation or administration of any labor organization or contribute financial or other support to it: *Provided,* That subject to rules and regulations made and published by the Board pursuant to section 6, an employer shall not be prohibited from permitting employees to confer with him during working hours without loss of time or pay;

(3) by discrimination in regard to hire or tenure of employment or any term or condition of employment to encourage or discourage membership in any labor organization: *Provided,* That nothing in this Act, or in any other statute of the United States, shall preclude an employer from making an agreement with a labor organization (not established, maintained, or assisted by any action defined in section 8(a) of this Act as an unfair labor practice) to require as a condition of employment membership therein on or after the thirtieth day following the beginning of such employment or the effective date of such agreement, whichever is the later, (i) if such labor organization is the representative of the employees as provided in section 9(a), in the appropriate collective-bargaining unit covered by such agreement when made, and (ii) unless following an election held as provided in section 9(e) within one year preceding the effective date of such agreement, the Board shall have certified that at least a majority of the employees eligible to vote in such election have voted to rescind the authority of such labor organization to make such an agreement: *Provided further,* That no employer shall justify any discrimination against an employee for non-membership in a labor organization (A) if he has reasonable grounds for believing that such membership was not available to the employee on the same terms and conditions generally applicable to other members, or (B) if he has reasonable grounds for believing that membership was denied or terminated for reasons other than the failure of the employee to tender the periodic dues and the initiation fees uniformly required as a condition of acquiring or retaining membership;

(4) to discharge or otherwise discriminate against an employee because he has filed charges or given testimony under this Act;

(5) to refuse to bargain collectively with the representatives of his employees, subject to the provisions of section 9(a).

(b) It shall be an unfair labor practice for a labor organization or its agents—

(1) to restrain or coerce (A) employees in the exercise of the rights guaranteed in section 7: *Provided,* That this paragraph shall not impair the right of a labor organization to prescribe its own rules with respect to the acquisition or retention of membership therein; or (B) an employer in the selection of his representatives for the purposes of collective bargaining or the adjustment of grievances;

(2) to cause or attempt to cause an employer to discriminate against an employee in violation of subsection (a)(3) or to discriminate against an employee with respect to whom membership in such organization has been denied or terminated on some ground other than his failure to tender the periodic dues and the initiation fees uniformly required as a condition of acquiring or retaining membership;

(3) to refuse to bargain collectively with an employer, provided it is the representative of his employees subject to the provisions of section 9(a);

(4) (i) to engage in, or to induce or encourage any individual employed by any person engaged in commerce or in an industry affecting commerce to engage in, a strike or a refusal in the course of his employment to use, manufacture, process, transport, or otherwise handle or work on any goods, articles, materials, or commodities or to perform any services; or (ii) to threaten, coerce, or restrain any person engaged in commerce or in an industry affecting commerce, where in either case an object thereof is:

(A) forcing or requiring any employer or self-employed person to join any labor or employer organization or to enter into any agreement which is prohibited by section 8(e);

(B) forcing or requiring any person to cease using, selling, handling, transporting, or otherwise dealing in the products of any other producer, processor, or manufacturer, or to cease doing business with any other person, or forcing or requiring any other employer to recognize or bargain with a labor organization as the representative of his employees unless such labor organization has been certified as the representative of such employees under the provisions of section 9: *Provided*, That nothing contained in this clause (B) shall be construed to make unlawful, where not otherwise unlawful, any primary strike or primary picketing;

(C) forcing or requiring any employer to recognize or bargain with a particular labor organization as the representative of his employees if another labor organization has been certified as the representative of such employees under the provisions of section 9;

(D) forcing or requiring any employer to assign particular work to employees in a particular labor organization or in a particular trade, craft, or class rather than to employees in another labor organization or in another trade, craft, or class, unless such employer is failing to conform to an order or certification of the Board determining the bargaining representative for employees performing such work:

Provided, That nothing contained in this subsection (b) shall be construed to make unlawful a refusal by any person to enter upon the premises of any employer (other than his own employer), if the employees of such employer are engaged in a strike ratified or approved by a representative of such employees whom such employer is required to recognize under this Act: *Provided further*, That for the purposes of this paragraph (4) only, nothing contained in such paragraph shall be construed to prohibit publicity, other than picketing, for the purpose of truthfully advising the public, including consumers and members of a labor organization, that a product or products are produced by an employer with whom the labor organization has a primary dispute and are distributed by another employer, as long as such publicity does not have an effect of inducing any individual employed by any person other than the primary employer in the course of his employment to refuse to pick up, deliver, or transport any goods, or not to perform any services, at the establishment of the employer engaged in such distribution;

(5) to require of employees covered by an agreement authorized under

subsection (a)(3) the payment, as a condition precedent to becoming a member of such organization, of a fee in an amount which the Board finds excessive or discriminatory under all the circumstances. In making such a finding, the Board shall consider, among other relevant factors, the practices and customs of labor organizations in the particular industry, and the wages currently paid to the employees affected;

(6) to cause or attempt to cause an employer to pay or deliver or agree to pay or deliver any money or other thing of value, in the nature of an exaction, for services which are not performed or not to be performed; and

(7) to picket or cause to be picketed, or threaten to picket or cause to be picketed, any employer where an object thereof is forcing or requiring an employer to recognize or bargain with a labor organization as the representative of his employees, or forcing or requiring the employees of an employer to accept or select such labor organization as their collective bargaining representative, unless such labor organization is currently certified as the representative of such employees:

(A) where the employer has lawfully recognized in accordance with this Act any other labor organization and a question concerning representation may not appropriately be raised under section 9(c) of this Act,

(B) where within the preceding twelve months a valid election under section 9(c) of this Act has been conducted, or

(C) where such picketing has been conducted without a petition under section 9(c) being filed within a reasonable period of time not to exceed thirty days from the commencement of such picketing: *Provided,* That when such a petition has been filed the Board shall forthwith, without regard to the provisions of section 9(c)(1) or the absence of a showing of a substantial interest on the part of the labor organization, direct an election in such unit as the Board finds to be appropriate and shall certify the results thereof: *Provided further,* That nothing in this subparagraph (C) shall be construed to prohibit any picketing or other publicity for the purpose of truthfully advising the public (including consumers) that an employer does not employ members of, or have a contract with, a labor organization, unless an effect of such picketing is to induce any individual employed by any other person in the course of his employment, not to pick up, deliver or transport any goods or not to perform any services.

Nothing in this paragraph (7) shall be construed to permit any act which would otherwise be an unfair labor practice under this section 8(b).

(c) The expressing of any views, argument, or opinion, or the dissemination thereof, whether in written, printed, graphic, or visual form, shall not constitute or be evidence of an unfair labor practice under any of the provisions of this Act, if such expression contains no threat of reprisal or force or promise of benefit.

(d) For the purposes of this section, to bargain collectively is the performance of the mutual obligation of the employer and the representative of the employees to meet at reasonable times and confer in good faith with respect to wages, hours, and other terms and conditions of employment, or the negotiation of an agreement, or any question arising thereunder, and the execution of a written contract incorporating any agreement reached if requested by either party, but such obligation does not compel either party to agree to a proposal or require the making of a concession: *Provided,* That where there is in effect a collective-bargaining contract covering employees in an industry affecting commerce, the duty to bargain collectively shall also mean that no party to such contract shall terminate or modify such contract, unless the party desiring such termination or modification—

(1) serves a written notice upon the other party to the contract of the proposed termination or modification sixty days prior to the expiration date thereof, or in the event such contract contains no expiration date, sixty days prior to the time it is proposed to make such termination or modification;

(2) offers to meet and confer with the other party for the purpose of negotiating a new contract or a contract containing the proposed modifications;

(3) notifies the Federal Mediation and Conciliation Service within thirty days after such notice of the existence of a dispute, and simultaneously therewith notifies any State or Territorial agency established to mediate and conciliate disputes within the State or Territory where the dispute occurred, provided no agreement has been reached by that time; and

(4) continues in full force and effect, without resorting to strike or lock-out, all the terms and conditions of the existing contract for a period of sixty days after such notice is given or until the expiration date of such contract, whichever occurs later:

The duties imposed upon employers, employees, and labor organizations by paragraphs (2), (3), and (4) shall become inapplicable upon an intervening certification of the Board, under which the labor organization or individual, which is a party to the contract, has been superseded as or ceased to be the representative of the employees subject to the provisions of section 9(a), and the duties so imposed shall not be construed as requiring either party to discuss or agree to any modification of the terms and conditions contained in a contract for a fixed period, if such modification is to become effective before such terms and conditions can be reopened under the provisions of the contract. Any employee who engages in a strike within any notice* period specified in this subsection, or who engages in any strike within the appropriate period specified in subsection (g) of this section* shall lose his status as an employee of the employer engaged in the particular labor dispute, for the purposes of sections 8, 9, and 10 of this Act, as amended, but such loss of status for such employee shall terminate if and when he is reemployed by such employer. Whenever the collective bargaining involves employees of a health care institution, the provisions of this section 8(d) shall be modified as follows:

(A) The notice of section 8(d)(1) shall be ninety days; the notice of section 8(d)(3) shall be sixty days; and the contract period of section 8(d)(4) shall be ninety days;

(B) Where the bargaining is for an initial agreement following certification or recognition, at least thirty days' notice of the existence of a dispute shall be given by the labor organization to the agencies set forth in section 8(d)(3).

(C) After notice is given to the Federal Mediation and Conciliation Service under either clause (A) or (B) of this sentence, the Service shall promptly communicate with the parties and use its best efforts, by mediation and conciliation, to bring them to agreement. The parties shall participate fully and promptly in such meetings as may be undertaken by the Service for the purpose of aiding in a settlement of the dispute.*

(e) It shall be an unfair labor practice for any labor organization and any employer to enter into any contract or agreement, express or implied, whereby such employer ceases or refrains or agrees to cease or refrain from handling, using, selling, transporting or otherwise dealing in any of the products of any other employer, or

---

* Pursuant to Public Law 93–360, 93d Cong., S. 3203, 88 Stat. 396, the last sentence of Sec. 8(d) is amended by striking the words "the sixty day" and inserting the words "any notice" and by inserting before the words "shall lose" the phrase ", or who engages in any strike within the appropriate period specified in subsection (g) of this section." In addition, the end of paragraph Sec. 8(d) is amended by adding a new sentence "Whenever the collective bargaining . . . aiding in a settlement of the dispute."

to cease doing business with any other person, and any contract or agreement entered into heretofore or hereafter containing such an agreement shall be to such extent unenforceable and void: *Provided*, That nothing in this subsection (e) shall apply to an agreement between a labor organization and an employer in the construction industry relating to the contracting or subcontracting of work to be done at the site of the construction, alteration, painting, or repair of a building, structure, or other work: *Provided further*, That for the purposes of this subsection (e) and section 8(b)(4) (B) the terms "any employer", "any person engaged in commerce or in industry affecting commerce", and "any person" when used in relation to the terms "any other producer, processor, or manufacturer", "any other employer", or "any other person" shall not include persons in the relation of a jobber, manufacturer, contractor, or sub-contractor working on the goods or premises of the jobber or manufacturer or per-forming parts of an integrated process of production in the apparel and clothing industry: *Provided further*, That nothing in this Act shall prohibit the enforcement of any agreement which is within the foregoing exception.

(f) It shall not be an unfair labor practice under subsections (a) and (b) of this section for an employer engaged primarily in the building and construction industry to make an agreement covering employees engaged (or who, upon their employment, will be engaged) in the building and construction industry with a labor organization of which building and construction employees are members (not established, main-tained, or assisted by any action defined in section 8(a) of this Act as an unfair labor practice) because (1) the majority status of such labor organization has not been established under the provisions of section 9 of this Act prior to the making of such agreement, or (2) such agreement requires as a condition of employment, member-ship in such labor organization after the seventh day following the beginning of such employment or the effective date of the agreement, whichever is later, or (3) such agreement requires the employer to notify such labor organization of opportunities for employment with such employer, or gives such labor organization an opportunity to refer qualified applicants for such employment, or (4) such agreement specifies minimum training or experience qualifications for employment or provides for priority in opportunities for employment based upon length of service with such employer, in the industry or in the particular geographical area: *Provided*, That nothing in this subsection shall set aside the final proviso to section 8(a)(3) of this Act: *Provided further*, That any agreement which would be invalid, but for clause (1) of this sub-section, shall not be a bar to a petition filed pursuant to section 9(c) or 9(e).*

(g) A labor organization before engaging in any strike, picketing, or other concerted refusal to work at any health care institution shall, not less than ten days prior to such action, notify the institution in writing and the Federal Mediation and Conciliation Service of that intention, except that in the case of bargaining for an initial agreement following certification or recogition the notice required by this subsection shall not be given until the expiration of the period specified in clause (B) of the last sentence of section 8(d) of this Act. The notice shall state the date and time that such action will commence. The notice, once given, may be extended by the written agreement of both parties.**

---

*Sec. 8(f) is inserted in the Act by subsec. (a) of Sec. 705 of Public Law 86–257. Sec. 705(b) provides:

Nothing contained in the amendment made by subsection (a) shall be construed as authorizing the execution or application of agreements requiring membership in a labor organization as a condition of employment in any State or Territory in which such execution or application is prohibited by State or Territorial law.

**Pursuant to Public Law 93–360, 93d Cong., S. 3203, 88 Stat. 396, Sec. 8 is amended by adding subsection (g).

REPRESENTATIVES AND ELECTIONS

SEC. 9. (a) Representatives designated or selected for the purposes of collective bargaining by the majority of the employees in a unit appropriate for such purposes, shall be the exclusive representatives of all the employees in such unit for the purposes of collective bargaining in respect to rates of pay, wages, hours of employment, or other conditions of employment: *Provided*, That any individual employee or a group of employees shall have the right at any time to present grievances to their employer and to have such grievances adjusted, without the intervention of the bargaining representative, as long as the adjustment is not inconsistent with the terms of a collective-bargaining contract or agreement then in effect: *Provided further*, That the bargaining representative has been given opportunity to be present at such adjustment.

(b) The Board shall decide in each case whether, in order to assure to employees the fullest freedom in exercising the rights guaranteed by this Act, the unit appropriate for the purposes of collective- bargaining shall be the employer unit, craft unit, plant unit, or subdivision thereof: *Provided*, That the Board shall not (1) decide that any unit is appropriate for such purposes if such unit includes both professional employees and employees who are not professional employees unless a majority of such professional employees vote for inclusion in such unit; or (2) decide that any craft unit is inappropriate for such purposes on the ground that a different unit has been established by a prior Board determination, unless a majority of the employees in the proposed craft unit vote against separate representation or (3) decide that any unit is appropriate for such purposes if it includes, together with other employees, any individual employed as a guard to enforce against employees and other persons rules to protect property of the employer or to protect the safety of persons on the employer's premises; but no labor organization shall be certified as the representative of employees in a bargaining unit of guards if such organization admits to membership, or is affiliated directly or indirectly with an organization which admits to membership, employees other than guards.

(c)(1) Wherever a petition shall have been filed, in accordance with such regulations as may be prescribed by the Board—

(A) by an employee or group of employees or any individual or labor organization acting in their behalf alleging that a substantial number of employees (i) wish to be represented for collective bargaining and that their employer declines to recognize their representative as the representative defined in section 9(a), or (ii) assert that the individual or labor organization, which has been certified or is being currently recognized by their employer as the bargaining representative, is no longer a representative as defined in section 9(a); or

(B) by an employer, alleging that one or more individuals or labor organizations have presented to him a claim to be recognized as the representative defined in section 9(a);

the Board shall investigate such petition and if it has reasonable cause to believe that a question of representation affecting commerce exists shall provide for an appropriate hearing upon due notice. Such hearing may be conducted by an officer or employee of the regional office, who shall not make any recommendations with respect thereto. If the Board finds upon the record of such hearing that such a question of representation exists, it shall direct an election by secret ballot and shall certify the results thereof.

(2) In determining whether or not a question of representation affecting commerce exists, the same regulations and rules of decision shall apply irrespective of

the identity of the persons filing the petition or the kind of relief sought and in no case shall the Board deny a labor organization a place on the ballot by reason of an order with respect to such labor organization or its predecessor not issued in conformity with section 10(c).

(3) No election shall be directed in any bargaining unit or any subdivision within which, in the preceding twelve-month period, a valid election shall have been held. Employees engaged in an economic strike who are not entitled to reinstatement shall be eligible to vote under such regulations as the Board shall find are consistent with the purposes and provisions of this Act in any election conducted within twelve months after the commencement of the strike. In any election where none of the choices on the ballot receives a majority, a run-off shall be conducted, the ballot providing for a selection between the two choices receiving the largest and second largest number of valid votes cast in the election.

(4) Nothing in this section shall be construed to prohibit the waiving of hearings by stipulation for the purpose of a consent election in conformity with regulations and rules of decision of the Board.

(5) In determining whether a unit is appropriate for the purposes specified in subsection (b) the extent to which the employees have organized shall not be controlling.

(d) Whenever an order of the Board made pursuant to section 10(c) is based in whole or in part upon facts certified following an investigation pursuant to subsection (c) of this section and there is a petition for the enforcement or review of such order, such certification and the record of such investigation shall be included in the transcript of the entire record required to be filed under section 10(e) or 10(f), and thereupon the decree of the court enforcing, modifying, or setting aside in whole or in part the order of the Board shall be made and entered upon the pleadings, testimony, and proceedings set forth in such transcript.

(e)(1) Upon the filing with the Board, by 30 per centum or more of the employees in a bargaining unit covered by an agreement between their employer and a labor organization made pursuant to section 8(a)(3), of a petition alleging they desire that such authority be rescinded, the Board shall take a secret ballot of the employees in such unit and certify the results thereof to such labor organization and to the employer.

(2) No election shall be conducted pursuant to this subsection in any bargaining unit or any subdivision within which, in the preceding twelve-month period, a valid election shall have been held.

PREVENTION OF UNFAIR LABOR PRACTICES

SEC. 10. (a) The Board is empowered, as hereinafter provided, to prevent any person from engaging in any unfair labor practice (listed in section 8) affecting commerce. This power shall not be affected by any other means of adjustment or prevention that has been or may be established by agreement, law, or otherwise: *Provided*, That the Board is empowered by agreement with any agency of any State or Territory to cede to such agency jurisdiction over any cases in any industry (other than mining, manufacturing, communications, and transportation except where predominantly local in character) even though such cases may involve labor disputes affecting commerce, unless the provision of the State or Territorial statute applicable to the determination of such cases by such agency is inconsistent with the corresponding provision of this Act or has received a construction inconsistent therewith.

(b) Whenever it is charged that any person has engaged in or is engaging in any such unfair labor practice, the Board, or any agent or agency designated by the Board for such purposes, shall have power to issue and cause to be served upon such person a complaint stating the charges in that respect, and containing a notice of hearing before the Board or a member thereof, or before a designated agent or agency, at a place therein fixed, not less than five days after the serving of said complaint: *Provided,* That no complaint shall issue based upon any unfair labor practice occurring more than six months prior to the filing of the charge with the Board and the service of a copy thereof upon the person against whom such charge is made, unless the person aggrieved thereby was prevented from filing such charge by reason of service in the armed forces, in which event the six-month period shall be computed from the day of his discharge. Any such complaint may be amended by the member, agent, or agency conducting the hearing or the Board in its discretion at any time prior to the issuance of an order based thereon. The person so complained of shall have the right to file an answer to the original or amended complaint and to appear in person or otherwise and give testimony at the place and time fixed in the complaint. In the discretion of the member, agent, or agency conducting the hearing or the Board, any other person may be allowed to intervene in the said proceeding and to present testimony. Any such proceeding shall, so far as practicable, be conducted in accordance with the rules of evidence applicable in the district courts of the United States under the rules of civil procedure for the district courts of the United States, adopted by the Supreme Court of the United States pursuant to the Act of June 19, 1934 (U. S. C., title 28, secs. 723–B, 723–C).

(c) The testimony taken by such member, agent, or agency or the Board shall be reduced to writing and filed with the Board. Thereafter, in its discretion, the Board upon notice may take further testimony or hear argument. If upon the preponderance of the testimony taken the Board shall be of the opinion that any person named in the complaint has engaged in or is engaging in any such unfair labor practice, then the Board shall state its findings of fact and shall issue and cause to be served on such person an order requiring such person to cease and desist from such unfair labor practice, and to take such affirmative action including reinstatement of employees with or without back pay, as will effectuate the policies of this Act: *Provided,* That where an order directs reinstatement of an employee, back pay may be required of the employer or labor organization, as the case may be, responsible for the discrimination suffered by him: *And provided further,* That in determining whether a complaint shall issue alleging a violation of section 8(a)(1) or section 8(a)(2), and in deciding such cases, the same regulations and rules of decision shall apply irrespective of whether or not the labor organization affected is affiliated with a labor organization national or international in scope. Such order may further require such person to make reports from time to time showing the extent to which it has complied with the order. If upon the preponderance of the testimony taken the Board shall not be of the opinion that the person named in the complaint has engaged in or is engaging in any such unfair labor practice, then the Board shall state its findings of fact and shall issue an order dismissing the said complaint. No order of the Board shall require the reinstatement of any individual as an employee who has been suspended or discharged, or the payment to him of any back pay, if such individual was suspended or discharged for cause. In case the evidence is presented before a member of the Board, or before an examiner or examiners thereof, such member, or such examiner or examiners, as the case may be, shall issue and cause to be served on the parties to the proceeding a proposed report, together with a recommended order, which shall be filed with the Board, and if no exceptions are filed within twenty days after service thereof upon such parties, or within such further period as the Board may authorize, such recommended order shall become the order of the Board and become effective as therein prescribed.

(d) Until the record in a case shall have been filed in a court, as hereinafter provided, the Board may at any time, upon reasonable notice and in such manner as it shall deem proper, modify or set aside, in whole or in part, any finding or order made or issued by it.

(e) The Board shall have power to petition any court of appeals of the United States, or if all the courts of appeals to which application may be made are in vacation, any district court of the United States, within any circuit or district, respectively, wherein the unfair labor practice in question occurred or wherein such person resides or transacts business, for the enforcement of such order and for appropriate temporary relief or.restraining order, and shall file in the court the record in the proceedings, as provided in section 2112 of title 28, United States Code. Upon the filing of such petition, the court shall cause notice thereof to be served upon such person, and thereupon shall have jurisdiction of the proceeding and of the question determined therein, and shall have power to grant such temporary relief or restraining order as it deems just and proper, and to make and enter a decree enforcing, modifying, and enforcing as so modified, or setting aside in whole or in part the order of the Board. No objection that has not been urged before the Board, its member, agent, or agency, shall be considered by the court, unless the failure or neglect to urge such objection shall be excused because of extraordinary circumstances. The findings of the Board with respect to questions of fact if supported by substantial evidence on the record considered as a whole shall be conclusive. If either party shall apply to the court for leave to adduce additional evidence and shall show to the satisfaction of the court that such additional evidence is material and that there were reasonable grounds for the failure to adduce such evidence in the hearing before the Board, its member, agent, or agency, the court may order such additional evidence to be taken before the Board, its member, agent, or agency, and to be made a part of the record. The Board may modify its findings as to the facts, or make new findings, by reason of additional evidence so taken and filed, and it shall file such modified or new findings, which findings with respect to questions of fact if supported by substantial evidence on the record considered as a whole shall be conclusive, and shall file its recommendations, if any, for the modification or setting aside of its original order. Upon the filing of the record with it the jurisdiction of the court shall be exclusive and its judgment and decree shall be final, except that the same shall be subject to review by the appropriate United States court of appeals if application was made to the district court as hereinabove provided, and by the Supreme Court of the United States upon writ of certiorari or certification as provided in section 1254 of title 28.

(f) Any person aggrieved by a final order of the Board granting or denying in whole or in part the relief sought may obtain a review of such order in any circuit court of appeals of the United States in the circuit wherein the unfair labor practice in question was alleged to have been engaged in or wherein such person resides or transacts business, or in the United States Court of Appeals for the District of Columbia, by filing in such court a written petition praying that the order of the Board be modified or set aside. A copy of such petition shall be forthwith transmitted by the clerk of the court to the Board, and thereupon the aggrieved party shall file in the court the record in the proceeding, certified by the Board, as provided in section 2112 of title 28, United States Code. Upon the filing of such petition, the court shall proceed in the same manner as in the case of an application by the Board under subsection (e) of this section, and shall have the same jurisdiction to grant to the Board such temporary relief or restraining order as it deems just and proper, and in like manner to make and enter a decree enforcing, modifying, and enforcing as so modified, or setting aside in whole or in part the order of the Board; the findings of the Board with respect to questions of fact if supported by substantial evidence on the record considered as a whole shall in like manner be conclusive.

(g) The commencement of proceedings under subsection (e) or (f) of this section shall not, unless specifically ordered by the court, operate as a stay of the Board's order.

(h) When granting appropriate temporary relief or a restraining order, or making and entering a decree enforcing, modifying, and enforcing as so modified, or setting aside in whole or in part an order of the Board, as provided in this section, the jurisdiction of courts sitting in equity shall not be limited by the Act entitled "An Act to amend the Judicial Code and to define and limit the jurisdiction of courts sitting in equity, and for other purposes," approved March 23, 1932 (U.S.C., Supp. VII, title 29, secs. 101–115).

(i) Petitions filed under this Act shall be heard expeditiously, and if possible within ten days after they have been docketed.

(j) The Board shall have power, upon issuance of a complaint as provided in subsection (b) charging that any person has engaged in or is engaging in an unfair labor practice, to petition any district court of the United States (including the District Court of the United States for the District of Columbia), within any district wherein the unfair labor practice in question is alleged to have occurred or wherein such person resides or transacts business, for appropriate temporary relief or restraining order. Upon the filing of any such petition the court shall cause notice thereof to be served upon such person, and thereupon shall have jurisdiction to grant to the Board such temporary relief or restraining order as it deems just and proper.

(k) Whenever it is charged that any person has engaged in an unfair labor practice within the meaning of paragraph (4)(D) of section 8(b), the Board is empowered and directed to hear and determine the dispute out of which such unfair labor practice shall have arisen, unless, within ten days after notice that such charge has been filed, the parties to such dispute submit to the Board satisfactory evidence that they have adjusted, or agreed upon methods for the voluntary adjustment of, the dispute. Upon compliance by the parties to the dispute with the decision of the Board or upon such voluntary adjustment of the dispute, such charge shall be dismissed.

(l) Whenever it is charged that any person has engaged in an unfair labor practice within the meaning of paragraph (4) (A), (B), or (C) of section 8(b), or section 8(e) or section 8(b)(7), the preliminary investigation of such charge shall be made forthwith and given priority over all other cases except cases of like character in the office where it is filed or to which it is referred. If, after such investigation, the officer or regional attorney to whom the matter may be referred has reasonable cause to believe such charge is true and that a complaint should issue, he shall, on behalf of the Board, petition any district court of the United States (including the District Court of the United States for the District of Columbia) within any district where the unfair labor practice in question has occurred, is alleged to have occurred, or wherein such person resides or transacts business, for appropriate injunctive relief pending the final adjudication of the Board with respect to such matter. Upon the filing of any such petition the district court shall have jurisdiction to grant such injunctive relief or temporary restraining order as it deems just and proper, notwithstanding any other provision of law: *Provided further,* That no temporary restraining order shall be issued without notice unless a petition alleges that substantial and irreparable injury to the charging party will be unavoidable and such temporary restraining order shall be effective for no longer than five days and will become void at the expiration of such period: *Provided further,* That such officer or regional attorney shall not apply for any restraining order under section 8(b)(7) if a charge against the employer under section 8(a)(2) has been filed and after the preliminary investigation, he has reasonable cause to believe that such charge is true and that a complaint should issue. Upon filing of any such petition the courts shall cause notice thereof to be served upon any person involved in the charge and such person, including the charging party, shall be given an opportunity to appear by counsel and present any relevant testimony: *Provided further,*

That for the purposes of this subsection district courts shall be deemed to have jurisdiction of a labor organization (1) in the district in which such organization maintains its principal office, or (2) in any district in which its duly authorized officers or agents are engaged in promoting or protecting the interests of employee members. The service of legal process upon such officer or agent shall constitute service upon the labor organization and make such organizations a party to the suit. In situations where such relief is appropriate the procedure specified herein shall apply to charges with respect to section 8(b)(4)(D).

(m) Whenever it is charged that any person has engaged in an unfair labor practice within the meaning of subsection (a)(3) or (b)(2) of section 8, such charge shall be given priority over all other cases except cases of like character in the office where it is filed or to which it is referred and cases given priority under subsection (l).

INVESTIGATORY POWERS

SEC. 11. For the purpose of all hearings and investigations, which, in the opinion of the Board, are necessary and proper for the exercise of the powers vested in it by section 9 and section 10—

(1) The Board, or its duly authorized agents or agencies, shall at all reasonable times have access to, for the purpose of examination, and the right to copy any evidence of any person being investigated or proceeded against that relates to any matter under investigation or in question. The Board, or any member thereof, shall upon application of any party to such proceedings, forthwith issue to such party subpenas requiring the attendance and testimony of witnesses or the production of any evidence in such proceeding or investigation requested in such application. Within five days after the service of a subpena on any person requiring the production of any evidence in his possession or under his control, such person may petition the Board to revoke, and the Board shall revoke, such subpena if in its opinion the evidence whose production is required does not relate to any matter under investigation, or any matter in question in such proceedings, or if in its opinion such subpena does not describe with sufficient particularity the evidence whose production is required. Any member of the Board, or any agent or agency designated by the Board for such purposes, may administer oaths and affirmations, examine witnesses, and receive evidence. Such attendance of witnesses and the production of such evidence may be required from any place in the United States or any Territory or possession thereof, at any designated place of hearing.

(2) In case of contumacy or refusal to obey a subpena issued to any person, any district court of the United States or the United States courts of any Territory or possession, or the District Court of the United States for the District of Columbia, within the jurisdiction of which the inquiry is carried on or within the jurisdiction of which said person guilty of contumacy or refusal to obey is found or resides or transacts business, upon application by the Board shall have jurisdiction to issue to such person an order requiring such person to appear before the Board, its member, agent, or agency, there to produce evidence if so ordered, or there to give testimony touching the matter under investigation or in question; and any failure to obey such order of the court may be punished by said court as a contempt thereof.

(3)*

(4) Complaints, orders, and other process and papers of the Board, its member, agent, or agency, may be served either personally or by registered mail or by telegraph or by leaving a copy thereof at the principal office or place of business of

---

*Sec. 11(3) is repealed by Sec. 234, Public Law 91–452, 91st Cong., S. 30, 84 Stat. 926, Oct. 15, 1970. See Title 18, U.S.C. Sec. 6001, *et seq.*

the person required to be served. The verified return by the individual so serving the same setting forth the manner of such service shall be proof of the same, and the return post office receipt or telegraph receipt therefor when registered and mailed or telegraphed as aforesaid shall be proof of service of the same. Witnesses summoned before the Board, its member, agent, or agency, shall be paid the same fees and mileage that are paid witnesses in the courts of the United States, and witnesses whose depositions are taken and the persons taking the same shall severally be entitled to the same fees as are paid for like services in the courts of the United States.

(5) All process of any court to which application may be made under this Act may be served in the judicial district wherein the defendant or other person required to be served resides or may be found.

(6) The several departments and agencies of the Government, when directed by the President, shall furnish the Board, upon its request, all records, papers, and information in their possession relating to any matter before the Board.

SEC. 12. Any person who shall willfully resist, prevent, impede, or interfere with any member of the Board or any of its agents or agencies in the performance of duties pursuant to this Act shall be punished by a fine of not more than $5,000 or by imprisonment for not more than one year, or both.

LIMITATIONS

SEC. 13. Nothing in this Act, except as specifically provided for herein, shall be construed so as either to interfere with or impede or diminish in any way the right to strike, or to affect the limitations or qualifications on that right.

SEC. 14. (a) Nothing herein shall prohibit any individual employed as a supervisor from becoming or remaining a member of a labor organization, but no employer subject to this Act shall be compelled to deem individuals defined herein as supervisors as employees for the purpose of any law, either national or local, relating to collective bargaining.

(b) Nothing in this Act shall be construed as authorizing the execution or application of agreements requiring membership in a labor organization as a condition of employment in any State or Territory in which such execution or application is prohibited by State or Territorial law.

(c)(1) The Board, in its discretion, may, by rule of decision or by published rules adopted pursuant to the Administrative Procedure Act, decline to assert jurisdiction over any labor dispute involving any class or category of employers, where, in the opinion of the Board, the effect of such labor dispute on commerce is not sufficiently substantial to warrant the exercise of its jurisdiction: *Provided,* That the Board shall not decline to assert jurisdiction over any labor dispute over which it would assert jurisdiction under the standards prevailing upon August 1, 1959.

(2) Nothing in this Act shall be deemed to prevent or bar any agency or the courts of any State or Territory (including the Commonwealth of Puerto Rico, Guam, and the Virgin Islands), from assuming and asserting jurisdiction over labor disputes over which the Board declines, pursuant to paragraph (1) of this subsection, to assert jurisdiction.

SEC. 15. Wherever the application of the provisions of section 272 of chapter 10 of the Act entitled "An Act to establish a uniform system of bankruptcy throughout the United States," approved July 1, 1898, and Acts amendatory thereof and supplementary thereto (U.S.C., title 11, sec. 672), conflicts with the application of the provisions of this Act, this Act shall prevail: *Provided,* That in any situation where the provisions of this Act cannot be validly enforced, the provisions of such other Acts shall remain in full force and effect.

SEC. 16. If any provision of this Act, or the application of such provision to any person or circumstances, shall be held invalid, the remainder of this Act, or the application of such provision to persons or circumstances other than those as to which it is held invalid, shall not be affected thereby.

SEC. 17. This Act may be cited as the "National Labor Relations Act."

SEC. 18. No petition entertained, no investigation made, no election held, and no certification issued by the National Labor Relations Board, under any of the provisions of section 9 of the National Labor Relations Act, as amended, shall be invalid by reason of the failure of the Congress of Industrial Organizations to have complied with the requirements of section 9(f), (g), or (h) of the aforesaid Act prior to December 22, 1949, or by reason of the failure of the American Federation of Labor to have complied with the provisions of section 9(f), (g), or (h) of the aforesaid Act prior to November 7, 1947: *Provided,* That no liability shall be imposed under any provision of this Act upon any person for failure to honor any election or certificate referred to above, prior to the effective date of this amendment: *Provided, however,* That this proviso shall not have the effect of setting aside or in any way affecting judgments or decrees heretofore entered under section 10(e) or (f) and which have become final.

INDIVIDUALS WITH RELIGIOUS CONVICTIONS*

SEC. 19. Any employee of a health care institution who is a member of and adheres to established and traditional tenets or teachings of a bona fide religion, body, or sect which has historically held conscientious objections to joining or financially supporting labor organizations shall not be required to join or financially support any labor organization as a condition of employment; except that such employee may be required, in lieu of periodic dues and initiation fees, to pay sums equal to such dues and initiation fees to a nonreligious charitable fund exempt from taxation under section 501(c)(3) of the Internal Revenue Code, chosen by such employee from a list of at least three such funds, designated in a contract between such institution and a labor organization, or if the contract fails to designate such funds, then to any such fund chosen by the employee.

EFFECTIVE DATE OF CERTAIN CHANGES**

SEC. 102. No provision of this title shall be deemed to make an unfair labor practice any act which was performed prior to the date of the enactment of this Act which did not constitute an unfair labor practice prior thereto, and the provisions of section 8(a)(3) and section 8(b)(2) of the National Labor Relations Act as amended by this title shall not make an unfair labor practice the performance of any obligation under a collective-bargaining agreement entered into prior to the date of the enactment of this Act, or (in the case of an agreement for a period of not more than one year) entered into on or after such date of enactment, but prior to the effective date of this title, if the performance of such obligation would not have constituted an unfair labor practice under section 8(3) of the National Labor Relations Act prior to the effective date of this title, unless such agreement was renewed or extended subsequent thereto.

SEC. 103. No provisions of this title shall affect any certification of representatives or any determination as to the appropriate collective-bargaining unit, which was made under section 9 of the National Labor Relations Act prior to the effective date of this title until one year after the date of such certification or if, in respect of any such certification, a collective-bargaining contract was entered into

---

*Pursuant to Public Law 93–360, 93d Cong., S. 3203, 88 Stat. 397, the National Labor Relations Act is amended by adding Sec. 19.

**The effective date referred to in Secs. 102, 103, and 104 is Aug. 22, 1947. For effective dates of 1959 and 1974 amendments, see footnotes on first page of this text.

prior to the effective date of this title, until the end of the contract period or until one year after such date, whichever first occurs.

SEC. 104.   The amendments made by this title shall take effect sixty days after the date of the enactment of this Act, except that the authority of the President to appoint certain officers conferred upon him by section 3 of the National Labor Relations Act as amended by this title may be exercised forthwith.

TITLE II—CONCILIATION OF LABOR DISPUTES IN INDUSTRIES AFFECTING COMMERCE; NATIONAL EMERGENCIES

SEC. 201.   That it is the policy of the United States that—

(a) sound and stable industrial peace and the advancement of the general welfare, health, and safety of the Nation and of the best interest of employers and employees can most satisfactorily be secured by the settlement of issues between employers and employees through the processes of conference and collective bargaining between employers and the representatives of their employees;

(b) the settlement of issues between employers and employees through collective bargaining may be advanced by making available full and adequate governmental facilities for conciliation, mediation, and voluntary arbitration to aid and encourage employers and the representatives of their employees to reach and maintain agreements concerning rates of pay, hours, and working conditions, and to make all reasonable efforts to settle their differences by mutual agreement reached through conferences and collective bargaining or by such methods as may be provided for in any applicable agreement for the settlement of disputes; and

(c) certain controversies which arise between parties to collective-bargaining agreements may be avoided or minimized by making available full and adequate governmental facilities for furnishing assistance to employers and the representatives of their employees in formulating for inclusion within such agreements provision for adequate notice of any proposed changes in the terms of such agreements, for the final adjustment of grievances or questions regarding the application or interpretation of such agreements, and other provisions designed to prevent the subsequent arising of such controversies.

SEC. 202.   (a) There is hereby created an independent agency to be known as the Federal Mediation and Conciliation Service (herein referred to as the "Service," except that for sixty days after the date of the enactment of this Act such term shall refer to the Conciliation Service of the Department of Labor). The Service shall be under the direction of a Federal Mediation and Conciliation Director (hereinafter referred to as the "Director"), who shall be appointed by the President by and with the advice and consent of the Senate. The Director shall receive compensation at the rate of $12,000* per annum. The Director shall not engage in any other business, vocation, or employment.

(b) The Director is authorized, subject to the civil-service laws, to appoint such clerical and other personnel as may be necessary for the execution of the functions of the Service, and shall fix their compensation in accordance with the Classification Act of 1923, as amended, and may, without regard to the provisions of the civil-service laws and the Classification Act of 1923, as amended, appoint and fix the compensation of such conciliators and mediators as may be necessary to carry out the functions of the Service. The Director is authorized to make such expenditures

---

*Pursuant to Public Law 90–206, 90th Cong., 81 Stat. 644, approved Dec. 16, 1967, and in accordance with Sec. 225(f)(ii) thereof, effective in 1969, the salary of the Director shall be $40,000 per year.

for supplies, facilities, and services as he deems necessary. Such expenditures shall be allowed and paid upon presentation of itemized vouchers therefor approved by the Director or by any employee designated by him for that purpose.

(c) The principal office of the Service shall be in the District of Columbia, but the Director may establish regional offices convenient to localities in which labor controversies are likely to arise. The Director may by order, subject to revocation at any time, delegate any authority and discretion conferred upon him by this Act to any regional director, or other officer or employee of the Service. The Director may establish suitable procedures for cooperation with State and local mediation agencies. The Director shall make an annual report in writing to Congress at the end of the fiscal year.

(d) All mediation and conciliation functions of the Secretary of Labor or the United States Conciliation Service under section 8 of the Act entitled "An Act to create a Department of Labor," approved March 4, 1913 (U.S.C., title 29, sec. 51), and all functions of the United States Conciliation Service under any other law are hereby transferred to the Federal Mediation and Conciliation Service, together with the personnel and records of the United States Conciliation Service. Such transfer shall take effect upon the sixtieth day after the date of enactment of this Act. Such transfer shall not affect any proceedings pending before the United States Conciliation Service or any certification, order, rule, or regulation theretofore made by it or by the Secretary of Labor. The Director and the Service shall not be subject in any way to the jurisdiction or authority of the Secretary of labor or any official or division of the Department of Labor.

FUNCTIONS OF THE SERVICE

SEC. 203. (a) It shall be the duty of the Service, in order to prevent or minimize interruptions of the free flow of commerce growing out of labor disputes, to assist parties to labor disputes in industries affecting commerce to settle such disputes through conciliation and mediation.

(b) The Service may proffer its services in any labor dispute in any industry affecting commerce, either upon its own motion or upon the request of one or more of the parties to the dispute, whenever in its judgment such dispute threatens to cause a substantial interruption of commerce. The Director and the Service are directed to avoid attempting to mediate disputes which would have only a minor effect on interstate commerce if State or other conciliation services are available to the parties. Whenever the Service does proffer its services in any dispute, it shall be the duty of the Service promptly to put itself in communication with the parties and to use its best efforts, by mediation and conciliation, to bring them to agreement.

(c) If the Director is not able to bring the parties to agreement by conciliation within a reasonable time, he shall seek to induce the parties voluntarily to seek other means of settling the dispute without resort to strike, lock-out, or other coercion, including submission to the employees in the bargaining unit of the employer's last offer of settlement for approval or rejection in a secret ballot. The failure or refusal of either party to agree to any procedure suggested by the Director shall not be deemed a violation of any duty or obligation imposed by this Act.

(d) Final adjustment by a method agreed upon by the parties is hereby declared to be the desirable method for settlement of grievance disputes arising over the application or interpretation of an existing collective-bargaining agreement. The Service is directed to make its conciliation and mediation services available in the settlement of such grievance disputes only as a last resort and in exceptional cases.

SEC. 204. (a) In order to prevent or minimize interruptions of the free flow of commerce growing out of labor disputes, employers and employees and their representatives, in any industry affecting commerce, shall—

(1) exert every reasonable effort to make and maintain agreements concerning rates of pay, hours, and working conditions, including provision for adequate notice of any proposed change in the terms of such agreements;

(2) whenever a dispute arises over the terms or application of a collective-bargaining agreement and a conference is requested by a party or prospective party thereto, arrange promptly for such a conference to be held and endeavor in such conference to settle such dispute expeditiously; and

(3) in case such dispute is not settled by conference, participate fully and promptly in such meetings as may be undertaken by the Service under this Act for the purpose of aiding in a settlement of the dispute.

SEC. 205. (a) There is hereby created a National Labor-Management Panel which shall be composed of twelve members appointed by the President, six of whom shall be selected from among persons outstanding in the field of management and six of whom shall be selected from among persons outstanding in the field of labor. Each member shall hold office for a term of three years, except that any member appointed to fill a vacancy occurring prior to the expiration of the term for which his predecessor was appointed shall be appointed for the remainder of such term, and the terms of office of the members first taking office shall expire, as designated by the President at the time of appointment, four at the end of the first year, four at the end of the second year, and four at the end of the third year after the date of appointment. Members of the panel, when serving on business of the panel, shall be paid compensation at the rate of $25 per day, and shall also be entitled to receive an allowance for actual and necessary travel and subsistence expenses while so serving away from their places of residence.

(b) It shall be the duty of the panel, at the request of the Director, to advise in the avoidance of industrial controversies and the manner in which mediation and voluntary adjustment shall be administered, particularly with reference to controversies affecting the general welfare of the country.

NATIONAL EMERGENCIES

SEC. 206. Whenever in the opinion of the President of the United States, a threatened or actual strike or lock-out affecting an entire industry or a substantial part thereof engaged in trade, commerce, transportation, transmission, or communication among the several States or with foreign nations, or engaged in the production cf goods for commerce, will, if permitted to occur or to continue, imperil the national health or safety, he may appoint a board of inquiry to inquire into the issues involved in the dispute and to make a written report to him within such time as he shall prescribe. Such report shall include a statement of the facts with respect to the dispute, including each party's statement of its position but shall not contain any recommendations. The President shall file a copy of such report with the Service and shall make its contents available to the public.

SEC. 207. (a) A board of inquiry shall be composed of a chairman and such other members as the President shall determine, and shall have power to sit and act in any place within the United States and to conduct such hearings either in public or in private, as it may deem necessary or proper, to ascertain the facts with respect to the causes and circumstances of the dispute.

(b) Members of a board of inquiry shall receive compensation at the rate of $50 for each day actually spent by them in the work of the board, together with necessary travel and subsistence expenses.

(c) For the purpose of any hearing·or inquiry conducted by any board appointed under this title, the provisions of sections 9 and 10 (relating to the attendance of witnesses and the production of books, papers, and documents) of the Federal Trade Commission Act of September 16, 1914, as amended (U.S.C. 19, title 15, secs. 49 and 50, as amended), are hereby made applicable to the powers and duties of such board.

SEC. 208. (a) Upon receiving a report from a board of inquiry the President may direct the Attorney General to petition any district court of the United States having jurisdiction of the parties to enjoin such strike or lock-out or the continuing thereof, and if the court finds that such threatened or actual strike or lock-out—

(i) affects an entire industry or a substantial part thereof engaged in trade, commerce, transportation, transmission, or communication among the several States or with foreign nations, or engaged in the production of goods for commerce; and

(ii) if permitted to occur or to continue, will mperil the national health or safety, it shall have jurisdiction to enjoin any such strike or lock-out, or the continuing thereof, and to make such other orders as may be appropriate.

(b) In any case, the provisions of the Act of March 23, 1932, entitled "An Act to amend the Judicial Code and to define and limit the jurisdiction of courts sitting in equity, and for other purposes," shall not be applicable.

(c) The order or orders of the court shall be subject to review by the appropriate circuit court of appeals and by the Supreme Court upon writ of certiorari or certification as provided in sections 239 and 240 of the Judicial Code, as amended (U.S.C., title 29, secs. 346 and 347).

SEC. 209. (a) Whenever a district court has issued an order under section 208 enjoining acts or practices which imperil or threaten to imperil the national health or safety, it shall be the duty of the parties to the labor dispute giving rise to such order to make every effort to adjust and settle their differences, with the assistance of the Service created by this Act. Neither party shall be under any duty to accept, in whole or in part, any proposal of settlement made by the Service.

(b) Upon the issuance of such order, the President shall reconvene the board of inquiry which has previously reported with respect to the dispute. At the end of a sixty-day period (unless the dispute has been settled by that time), the board of inquiry shall report to the President the current position of the parties and the efforts which has been made for settlement, and shall include a statement by each party of its position and a statement of the employer's last offer of settlement. The President shall make such report available to the public. The National Labor Relations Board, within the succeeding fifteen days, shall take a secret ballot of the employees of each employer involved in the dispute on the question of whether they wish to accept the final offer of settlement made by their employer as stated by him and shall certify the results thereof to the Attorney General within five days thereafter.

SEC. 210. Upon the certification of the results of such ballot or upon a settlement being reached, whichever happens sooner, the Attorney General shall move the court to discharge the injunction, which motion shall then be granted and the injunction discharged. When such motion is granted, the President shall submit to the Congress a full and comprehensive report of the proceedings, including the findings of the board of inquiry and the ballot taken by the National Labor Relations Board, together with such recommendations as he may see fit to make for consideration and appropriate action.

COMPILATION OF COLLECTIVE-BARGAINING AGREEMENTS, ETC.

SEC. 211. (a) For the guidance and information of interested representatives of employers, employees, and the general public, the Bureau of Labor Statistics of the Department of Labor shall maintain a file of copies of all available collective-bargaining agreements and other available agreements and actions thereunder settling or adjusting labor disputes. Such file shall be open to inspection under appropriate conditions prescribed by the Secretary of Labor, except that no specific information submitted in confidence shall be disclosed.

(b) The Bureau of Labor Statistics in the Department of Labor is authorized to furnish upon request of the Service, or employers, employees, or their representatives, all available data and factual information which may aid in the settlement of any labor dispute, except that no specific information submitted in confidence shall be disclosed.

EXEMPTION OF RAILWAY LABOR ACT

SEC. 212. The provisions of this title shall not be applicable with respect to any matter which is subject to the provisions of the Railway Labor Act, as amended from time to time.

CONCILIATION OF LABOR DISPUTES IN THE HEALTH CARE INDUSTRY*

SEC. 213. (a) If, in the opinion of the Director of the Federal Mediation and Conciliation Service a threatened or actual strike or lockout affecting a health care institution will, if permitted to occur or to continue, substantially interrupt the delivery of health care in the locality concerned, the Director may further assist in the resolution of the impasse by establishing within 30 days after the notice to the Federal Mediation and Conciliation Service under clause (A) of the last sentence of section 8(d) (which is required by clause (3) of such section 8(d)), or within 10 days after the notice under clause (B), an impartial Board of Inquiry to investigate the issues involved in the dispute and to make a written report thereon to the parties within fifteen (15) days after the establishment of such a Board. The written report shall contain the findings of fact together with the Board's recommendations for settling the dispute, with the objective of achieving a prompt, peaceful and just settlement of the dispute. Each such Board shall be composed of such number of individuals as the Director may deem desirable. No member appointed under this section shall have any interest or involvement in the health care institutions or the employee organizations involved in the dispute.

(b) (1) Members of any board established under this section who are otherwise employed by the Federal Government shall serve without compensation but shall be reimbursed for travel, subsistence, and other necessary expenses incurred by them in carrying out its duties under this section.

(2) Members of any board established under this section who are not subject to paragraph (1) shall receive compensation at a rate prescribed by the Director but not to exceed the daily rate prescribed for GS-18 of the General Schedule under section 5332 of title 5, United States Code, including travel for each day they are engaged in the performance of their duties under this section and shall be entitled to reimbursement for travel, subsistence, and other necessary expenses incurred by them in carrying out their duties under this section.

(c) After the establishment of a board under subsection (a) of this section and for 15 days after any such board has issued its report, no change in the

---

*Pursuant to Public Law 93-360, 93d Cong., S. 3203, 88 Stat. 396-397, Title II of the Labor Management Relations Act, 1947, is amended by adding Sec. 213.

status quo in effect prior to the expiration of the contract in the case of negotiations for a contract renewal, or in effect prior to the time of the impasse in the case of an initial bargaining negotiation, except by agreement, shall be made by the parties to the controversy.

(d) There are authorized to be appropriated such sums as may be necessary to carry out the provisions of this section.

TITLE III

SUITS BY AND AGAINST LABOR ORGANIZATIONS

SEC. 301. (a) Suits for violation of contracts between an employer and a labor organization representing employees in an industry affecting commerce as defined in this Act, or between any such labor organizations, may be brought in any district court of the United States having jurisdiction of the parties, without respect to the amount in controversy or without regard to the citizenship of the parties.

(b) Any labor organization which represents employees in an industry affecting commerce as defined in this Act and any employer whose activities affect commerce as defined in this Act shall be bound by the acts of its agents. Any such labor organization may sue or be sued as an entity and in behalf of the employees whom it represents in the courts of the United States. Any money judgment against a labor organization in a district court of the United States shall be enforceable only against the organization as an entity and against its assets, and shall not be enforceable against any individual member or his assets.

(c) For the purposes of actions and proceedings by or against labor organizations in the district courts of the United States, district courts shall be deemed to have jurisdiction of a labor organization (1) in the district in which such organization maintains its principal offices, or (2) in any district in which its duly authorized officers or agents are engaged in representing or acting for employee members.

(d) The service of summons, subpena, or other legal process of any court of the United States upon an officer or agent of a labor organization, in his capacity as such, shall constitute service upon the labor organization.

(e) For the purposes of this section, in determining whether any person is acting as an "agent" of another person so as to make such other person responsible for his acts, the question of whether the specific acts performed were actually authorized or subsequently ratified shall not be controlling.

RESTRICTIONS ON PAYMENTS TO EMPLOYEE REPRESENTATIVES

SEC. 302. (a) It shall be unlawful for any employer or association of employers or any person who acts as a labor relations expert, adviser, or consultant to an employer or who acts in the interest of an employer to pay, lend, or deliver, or agree to pay, lend, or deliver, any money or other thing of value—

(1) to any representative of any of his employees who are employed in an industry affecting commerce; or

(2) to any labor organization, or any officer or employee thereof, which represents, seeks to represent, or would admit to membership, any of the employees of such employer who are employed in an industry affecting commerce; or

(3) to any employee or group or committee of employees of such employer employed in an industry affecting commerce in excess of their normal compensation for the purpose of causing such employee or group or committee directly or indirectly to influence any other employees in the exercise of the right to organize and bargain collectively through representatives of their own choosing; or

(4) to any officer or employee of a labor organization engaged in an industry affecting commerce with intent to influence him in respect to any of his actions, decisions, or duties as a representative of employees or as such officer or employee of such labor organization.

(b)(1) It shall be unlawful for any person to request, demand, receive, or accept, or agree to receive or accept, any payment, loan, or delivery of any money or other thing of value prohibited by subsection (a).

(2) It shall be unlawful for any labor organization, or for any person acting as an officer, agent, representative, or employee of such labor organization, to demand or accept from the operator of any motor vehicle (as defined in part II of the Interstate Commerce Act) employed in the transportation of property in commerce, or the employer of any such operator, any money or other thing of value payable to such organization or to an officer, agent, representative or employee thereof as a fee or charge for the unloading, or the connection with the unloading, of the cargo of such vehicle: *Provided,* That nothing in this paragraph shall be construed to make unlawful any payment by an employer to any of his employees as compensation for their services as employees.

(c) The provisions of this section shall not be applicable (1) in respect to any money or other thing of value payable by an employer to any of his employees whose established duties include acting openly for such employer in matters of labor relations or personnel administration or to any representative of his employees, or to any officer or employee of a labor organization, who is also an employee or former employee of such employer, as compensation for, or by reason of, his service as an employee of such employer; (2) with respect to the payment or delivery of any money or other thing of value in satisfaction of a judgment of any court or a decision or award of an arbitrator or impartial chairman or in compromise, adjustment, settlement, or release of any claim, complaint, grievance, or dispute in the absence of fraud or duress; (3) with respect to the sale or purchase of an article or commodity at the prevailing market price in the regular course of business; (4) with respect to money deducted from the wages of employees in payment of membership dues in a labor organization: *Provided,* That the employer has received from each employee, on whose account such deductions are made, a written assignment which shall not be irrevocable for a period of more than one year, or beyond the termination date of the applicable collective agreement, whichever occurs sooner; (5) with respect to money or other thing of value paid to a trust fund established by such representative, for the sole and exclusive benefit of the employees of such employer, and their families and dependents (or of such employees, families, and dependents jointly with the employees of other employers making similar payments, and their families and dependents): *Provided,* That (A) such payments are held in trust for the purpose of paying, either from principal or income or both, for the benefit of employees, their families and dependents, for medical or hospital care, pensions on retirement or death of employees, compensation for injuries or illness resulting from occupational activity or insurance to provide any of the foregoing, or unemployment benefits or life insurance, disability and sickness insurance, or accident insurance; (B) the detailed basis on which such payments are to be made is specified in a written agreement with the employer, and employees and employers are equally represented in the administration of such fund, together with such neutral persons as the representatives of the employers and the representatives of employees may agree upon and in the event the employer and employee groups deadlock on the administration of such fund and there are no neutral persons empowered to break such deadlock, such agreement provides that the two groups shall agree on an impartial umpire to decide such dispute, or in event of their failure to agree within a reasonable length of time, an impartial umpire to decide such dispute shall, on petition of either group, be appointed by the district court of the United States for the district where the trust fund has its principal office, and shall also contain provisions for an annual audit of the trust fund, a statement of the results of which shall be available for inspection by interested persons at the principal office of the trust fund and at such other places as may be designated in such written agreement; and (C) such payments as are intended to be used for the purpose of providing pensions or annuities for employees are made to a separate trust which provides that the funds held therein cannot be used for any purpose other than paying such pensions or annuities; (6) with respect to money or other thing of value paid by any employer to a trust fund established by such representative for the purpose of pooled vacation, holiday, severance or similar benefits, or defraying costs of apprenticeship or other training program: *Provided,* That the requirements of clause (B) of the proviso to clause (5) of this subsection shall apply to such trust funds; or (7) with respect to money or other thing of value paid by any employer to a pooled or individual trust fund established by such representative for the purpose of (A) scholarships for the benefit of employees, their families, and dependents for study at educational institutions, or (B) child care centers for preschool and school age dependents of employees: *Provided,* That no labor organization or employer shall be required to bargain on the establishment of any such trust fund, and refusal to do so shall not constitute an unfair labor practice: *Provided further,* That the requirements of clause (B) of the proviso to clause (5) of this subsection shall apply to such trust funds*; or (8) with respect to money or any other thing of value paid by any employer to a trust fund established by such representative for the purpose of defraying the costs of legal services for employees, their families, and dependents for counsel or plan of their choice: *Provided,* That the requirements of clause (B) of the proviso to clause (5) of this subsection shall apply to such trust funds: *Provided further,* That no such legal services shall be furnished: (A) to initiate any proceeding directed (i) against any such employer or its officers or agents except in workman's compensation cases, or (ii) against such labor organization, or its parent or subordinate bodies, or their officers or agents, or (iii) against any other employer or labor organization, or their officers or agents, in any matter arising under the National Labor Relations Act, as amended, or this Act; and (B) in any proceeding where a labor organization would be prohibited from defraying the costs of legal services by the provisions of the Labor-Management Reporting and Disclosure Act of 1959.*

(d) Any person who willfully violates any of the provisions of this section shall, upon conviction thereof, be guilty of a misdemeanor and be subject to a fine of not more than $10,000 or to imprisonment for not more than one year, or both.

(e) The district courts of the United States and the United States courts of the Territories and possessions shall have jurisdiction, for cause shown, and subject to the provisions of section 17 (relating to notice to opposite party) of the Act entitled "An Act to supplement existing laws against unlawful restraints and monopolies, and for other purposes," approved October 15, 1914, as amended (U.S.C., title 28, sec. 381), to restrain violations of this section, without regard to the provisions of sections 6 and 20 of such Act of October 15, 1914, as amended (U.S.C., title 15, sec. 17, and title 29, sec. 52), and the provisions of the Act entitled "An Act to amend the Judicial Code and to define and limit the jurisdiction of courts sitting in equity, and for other purposes," approved March 23, 1932 (U.S.C., title 29, secs. 101–115).

(f) This section shall not apply to any contract in force on the date of enactment of this Act, until the expiration of such contract, or until July 1, 1948, whichever first occurs.

---

*Sec. 302(c)(7) has been added by Public Law 91–86, 91st Cong., S. 2068, 83 Stat. 133, approved Oct. 14, 1969; Sec. 302(c)(8) was added by Public Law 93–95, 93d Cong., S. 1423, 87 Stat. 314–315, approved Aug. 15, 1973.

(g) Compliance with the restrictions contained in subsection (c)(5)(B) upon contributions to trust funds, otherwise lawful, shall not be applicable to contributions to such trust funds established by collective agreement prior to January 1, 1946, nor shall subsection (c)(5)(A) be construed as prohibiting contributions to such trust funds if prior to January 1, 1947, such funds contained provisions for pooled vacation benefits.

BOYCOTTS AND OTHER UNLAWFUL COMBINATIONS

SEC. 303. (a) It shall be unlawful, for the purpose of this section only, in an industry or activity affecting commerce, for any labor organization to engage in any activity or conduct defined as an unfair labor practice in section 8(b)(4) of the National Labor Relations Act, as amended.

(b) Whoever shall be injured in his business or property by reason of any violation of subsection (a) may sue therefore in any district court of the United States subject to the limitations and provisions of section 301 hereof without respect to the amount in controversy, or in any other court having jurisdiction of the parties, and shall recover the damages by him sustained and the cost of the suit.

RESTRICTION ON POLITICAL CONTRIBUTIONS

SEC. 304. Section 313 of the Federal Corrupt Practices Act, 1925 (U.S.C., 1940 edition, title 2, sec. 251; Supp. V, title 50, App., sec. 1509), as amended, is amended to read as follows:

SEC. 313. It is unlawful for any national bank, or any corporation organized by authority of any law of Congress to make a contribution or expenditure in connection with any election to any political office, or in connection with any primary election or political convention or caucus held to select candidates for any political office, or for any corporation whatever, or any labor organization to make a contribution or expenditure in connection with any election at which Presidential and Vice Presidential electors or a Senator or Representative in, or a Delegate or Resident Commissioner to Congress are to be voted for, or in connection with any primary election or political convention or caucus held to select candidates for any of the foregoing offices, or for any candidate, political committee, or other person to accept or receive any contribution prohibited by this section. Every corporation or labor organization which makes any contribution or expenditure in violation of this section shall be fined not more than $5,000; and every officer or director of any corporation, or officer of any labor organization, who consents to any contribution or expenditure by the corporation or labor organization, as the case may be, in violation of this section shall be fined not more than $1,000 or imprisoned for not more than one year, or both. For the purposes of this section "labor organization" means any organization of any kind, or any agency or employee representation committee or plan, in which employees participate and which exists for the purpose, in whole or in part, of dealing with employers concerning grievances, labor disputes, wages, rates of pay, hours of employment, or conditions of work.

TITLE IV

CREATION OF JOINT COMMITTEE TO STUDY AND REPORT ON BASIC PROBLEMS AFFECTING FRIENDLY LABOR RELATIONS AND PRODUCTIVITY

*   *   *   *   *   *   *

TITLE V

DEFINITIONS

SEC. 501. When used in this Act—

(1) The term "industry affecting commerce" means any industry or activity in commerce or in which a labor dispute would burden or obstruct commerce or tend to burden or obstruct commerce or the free flow of commerce.

(2) The term "strike" includes any strike or other concerted stoppage of work by employees (including a stoppage by reason of the expiration of a collective-bargaining agreement) and any concerted slow-down or other concerted interruption of operations by employees.

(3) The terms "commerce," "labor disputes," "employer," "employee," "labor organization," "representative," "person," and "supervisor" shall have the same meaning as when used in the National Labor Relations Act as amended by this Act.

SAVING PROVISION

SEC. 502. Nothing in this Act shall be construed to require an individual employee to render labor or service without his consent, nor shall anything in this Act be construed to make the quitting of his labor by an individual employee an illegal act; nor shall any court issue any process to compel the performance by an individual employee of such labor or service, without his consent; nor shall the quitting of labor by an employee or employees in good faith because of abnormally dangerous conditions for work at the place of employment of such employee or employees be deemed a strike under this Act.

SEPARABILITY

SEC. 503. If any provision of this Act, or the application of such provision to any person or circumstance, shall be held invalid, the remainder of this Act, or the application of such provision to persons or circumstances other than those as to which it is held invalid, shall not be affected thereby.

Table of Cases

KEY: (1) The principal cases are designated by an asterisk (*) after the page which is the primary source for the case.

(2) If only one name is given for a case, the other party was the NLRB. For example, if a cite is for Smith, the actual case name is either Smith v. NLRB or NLRB v. Smith.